Waiting on God

by

Andrew Murray

Rickfords Hill Publishing Ltd.

Published by

RICKFORDS HILL PUBLISHING LTD.

24 High Street, Winslow, Buckingham, MK18 3HF, UK.

www.rhpbooks.co.uk

First Published 1895
This edition 2015

ISBN: 978-1-905044-44-3

Printed and bound in Great Britain
by CPI Group (UK) Ltd, Croydon CR0 4YY

Contents

Extract from
Address in Exeter Hall

I have been surprised at nothing more than at the letters that have come to me from missionaries and others from all parts of the world, devoted men and women, testifying to the need they feel in their work of being helped to a deeper and a clearer insight into all that Christ could be to them. Let us look to God to reveal Himself among His people in a measure very few have realized. Let us expect great things of our God. At all our conventions and assemblies too little time is given to waiting on God. Is He not willing to put things right in His own divine way? Has the life of God's people reached the utmost limit of what God is willing to do for them? Surely not. We want to wait on Him; to put away our experiences, however blessed they have been; our conceptions of truth, however sound and scriptural we think they seem; our plans, however needful and suitable they appear; and give God time and place to show us what He could do, what He will do. God has new developments and new resources. He can do new things, unheard of things, hidden things. Let us enlarge our hearts and not limit Him. "When thou camest down, thou didst terrible things we looked not for; the mountains flowed down at thy presence."

A. M.
May 31, 1895

Preface

Previous to my leaving home for England, I had been very much impressed by the thought of how, in all our religion, personal and public, we need more of God. I had felt that we needed to train our people in their worship more to wait on God, and to make the cultivation of a deeper sense of His presence, of more direct contact with Him, of entire dependence on Him, a definite aim of our ministry. At a "welcome" breakfast in Exeter Hall, I gave very simple expression to this thought in connection with all our religious work. I have already said elsewhere that I was surprised at the response the sentiment met with. I saw that God's Spirit had been working the same desire in many hearts.

The experiences of the past year, both personal and public, have greatly deepened the conviction. It is as if I myself am only beginning to see the deepest truth concerning God, and our relation to Him, centre in this waiting on God, and how very little, in our life and work, we have been surrounded by its spirit. The following pages are the outcome of my conviction, and of the desire to direct the attention of all God's people to the one great remedy for all our needs. More than half the pieces were written on board ship. I fear they bear the marks of being somewhat crude and hasty. I have felt that I should write them over again. But this I cannot now do. And so I send them out with the prayer that He who loves to use the feeble may give His blessing with them.

I do not know if it will be possible for me to put into a few words what are the chief things we need to learn. In a note at the close of the book on Law I have mentioned some. But what I want to say here is this: The great lack of our religion is, *we do not know God.* The answer to every complaint of feebleness and failure, the message to every congregation or convention seeking instruction on holiness, ought to be simply, What is the matter: *Have you not God?* If you really believe in God, He will put all right. God is willing and able by His Holy Spirit. Cease from expecting the least good from yourself, or the least help from anything there is in man, and just yield yourself unreservedly to God to work in you. He will do all for you.

How simple this looks! And yet this is the Gospel we so little know. I feel ashamed as I send forth these very defective meditations; I can only cast them on the love of my brethren, and of our God. May He use them to draw us all to Himself, to learn in practice and experience the blessed art of *waiting only upon God.* Would God that we might get some right conception of what the influence would be on a life spent, not in thought, or imagination, or effort, but in the power of the Holy Spirit, wholly waiting upon God.

With my greeting in Christ to all God's saints it has been my privilege to meet, and no less to those I have not met, I subscribe myself, your brother and servant,

Andrew Murray

First Day

The God of Our Salvation

My soul waiteth only upon God [marg. *is silent unto God*]; *from him cometh my salvation.*
—Psalm 62:1 (A.S.V.)

If Salvation indeed comes from God, and is entirely His work, just as our creation was, it follows, as a matter of course, that our first and highest duty is to wait on Him to do that work as pleases Him. Waiting becomes then the only way to the experience of a full salvation, the only way, truly to know God as the God of our salvation. All the difficulties that are brought forward, as keeping us back from full salvation, have their cause in this one thing: the defective knowledge and practice of waiting upon God. All that the Church and its members need for the manifestation of the mighty power of God in the world is the return to our true place, the place that belongs to us, both in creation and redemption, the place of absolute and unceasing dependence upon God. Let us strive to see what the elements are that make up this most blessed and needful waiting upon God. It may help us to discover the reasons why this grace is so little cultivated, and to feel how infinitely desirable it is that the Church, that we ourselves, should at any price learn its blessed secret.

The deep need for this waiting on God lies equally in the nature of man and the nature of God. God, as Creator, formed man, to be a vessel in which He could show forth His power and goodness. Man was not to have in himself a fountain of life, or strength, or happiness. The ever-living and only living One was each moment to be the Communicator to him of all that he needed. Man's glory and blessedness was not to be independent, or dependent upon himself, but dependent on a God of such infinite riches and love. Man was to have the joy of receiving every moment out of the fullness of God. This was his blessedness as an unfallen creature.

When he fell from God, he was still more absolutely dependent on Him. There was not the slightest hope of his recovery out of his state of death, but in God, His power and mercy. It is God alone who began the work of redemption. It is God alone who continues and carries it on each moment in each individual believer. Even in the regenerate man there is no power of goodness in himself. He has and can have nothing that he does not each moment receive; and waiting on God is just as indispensable, and must be just as continuous and unbroken, as the breathing that maintains his natural life.

It is then because Christians do not know their relation to God of absolute poverty and helplessness, that they have no sense of the need of absolute and unceasing dependence, or the unspeakable blessedness of continual waiting on God. But when once a believer begins to see it, and consent to it, that he by the Holy Spirit must each moment receive what God each moment works, waiting on God becomes his brightest hope and joy. As he apprehends how God, as God, as infinite Love, delights to impart His own nature to His child as fully as He can, how God is not weary of each moment keeping charge of his life and strength, he wonders that he ever thought otherwise of God than as a God to be waited on all the day. God unceasingly giving and working; His child unceasingly waiting and receiving; this is the blessed life.

"Truly my soul waiteth upon God; from him cometh my salvation." First we wait on God for salvation. Then we learn that salvation is only to bring us to God, and teach us to wait on Him. Then we find what is better still, that waiting on God is itself the highest salvation. It is the ascribing to Him the glory of being All; it is the experiencing that He is All to us. May God teach us the blessedness of waiting on Him!

My soul, wait thou only upon God!

Second Day

The Keynote of Life

I have waited for thy salvation, O LORD.

—Genesis 49:18

It is not easy to say exactly in what sense Jacob used these words, in the midst of his prophecies in regard to the future of his sons. But they do certainly indicate that both for himself and for them his expectation was from God alone. It was God's salvation he waited for; a salvation which God had promised and which God Himself alone could work out. He knew himself and his sons to be under God's charge. Jehovah the everlasting God would show in them what His saving power is and does. The words point forward to that wonderful history of redemption which is not yet finished, and to the glorious future in eternity whither it is leading. They suggest to us how there is no salvation but God's salvation, and how waiting on God for that, whether for our personal experience, or in wider circles, is our first duty, our true blessedness.

Let us think of ourselves, and the inconceivably glorious salvation God has wrought for us in Christ, and is now purposing to work out and to perfect in us by His Spirit. Let us meditate until we somewhat realize that every participation of this great salvation, from moment to moment, must be the work of God Himself. God cannot part with His grace, or goodness, or strength, as an external thing that He gives us, as He gives the raindrops from Heaven. No, He can only give it, and we can only enjoy it, as He works it Himself directly and unceasingly. And the only reason that He does not work it more effectually and continuously is that we do not let Him. We hinder Him either by our indifference or by our self effort, so that He cannot do what He would. What He asks of us, in the way of surrender, and obedience, and desire, and trust, is all comprised in this one word: waiting on Him, waiting for His salvation. It combines the deep sense of our entire helplessness of ourselves to work what is divinely good, and our perfect confidence that our God will work it all in His divine power.

Again, I say, let us meditate on the divine glory of the salvation God purposes working out in us, until we know the truths it implies. Our heart is the scene of a divine operation more wonderful than Creation. We can do as little toward the work as toward creating the world, except as God works in us to will and to do. God only asks of us to yield, to consent, to wait upon Him, and He will do it all. Let us meditate and be still, until we see how meet and right and blessed it is that God alone do all, and our soul will of itself sink down in deep humility to say: "I have waited for thy salvation, O LORD." And the deep blessed background of all our praying and working will be: "Truly my soul waiteth upon God."

The application of the truth to wider circles, to those we labour among or intercede for, to the Church of Christ around us, or throughout the world is not difficult. There can be no good but what God works; to wait upon God, and have the heart filled with faith in His working, and in that faith to pray for His mighty power to come down, is our only wisdom. Oh, for the eyes of our heart to be opened to see God working in ourselves and in others, and to see how blessed it is to worship and just to wait for His salvation!

Our private and public prayer is our chief expression of our relation to God. It is in them chiefly that our waiting upon God must be exercised. If our waiting begin by quieting the activities of nature, and being still before God; if it bows and seeks to see God in His universal and almighty operation, alone able and always ready to work all good; if it yields itself to Him in the assurance that He is working and will work in us; if it maintains the place of humility and stillness, and surrenders until God's Spirit has quickened the faith that He will perfect His work: it will indeed become the strength and the joy of the soul. Life will become one deep blessed cry: "I have waited for thy salvation, O Lord."

My soul, wait thou only upon God!

Third Day

The True Place of the Creature

These wait all upon thee,
That thou mayest give them their meat in due season.
That thou givest unto them, they gather;
Thou openest thine hand, they are satisfied with good.
—Psalm 104:27, 28 (A.S.V.)

This Psalm, in praise of the Creator, has been speaking of the birds and the beasts of the forest; of the young lions, and man going forth to his work; of the great sea, wherein are things creeping innumerable, both small and great beasts. And it sums up the whole relation of all creation to its Creator, and its continuous and universal dependence upon Him in the one word: "These all wait upon thee!" Just as much as it was God's work to create, it is His work to maintain. As little as the creature could create itself, is it left to provide for itself. The whole creation is ruled by the one unalterable law of—waiting upon God!

The word is the simple expression of that for the sake of which alone the creature was brought into existence, the very groundwork of its constitution. The one object for which God gave life to creatures was that in them He might prove and show forth His wisdom, power,

and goodness, in His being each moment their life and
happiness, and pouring forth unto them, according to
their capacity, the riches of His goodness and power.
And just as this is the very place and nature of God, to
be unceasingly the supplier of every want in the creature,
so the very place and nature of the creature is nothing but
this—to wait upon God and receive from Him what He
alone can give, what He delights to give. (See note on
Law, *The Power of the Spirit.*)

If we are in this little book at all to apprehend what
waiting on God is to be to the believer, to practice it and
to experience its blessedness, it is of consequence that
we begin at the very beginning, and see the deep reasonableness of the call that comes to us. We shall understand
how the duty is no arbitrary command. We shall see how it
is not only rendered necessary by our sin and helplessness.
It is simply and truly our restoration to our original destiny
and our highest nobility, to our true place and glory as
creatures blessedly dependent on the All-Glorious God.

If once our eyes are opened to this precious truth,
all Nature will become a preacher, reminding us of the
relationship which, founded in creation, is now taken up
in grace. As we read this psalm, and learn to look upon all
life in Nature as continually maintained by God Himself,
waiting on God will be seen to be the very necessity of
our being. As we think of the young lions and the ravens
crying to Him, of the birds and the fishes and every insect
waiting on Him, till He give them their meat in due season,
we shall see that it is the very nature and glory of God that
He is a God who is to be waited on. Every thought of what
Nature is, and what God is, will give new force to the call:

"Wait thou only upon God."

"These all wait upon thee, that thou mayest *give*." It is God who gives all: let this faith enter deeply into our hearts. Ere yet we fully understand all that is implied in our waiting upon God, and ere we have even been able to cultivate the habit, let the truth enter our souls. Waiting on God, unceasing and entire dependence upon Him, is, in Heaven and earth, the one only true religion, the one unalterable and all-comprehensive expression for the true relationship to the ever-blessed One in whom we live.

Let us resolve at once that it shall be the one characteristic of our life and worship, a continual, humble, truthful waiting upon God. We may rest assured that He who made us for Himself, that He might give Himself to us and in us, that *He* will never disappoint us. In waiting on Him we shall find rest and joy and strength, and the supply of every need.

My soul, wait thou only upon God!

Fourth Day

For Supplies

The LORD upholdeth all that fall,
And raiseth up all those that be bowed down.
The eyes of all wait upon thee;
And thou givest them their meat in due season.
                                        —Psalm 145:14, 15

Psalm 104 is a psalm of Creation, and the words, "These all wait upon thee," were used with reference to the animal creation. Here we have a psalm of the Kingdom, and "the eyes of all wait upon thee" appears specially to point to the needs of God's saints, of all that fall and them that be bowed down. What the universe and the animal creation does unconsciously, God's people are to do intelligently and voluntarily. Man is to be the interpreter of Nature. He is to prove that there is nothing nobler or more blessed in the exercise of our free will than to use it in waiting upon God.

If an army has been sent out to march into an enemy's country, and tidings are received that it is not advancing, the question is at once asked, what may be the cause of delay. The answer will very often be: "Waiting for supplies." All the stores of provisions or clothing or ammunition have not arrived; without these it dare not proceed. It is not otherwise in the Christian life: day by day, at every step, we need our supplies from above. And there is nothing so needful as to cultivate that spirit of dependence on God and of confidence in Him, which refuses to go on without the needed supply of grace and strength.

If the question be asked, whether this be anything different from what we do when we pray, the answer is that there may be much praying with but very little waiting on God. In praying we are often occupied with ourselves, with our own needs, and our own efforts in the presentation of them. In waiting upon God, the first thought is of *the God upon whom we wait*. We enter His presence, and feel we need just to be quiet, so that He, as God, can overshadow us with Himself. God longs to reveal Himself, to fill us with Himself. Waiting on God gives Him time in His own way and divine power to come to us.

It is specially at the time of prayer that we ought to set ourselves to cultivate this spirit.

Before you pray, bow quietly before God, just to remember and realize who He is, how near He is, how certainly He can and will help. Just be still before Him, and allow His Holy Spirit to waken and stir up in your soul the childlike disposition of absolute dependence and confident expectation. Wait upon God as a living Being, as the living God, who notices you, and is just longing to fill you with His salvation. Wait on God till you know you have met Him; prayer will then become so different.

And when you are praying, let there be intervals of silence, reverent stillness of soul, in which you yield yourself to God, in case He may have aught He wishes to teach you or to work in you. Waiting on Him will become the most blessed part of prayer, and the blessing thus obtained will be doubly precious as the fruit of such fellowship with the Holy One. God has so ordained it, in harmony with His holy nature, and with ours, that waiting on Him should be the honour we give Him. Let us bring Him the service gladly and truthfully; He will reward it abundantly.

"The eyes of all wait upon thee; and thou givest them their meat in due season." Dear soul, God provides in Nature for the creatures He has made. How much more will He provide in grace for those He has redeemed! Learn to say of every want, and every failure, and every lack of needful grace: I have waited too little upon God, or He would have given me in due season all I needed. And say then too –

My soul, wait thou only upon God!

Fifth Day

For Instruction

Show me thy ways, O LORD;
Teach me thy paths.
Lead me in thy truth, and teach me:
For thou art the God of my salvation;
On thee do I wait all the day.

—Psalm 25:4, 5

I spoke of an army on the point of entering an enemy's territories. Answering the question as to the cause of delay: "Waiting for supplies." The answer might also have been: "Waiting for instructions," or "Waiting for orders." If the last dispatch had not been received, with the final orders of the commander in chief, the army dared not move. Even so in the Christian life—as deep as the need of *waiting for supplies*, is that *of waiting for instructions*.

See how beautifully this comes out in Psalm 25. The writer knew and loved God's laws exceedingly, and meditated in that law day and night. But he knew that this was not enough. He knew that for the right spiritual apprehension of the truth, and for the right personal application of it to his own peculiar circumstances, he needed a direct divine teaching.

The psalm has at all times been a very peculiar one,

because of its reiterated expression of the felt need of the divine teaching, and of the childlike confidence that that teaching would be given. Study the psalm until your heart is filled with the two thoughts—the absolute need, the absolute certainty of divine guidance. And with these how entirely it is in this connection that he speaks: "On thee do I wait all the day." Waiting for guidance, waiting for instruction, all the day, is a very blessed part of waiting upon God.

The Father in Heaven is so interested in His child, and so longs to have his life at every step in His will and His love, that He is willing to keep his guidance entirely in His own hand. He knows so well that we are unable to do what is really holy and heavenly, except as He works it in us, that He means His very demands to become promises of what He will do, in watching over and leading us all the day. Not only in special difficulties and times of perplexity, but in the common course of everyday life, we may count upon Him to teach us *His* way, and show us *His* path.

And what is needed in us to receive this guidance? One thing: waiting for instructions, waiting on God. "On thee do I wait all the day." We want in our times of prayer to give clear expression to our sense of need, and our faith in His help. We want definitely to become conscious of our ignorance as to what God's way may be, and the need of the divine light shining within us, if our way is to be as of the sun, shining more and more unto the perfect day. And we want to wait quietly before God in prayer, until the deep, restful assurance fills us. It will be given—"the meek will he guide in the way."

"On thee do I wait all the day." The special surrender

to the divine guidance in our seasons of prayer must cultivate, and be followed up by, the habitual looking upward "all the day." As simple as it is, to one who has eyes, to walk all the day in the light of the sun, so simple and delightful can it become to a soul practiced in waiting on God, to walk all the day in the enjoyment of God's light and leading. What is needed to help us to such a life is just one thing—the real knowledge and faith of God as the one only source of wisdom and goodness, as ever ready, and longing much to be to us all that we can possibly require. Yes, this is the one thing we need! If we but saw our God in His love, if we but believed that He waits to be gracious, that He waits to be our life and to work all in us—how this waiting on God would become our highest joy, the natural and spontaneous response of our hearts to His great love and glory!

My soul, wait thou only upon God!

Sixth Day

For All Saints

Let none that wait on thee be ashamed.—Psalm 25:3

Let us now, in our meditation of today, each one forget himself, to think of the great company of God, saints throughout the world, who are all with us waiting on Him. And let us all join in the fervent prayer for each other: "Let none that wait on thee be ashamed."

Just think for a moment of the multitude of waiting ones who need that prayer; how many there are, sick and weary and solitary, to whom it is as if their prayers are not answered, and who sometimes begin to fear that their hope will be put to shame. And then, how many servants of God, ministers or missionaries, teachers or workers, of various name, whose hopes in their work have been disappointed, and whose longing for power and blessing remains unsatisfied. And then too, how many who have heard of a life of rest and perfect peace, of abiding light and fellowship, of strength and victory, and who cannot find the path. With all these, it is nothing but that they have not yet learned the secret of full waiting upon God. They just need, what we all need, the living assurance that waiting on God can never be in vain. Let us remember all who are in danger of fainting or being weary, and all unite in the cry, "Let none that wait on thee be ashamed!"

If this intercession for all who wait on God becomes part of our waiting on Him for ourselves, we shall help to bear each other's burdens, and so fulfil the law of Christ.

There will be introduced into our waiting on God that element of unselfishness and love, which is the path to the highest blessing and the fullest communion with God. Love to the brethren and love to God are inseparably linked. In God, the love to His Son *and to us* are one: "That the love wherewith thou hast loved me may be in them." In Christ, the love of the Father to Him, and *His love to us, are one*: "As the Father loved me, so have I loved you." In us, He asks that His love to us shall be *ours* to the brethren: "As I have loved you, that ye love one another." All the love of God, and of Christ, are inseparably linked with love to the brethren. And how can we, day by day, prove and cultivate this love otherwise than by daily praying for each other? Christ did not seek to enjoy the Father's love for Himself; He passed it all on to us. All true seeking of God, and His love for ourselves, will be inseparably linked with the thought and the love of our brethren in prayer for them.

"Let none that wait on thee be ashamed." Twice in the psalm David speaks of his waiting on God for himself; here he thinks of *all* who wait on Him. Let this page take the message to all God's tried and weary ones, that there are more praying for them than they know. Let it stir them and us in our waiting to make a point of at times forgetting ourselves, and to enlarge our hearts, and say to the Father: "*These all wait upon thee*, and thou givest them their meat in due season." Let it inspire us all with new courage—

for who is there who is not at times ready to faint and be weary? "Let none that wait on thee be ashamed" is a promise in a prayer, "They that wait on thee shall not be ashamed!" From many and many a witness the cry comes to everyone who needs the help, brother, sister, tried one, "Wait on the LORD; be of good courage, and he shall strengthen your heart; wait, I say, on the LORD. Be of good courage, and he shall strengthen your heart, all ye that wait on the LORD."

Blessed Father, we humbly beseech Thee, let none that wait on Thee be ashamed; no, not one. Some are weary, and the time of waiting appears long. And some are feeble, and scarcely know how to wait. And some are so entangled in the effort of their prayers and their work, they think that they can find no time to wait continually. Father, teach us all how to wait! Teach us to think of each other, and pray for each other. Teach us to think of Thee, the God of all waiting ones. Father, let none that wait on Thee be ashamed! For Jesus' sake. Amen.

My soul, wait thou only upon God!

Seventh Day

A Plea in Prayer

Let integrity and uprightness preserve me; for I wait on thee.—Psalm 25:21

For the third time in this psalm we have the word *wait*. As before in verse 5, "On thee do I wait all the day," so here too, the believing supplicant appeals to God to remember that he is waiting on Him, looking for an answer. It is a great thing for a soul not only to wait upon God, but to be filled with such a consciousness that its whole spirit and position is that of a waiting one, that it can, in childlike confidence, say, Lord, Thou knowest, I wait on Thee! It will prove a mighty plea in prayer, giving ever-increasing boldness of expectation to claim the promise: "They that wait on me shall not be ashamed!"

The prayer in connection with which the plea is put forth here is one of great importance in the spiritual life. If we draw nigh to God, it must be with a true heart. There must be perfect integrity, wholeheartedness in our dealing with God. As we read in the next psalm (26:1, 11): "Judge me, O LORD; for I have walked in mine integrity.... As for me, I will walk in mine integrity," there must be perfect uprightness or single-heartedness before God, as it is written: "His righteousness is for the upright in heart."

The soul must know that it allows nothing sinful, nothing doubtful; if it is indeed to meet the Holy One and receive His full blessing, it must be with a heart wholly and singly given up to His will. The whole spirit that animates us in the waiting must be, "Let integrity and uprightness"— Thou seest that I desire to come so to Thee, Thou knowest I am looking to Thee to work them perfectly in me—let them "preserve me; for I wait on thee."

And if at our first attempt truly to live the life of fully and always waiting on God, we begin to discover how much that perfect integrity is wanting, this will just be one of the blessings which the waiting was meant to work. *A soul cannot seek close fellowship with God, or attain the abiding consciousness of waiting on Him all the day, without a very honest and entire surrender to all His will.*

"For I wait on thee." It is not only in connection with the prayer of our text but with every prayer that this plea may be used. To use it often will be a great blessing to ourselves. Let us therefore study the words well until we know all their bearings. It must be clear to us *what we are waiting for.* There may be very different things. It may be waiting for God in our times of prayer to take His place as God, and to work in us the sense of His holy presence and nearness. It may be a special petition, to which we are expecting an answer. It may be our whole inner life, in which we are on the lookout for God's putting forth of His power. It may be the whole state of His Church and saints, or some part of His work, for which our eyes are ever toward Him. It is good that we sometimes count up to ourselves exactly what the things are we are waiting for, and as we say definitely to each of them, "On thee do

I wait," we shall be emboldened to claim the answer, "*For* on thee do I wait."

It must also be clear to us, *on whom we are waiting*. Not an idol, a God of whom we have made an image by our conceptions of what He is. No, but the living God, such as He really is in His great glory, His infinite holiness, His power, wisdom, and goodness, in His love and nearness. It is the presence of a beloved or a dreaded master that wakens up the whole attention of the servant who waits on him. It is *the presence of God, as He can in Christ by His Holy Spirit make Himself known*, and keep the soul under its covering and shadow, that will waken and strengthen the true waiting spirit. Let us be still and wait and worship till we know how near He is, and then say, "*On thee* do I wait."

And then, let it be very clear too that *we are waiting*. Let that become so much our consciousness that the utterance comes spontaneously, "On thee *I do wait* all the day; *I wait* on thee." This will indeed imply sacrifice and separation, a soul entirely given up to God as its all, it's only joy. This waiting on God has hardly yet been acknowledged as the only true Christianity. And yet if it be true that God alone is goodness and joy and love; if it be true that our highest blessedness is in having as much of God as we can; if it be true that Christ has redeemed us wholly for God, and made a life of continual abiding in His presence possible, nothing less ought to satisfy than to be ever breathing this blessed atmosphere, "I wait on thee."

My soul, wait thou only upon God!

Eighth Day

Strong and of Good Courage

Wait on the LORD: be strong,
And let thine heart take courage;
Yea, wait thou on the LORD.—Psalm 27:14 (Eng. Rev.)

The Psalmist had just said: "I had fainted, unless I had believed to see the goodness of the LORD in the land of the living." If it had not been for his faith in God, his heart had fainted. But in the confident assurance in God which faith gives, he urges himself and us to remember one thing above all—to wait upon God. "Wait on the LORD: be strong, and let your heart take courage: yea, wait thou on the LORD." One of the chief needs in our waiting upon God, one of the deepest secrets of its blessedness and blessing, is a quiet, confident persuasion that it is not in vain; courage to believe that God will hear and help; we are waiting on a God who never could disappoint His people.

"Be strong and of good courage." These words are frequently found in connection with some great and difficult enterprise, in prospect of the combat with the power of strong enemies, and the utter insufficiency of all human strength. Is waiting on God a work so difficult, that such words are needed: "Be strong, and let your heart take courage"? Yes, indeed. The deliverance for which we often have to wait is from enemies, in whose presence we are impotent. The blessings for which we plead are spiritual and all unseen; things impossible with men; heavenly, supernatural, divine realities. Our heart may well faint and fail. Our souls are so little accustomed to hold fellowship with God, the God on whom we wait so often *appears* to hide Himself. We who have to wait are often tempted to fear that we do not wait aright, that our faith is too feeble, that our desire is not as upright or as earnest as it should be, that our surrender is not complete. Amid all these causes of fear or doubt, how blessed to hear the voice of God: "Wait on the LORD! Be strong, and let thine heart take courage! Yea, wait thou on the LORD"! Let nothing in Heaven or earth or Hell—let nothing keep you from waiting on your God in full assurance that it cannot be in vain.

The one lesson our text teaches us is this, that when we set ourselves to wait on God we ought beforehand to resolve that it shall be with the most confident expectation of God's meeting and blessing us. We ought to make up our minds to this, that nothing was ever so sure, as that waiting on God will bring us untold and unexpected blessing. We are so accustomed to judge of God and His work in us by *what we feel*, that the great probability is that when we begin more to cultivate the waiting on Him, we shall be discouraged because we do not find any special blessing from it. The message comes to us: "Above everything, when you wait on God, do so in the spirit of abounding hopefulness. It is God in His glory, in His power, in His love, longing to bless you that you are waiting on."

If you say that you are afraid of deceiving yourself with vain hope, because you do not see or feel any warrant in your present state for such special expectations, my answer is, It is God who is the warrant for your expecting great things. Oh, do learn the lesson! You are not going to wait on yourself to see what you feel and what changes come to you. You are going to WAIT ON GOD, to know *first* WHAT HE IS, and then after that, what He will do. The whole duty and blessedness of waiting on God has its root in this, that He is such a blessed Being, full, to overflowing, of goodness and power and life and joy, that we, however wretched, cannot for any time come into contact with Him, without that life and power secretly, silently beginning to enter into us and blessing us. God is love! That is the one only and all-sufficient warrant of your expectation. Love seeketh out its own: God's love is just *His delight to impart Himself and His blessedness* to His children. Come, and however feeble you feel, just wait in His presence. As a feeble, sickly invalid is brought out into the sunshine to let its warmth go through him, come with all that is dark and cold in you *into the sunshine of God's holy, omnipotent love*, and sit and wait there, with the one thought: Here I am, in the sunshine of His love. As the sun does its work in the weak one who seeks its rays, *God will do His work in you*. Oh, do trust Him fully! "Wait on the LORD! Be strong, and let your heart take courage! Yea, wait thou on the LORD"!

My soul, wait thou only upon God!

Ninth Day

With the Heart

Be strong, and let your heart take courage, All ye that wait for [marg.] *the LORD.*—Psalm 31:24 (Eng. Rev.)

The words are nearly the same as in our last meditation. But I gladly avail myself of them again to press home a much-needed lesson for all who desire to learn truly and fully what waiting on God is. The lesson is this: It is *with the heart* we must wait upon God. "Let *your heart* take courage." All our waiting depends upon the state of the heart. As a man's heart is, so is he before God. We can advance no further or deeper into the holy place of God's presence to wait on Him there, than our heart is prepared for it by the Holy Spirit. The message is: "Let *your heart* take courage, all ye that wait on the LORD."

The truth appears so simple that some may ask, Do not all admit this? Where is the need of insisting on it so specially? Because very many Christians have no sense of the great difference between the religion of the mind and the religion of the heart, and the former is far more diligently cultivated than the latter. They know not how infinitely greater the heart is than the mind. It is in this that one of the chief causes must be sought of the feebleness of our Christian life, and it is only as this is understood that waiting on God will bring its full blessing.

A text in Proverbs (3:5) may help to make my meaning plain. Speaking of a life in the fear and favour of God, it says: "Trust in the LORD with all thine heart; and lean not unto thine own understanding." In all religion we have to use these two powers. The mind has to gather knowledge from God's Word, and prepare the food by which the heart with the inner life is to be nourished. But here comes a terrible danger of our leaning to our own understanding, and trusting in our apprehension of divine things. People imagine that if they are occupied with the truth, the spiritual life will as a matter of course be strengthened. And this is by no means the case. The understanding deals with conceptions and images of divine things, but it cannot reach the real life of the soul. Hence the command: "Trust in the LORD with all thine heart, and lean not upon thine own understanding." It is with the heart man believes, and comes into touch with God. It is in the heart God has given His Spirit, to be there to us the presence and the power of God working in us. In all our religion it is the heart that must trust and love and worship and obey. My mind is utterly impotent in creating or maintaining the spiritual life within me. The heart must wait on God for Him to work it in me.

It is in this even as in the physical life. My reason may tell me what to eat and drink, and how the food nourishes me. But in the eating and feeding my reason can do nothing—the body has its organs for that special purpose. Just so, reason may tell me what God's Word says, but it can do nothing to the feeding of the soul on the bread of life—this the heart alone can do by its faith and trust in God. A man may be studying the nature and effects of food or sleep; when he wants to eat or sleep he sets aside his thoughts and study, and uses the power of eating or sleeping. And so the Christian needs ever, when he has studied or heard God's Word, to cease from his thoughts, to put no trust in them, and to waken up his heart to open itself before God, and seek the living fellowship with Him.

This is now the blessedness of waiting upon God, that I confess the impotence of all my thoughts and efforts, and set myself still to bow my heart before Him in holy silence, and to trust Him to renew and strengthen His own work in me. And this is just the lesson of our text: "Let *your heart* take courage, all ye that wait on the LORD." Remember the difference between knowing with the mind and believing with the heart. Beware of the temptation of leaning upon your understanding, with its clear strong thoughts. They only help you to know what the heart must get from God—in themselves they are only images and shadows. "Let *your heart* take courage, all ye that wait on the LORD." Present it before Him as that wonderful part of your spiritual nature in which God reveals Himself, and by which you can know Him. Cultivate the greatest confidence that though you cannot see into your heart, God is working there by His Holy Spirit. Let the heart wait at times in perfect silence and quiet; in its hidden depths God will work. Be sure of this, and just wait on Him. Give your whole heart, with its secret workings, into God's hands continually. He wants the heart, and takes it, and as God dwells in it. "Be strong, and let your heart take courage, all ye that wait on the LORD."

My soul, wait thou only upon God!

Tenth Day

In Humble Fear and Hope

Behold, the eye of the LORD is upon them that fear him,
Upon them that hope in his mercy;
To deliver their soul from death,
And to keep them alive in famine.
Our soul hath waited for the LORD:
He is our help and our shield.
For our heart shall rejoice in him,
Because we have trusted in his holy name.
Let thy mercy, O LORD, be upon us,
According as we wait for [marg.] *thee.*

—Psalm 33:18–22 (Eng. Rev.)

God's eye is upon His people; their eye is upon Him. In waiting upon God, our eye, looking up to Him, meets His looking down upon us. This is the blessedness of waiting upon God, that it takes our eyes and thoughts away from ourselves, even our needs and desires, and occupies us with our God. We worship Him in His glory and love, with His all-seeing eye watching over us, that He may supply our every need. Let us consider this wonderful meeting between God and His people, and mark well what we are taught here of them on whom God's eye rests, and of Him on whom our eye rests.

"The eye of the LORD is on them that *fear* him, on them that *hope* in his mercy." Fear and hope are generally thought to be in conflict with each other. In the presence and worship of God they are found side by side in perfect and beautiful harmony. And this because in God Himself all apparent contradictions are reconciled. Righteousness and peace, judgment and mercy, holiness and love, infinite power and infinite gentleness, a majesty that is exalted above all Heaven, and a condescension that bows very low, meet and kiss each other. There is indeed a fear that has torment, that is cast out entirely by perfect love. But there is a fear that is found in the very heavens. In the song of Moses and the Lamb they sing: "Who shall not fear thee, O LORD, and glorify thy name?" And out of the very throne the voice came: "Praise our God, all ye his servants, and ye that fear him." Let us in our waiting ever seek "to fear the glorious and fearful name, the LORD thy God." The deeper we bow before His holiness in holy fear and adoring awe, in deep reverence and humble self-abasement, even as the angels veil their faces before the throne, the more will His holiness rest upon us, and the soul be filled to have God reveal Himself; the deeper we enter into the truth "that no flesh glory in his presence," will it be given us to see His glory. "The eye of the LORD is on them that fear him."

"On them that hope in his mercy." So far will the true fear of God be from keeping us back from hope, it will stimulate and strengthen it. The lower we bow, the deeper we feel we have nothing to hope in but His mercy. The lower we bow, the nearer God will come, and make our hearts bold to trust Him. Let every exercise of waiting, let our whole habit of waiting on God, be pervaded by abounding hope—a hope as bright and boundless as God's mercy. The fatherly kindness of God is such that, in whatever state we come to Him, we may confidently hope in His mercy.

Such are God's waiting ones. And now, think of the God on whom we wait. "The eye of the LORD is on them that fear him, on them that hope in his mercy; to deliver their soul from death, and to keep them alive in famine." Not to prevent the danger of death and famine—this is often needed to stir up to wait on Him—but to deliver and keep alive. For the dangers are often very real and dark; the situation, whether in the temporal or spiritual life, may appear to be utterly hopeless. There is always one hope: *God's eye is on them.*

That eye sees the danger, and sees in tender love His trembling waiting child, and sees the moment when the heart is ripe for the blessing, and sees the way in which it is to come. This living, mighty God, oh, let us fear Him and hope in His mercy! And let us humbly but boldly say: "Our soul waiteth for the LORD; he is our help and our shield. Let thy mercy be upon us, O LORD, according as we wait for thee."

Oh, the blessedness of waiting on such a God! A very present help in every time of trouble; a shield and defense against every danger. Children of God, will you not learn to sink down in entire helplessness and impotence and in stillness to wait and see the salvation of God? In the utmost spiritual famine, and when death appears to prevail, oh, wait on God! He does deliver, He does keep alive. Say it not only in solitude, but say it to each other—the psalm speaks not of one but of God's people—"*Our* soul waiteth on the LORD: He is *our* help and *our* shield." Strengthen and encourage each other in the holy exercise of waiting, that each may not only say of himself, but of his brethren, "*We* have waited for him; *we* will be glad and rejoice in his salvation."

My soul, wait thou only upon God!

Eleventh Day

Patiently

Rest in the LORD, and wait patiently for him.... Those that wait upon the LORD, they shall inherit the land.
—Psalm 37:7, 9 (Eng. Rev.)

In patience possess your souls." "Ye have need of patience." "Let patience have its perfect work, that ye may be perfect and entire." Such words of the Holy Spirit show us what an important element in the Christian life and character patience is. And nowhere is there a better place for cultivating or displaying it than in waiting on God. There we discover how impatient we are, and what our impatience means. We confess at times that we are impatient with men and circumstances that hinder us, or with ourselves and our slow progress in the Christian life. If we truly set ourselves to wait upon God, we shall find that it is with Him we are impatient, because He does not at once, or as soon as we could wish, do our bidding. It is in waiting upon God that our eyes are opened to believe in His wise and sovereign will, and to see that the sooner and the more completely we yield absolutely to it, the more surely His blessing can come to us.

"It is not of him that willeth, nor of him that runneth, but of God that showeth mercy." We have as little power to increase or strengthen our spiritual life, as we had to originate it. We "were born not of the will of the flesh, nor of the will of man, but of the will of God." Even so, our willing and running, our desire and effort, avail nought; all is "of God that showeth mercy." All the exercises of the spiritual life, our reading and praying, our willing and doing, have their very great value. But they can go no farther than this, that they point the way and prepare us in humility to look to and depend alone upon God Himself, and in patience to wait His good time and mercy. The waiting is to teach us our absolute dependence upon God's mighty working, and to make us in perfect patience place ourselves at His disposal. They that wait on the Lord shall inherit the land; the promised land and its blessing. The heirs must wait; they can afford to wait.

"Rest in the LORD, and wait patiently for him." The margin gives for "Rest in the LORD," "Be silent to the LORD," or "Be still before the LORD" (A.S.V.). It is resting in the Lord, in His will, His promise, His faithfulness, and His love, that makes patience easy. And the resting in Him is nothing but being silent unto Him, still before Him. Having our thoughts and wishes, our fears and hopes, hushed into calm and quiet in that great peace of God which passes all understanding. That peace keeps the heart and mind when we are anxious for anything, because we have made our request known to Him. The rest, the silence, the stillness, and the patient waiting, all find their strength and joy in God Himself.

The need for patience, and the reasonableness, and the blessedness of patience will be opened up to the waiting soul. Our patience will be seen to be the counterpart of

God's patience. He longs far more to bless us fully than we can desire it. But as the husbandman has long patience till the fruit be ripe, so God bows Himself to our slowness and bears long with us. Let us remember this, and wait patiently. Of each promise and every answer to prayer the word is true: "I the LORD will hasten it *in its time*."

"Rest in the LORD, and wait patiently for him." Yes, *for* Him. Seek not only the help, the gift, seek Himself; wait for Him. Give God His glory by resting in Him, by trusting Him fully, by waiting patiently for Him. This patience honors Him greatly; it leaves Him, as God on the throne, to do His work; it yields self wholly into His hands. It lets God *be God*. If your waiting be for some special request, wait patiently. If your waiting be more the exercise of the spiritual life seeking to know and have more of God, wait patiently. Whether it be in the shorter specific periods of waiting, or as the continuous habit of the soul, rest in the Lord, be still before the Lord, and wait patiently. "They that wait on the LORD shall inherit the land."

My soul, wait thou only upon God!

Twelfth Day

Keeping His Ways

Wait on the Lord, and keep his way,
And he shall exalt thee to inherit the land.

—Psalm 37:34

If we desire to find a man whom we long to meet, we inquire where the places and the ways are where he is to be found. When waiting on God, we need to be very careful that we keep His ways; outside of these we never can expect to find Him. "Thou meetest him that rejoiceth and worketh righteousness; those that remember *thee in thy ways*." We may be sure that God is never and nowhere to be found but in His way. And that there, by the soul who seeks and patiently waits, He is always most surely to be found. "Wait on the Lord, and keep his way, and he shall exalt thee."

How close is the connection between the two parts of the injunction, "Wait on the Lord"—that has to do with worship and disposition—"and keep his way"—that deals with walk and work. The outer life must be in harmony with the inner; the inner must be the inspiration and the strength for the outer. It is our God who has made known His way in His Word for our conduct, and invites our confidence for His grace and help in our heart. If we do not keep His way, our waiting on Him can bring no blessing. The surrender to a full obedience to all His will is the secret of full access to all the blessings of His fellowship.

Notice how strongly this comes out in the psalm. It speaks of the evildoer who prospers in his way, and calls on the believer not to fret himself. When we see men around us prosperous and happy while they forsake God's ways, and ourselves left in difficulty or suffering, we are in danger of first fretting at what appears so strange, and then gradually yielding to seek our prosperity in their path. The psalm says: "Fret not thyself.... Trust in the LORD, and do good.... Rest in the LORD, and wait patiently for him.... Cease from anger, and forsake wrath.... Depart from evil, and do good.... The LORD... forsaketh not his saints.... The righteous shall inherit the land.... The law of his God is in his heart; none of his steps shall slide." And then follows —the word occurs for the third time in the psalm—"*Wait* on the LORD, *and keep His way*." Do what God asks you to do; God will do more than you can ask Him to do.

And let no one give way to the fear: I cannot keep His way. It is this that robs of every confidence. It is true you have not the strength yet to keep all His ways. But keep carefully those for which you have received strength already. Surrender yourself willingly and trustingly to keep all God's ways, in the strength which will come in waiting on Him. Give up your whole being to God without reserve and without doubt. He will prove Himself God to you, and work in you that which is pleasing in His sight through Jesus Christ. Keep His ways as you know them in the Word. Keep His ways, as nature teaches them, in always doing what appears right. Keep His ways as providence points them out. Keep His ways as the Holy Spirit suggests. Do not think of waiting on God while you say you are not willing to work in His path. However weak you feel, only be willing, and He who has worked to will, will work to *do* by His power.

"Wait on the LORD, and keep his way." It may be that the consciousness of shortcoming and sin makes our text look more like a hindrance than a help in waiting on God. Let it not be so. Have we not said more than once, the very starting point and groundwork of this waiting is utter and absolute impotence? Why then not come with everything evil you feel in yourself, every memory of unwillingness, unwatchfulness, unfaithfulness, and all that causes such unceasing self-condemnation? Put your power in God's omnipotence, and find in waiting on God your deliverance. Your failure has been owing to only one thing. You sought to conquer and obey in your own strength. Come and bow before God until you learn that He is the God who alone is good, and alone can work any good thing. Believe that in you, and all that nature can do, there is no true power. Be content to receive from God each moment the in-working of His mighty grace and life, and waiting on God will become the renewal of your strength to run in His ways and not be weary, to walk in His paths and never faint. "Wait on the LORD, and keep his way" will be command and promise in one.

My soul, wait thou only upon God!

Thirteenth Day

For More Than We Know

And now, Lord, what wait I for? My hope is in thee. Deliver me from all my transgressions.

—Psalm 39:7, 8

There may be times when we feel as if we knew not what we are waiting for. There may be other times when we think we do know, and when it would be good for us to realize that we do not know what to ask as we ought. God is able to do for us exceeding abundantly above what we ask or think, and we are in danger of limiting Him, when we confine our desires and prayers to our own thoughts of them. It is a great thing at times to say, as our psalm says: "And now, Lord, what wait I for?" I scarcely know or can tell; this only I can say—"My hope is in thee."

How we see this limiting of God in the case of Israel! When Moses promised them meat in the wilderness, they doubted, saying: "Can God furnish a table in the wilderness? He smote the rock that the water gushed out; can he give bread also? Can he provide flesh for his people?" If they had been asked whether God could provide streams in the desert, they would have answered, Yes. God had done it; He could do it again. But when the thought came of God doing something new, they limited

Him. Their expectation could not rise beyond their past experience, or their own thoughts of what was possible. Even so we may be limiting God by our conceptions of what He has promised or is able to do. Do let us beware of limiting the Holy One of Israel in our very prayer. Let us believe that the very promises of God we plead have a divine meaning, infinitely beyond our thoughts of them. Let us believe that His fulfillment of them can be, in a power and an abundance of grace, beyond our largest grasp of thought. And let us therefore cultivate the habit of waiting on God, not only for what we think we need, but for all His grace and power are ready to do for us.

In every true prayer there are two hearts in exercise. The one is your heart, with its little, dark, human thoughts of what you need and God can do. The other is God's great heart, with its infinite, its divine purposes of blessing. What think you? To which of these two ought the larger place to be given in your approach to Him? Undoubtedly, to the heart of God. Everything depends upon knowing and being occupied with that. But how little this is done. This is what waiting on God is meant to teach you. Just think of God's wonderful love and redemption, in the meaning these words must have to Him. Confess how little you understand what God is willing to do for you, and say each time as you pray: "And now, LORD, what wait I for?" My heart cannot say. God's heart knows and waits to give. "My hope is in thee." Wait on God to do for you more than you can ask or think.

Apply this to the prayer that follows: "Deliver me from all my transgressions." You have prayed to be delivered from temper, or pride, or self-will. It is as if it is in vain.

May it not be that you have had your own thoughts about the way or the extent of God's doing it, and have never waited on the God of glory, according to the riches of His glory, to do for you what has not entered the heart of man to conceive? Learn to worship God as the God who does wonders, who wishes to prove in you that He can do something supernatural and divine. Bow before Him, wait upon Him, until your soul realizes that you are in the hands of a divine and almighty worker. Consent but to know what and how He will work. Expect it to be something altogether godlike, something to be waited for in deep humility, and received only by His divine power. Let the, "And now, Lord, what wait I for? My hope is in thee" become the spirit of every longing and every prayer. He will in His time do His work.

Dear soul, in waiting on God you may often be weary, because you hardly know what to expect. I pray you, be of good courage—this ignorance is often one of the best signs. He is teaching you to leave all in His hands, and to wait on Him alone. "Wait on the Lord! Be strong, and let your heart take courage. Yea, wait thou on the Lord."

My soul, wait thou only upon God!

Fourteenth Day

The Way to the New Song

I waited patiently for the LORD; *and he inclined unto me, and heard my cry.... And he hath put a new song in my mouth, even praise unto our God.*

—Psalm 40:1, 3

Come and listen to the testimony of one who can speak from experience of the sure and blessed outcome of patient waiting upon God. True patience is so foreign to our self-confident nature, it is so indispensable in our waiting upon God, it is such an essential element of true faith, that we may well once again meditate on what the Word has to teach us.

The word patience is derived from the Latin word for suffering. It suggests the thought of being under the constraint of some power from which we fain would be free. At first we submit against our will. Experience teaches us that when it is vain to resist, patient endurance is our wisest course. In waiting on God it is of infinite consequence that we not only submit, because we are compelled to, but because we lovingly and joyfully consent to be in the hands of our blessed Father. Patience then becomes our highest blessedness and our highest grace. It honours God, and gives Him time to have His way with us. It is the highest expression of our faith in His goodness and faithfulness. It brings the soul perfect rest in the assurance that God is carrying on His work. It is the token of our full consent that God should deal with us in such a way and time as He thinks best. True patience is the losing of our self-will in His perfect will.

Such patience is needed for the true and full waiting on God. Such patience is the growth and fruit of our first lessons in the school of waiting. To many a one it will appear strange how difficult it is truly to wait upon God. The great stillness of soul before God that sinks into its own helplessness and waits for Him to reveal Himself; the deep humility that is afraid to let own will or own strength work aught except as God works to will and to do; the meekness that is content to be and to know nothing except as God gives His light; the entire resignation of the will that only wants to be a vessel in which His holy will can move and mold—all these elements of perfect patience are not found at once. But they will come in measure as the soul maintains its position, and ever again says: "Truly my soul waiteth upon God; from him cometh my salvation: he only is my rock and my salvation."

Have you ever noticed what proof we have that patience is a grace for which very special grace is given, in these words of Paul: *"Strengthened with all might, according to his glorious power, unto all"*—what? *"patience and long suffering with joyfulness."* Yes, we need to be strengthened with all God's might, and that according to the measure of His glorious power, if we are to wait on God in all patience. It is God revealing Himself in us as our life and strength, that will enable us with perfect patience to leave all in His hands. If any are inclined to despond, because they have not such patience, let them be of good courage. It is in the course of our feeble and very imperfect waiting that God Himself by His hidden power strengthens us and works out in us the patience of the saints, the patience of Christ Himself.

Listen to the voice of one who was deeply tried: "I waited patiently for the LORD; and he inclined unto me, and heard my cry." Hear what he passed through: "He brought me up also out of an horrible pit, out of the miry clay, and set my feet upon a rock, and established my goings. And he hath put a new song in my mouth, even praise unto our God." Patient waiting upon God brings a rich reward; the deliverance is sure; God Himself will put a new song into your mouth. O soul, be not impatient, whether it be in the exercise of prayer and worship that you find it difficult to wait, or in the delay of definite requests, or in the fulfilling of your heart's desire for the revelation of God Himself in a deeper spiritual life! Fear not, but rest in the Lord, and wait patiently for Him. And if you sometimes feel as if patience is not your gift, then remember it is God's gift, and take that prayer (2 Thess. 3:5, A.S.V.): "The Lord direct your hearts into the.... patience of Christ." Into the patience with which you are to wait on God, He Himself will guide you.

My soul, wait thou only upon God!

Fifteenth Day

For His Counsel

They soon forgot his works: they waited not for his counsel.

—Psalm 106:13

This is said of the sin of God's people in the wilderness. He had wonderfully redeemed them, and was prepared as wonderfully to supply their every need. But, when the time of need came, "they waited not for his counsel." They thought not that the Almighty God was their Leader and Provider; they asked not what His plans might be. They simply thought the thoughts of their own hearts, and tempted and provoked God by their unbelief. "They waited not for his counsel."

How this has been the sin of God's people in all ages! In the land of Canaan, in the days of Joshua, the only three failures of which we read were owing to this one sin. In going up against Ai, in making a covenant with the Gibeonites, in settling down without going up to possess the whole land, they waited not for His counsel. And so even the advanced believer is in danger from this most subtle of temptations—taking God's Word and thinking his own thoughts of them, and not waiting for His counsel. Let us take the warning and see what Israel teaches us.

And let us very specially regard it not only as a danger to which the individual is exposed, but as one against which God's people, in their collective capacity, need to be on their guard.

Our whole relation to God is ruled in this, that His will is to be done in us and by us as it is in Heaven. He has promised to make known His will to us by His Spirit, the Guide into all truth. And our position is to be that of waiting for His counsel as the only guide of our thoughts and actions. In our church worship, in our prayer meetings, in our conventions, in all our gatherings as managers, or directors, or committees, or helpers in any part of the work for God, our first object ought ever to be to ascertain the mind of God. God always works according to the counsel of His will. The more that counsel of His will is sought and found and honoured, the more surely and mightily will God do His work for us and through us.

The great danger in all such assemblies is that in our consciousness of having our Bible, and our past experience of God's leading, and our sound creed, and our honest wish to do God's will, we trust in these, and do not realize that with every step we need and may have a heavenly guidance. There may be elements of God's will, application of God's Word, experience of the close presence and leading of God, manifestations of the power of His Spirit, of which we know nothing as yet. God may be willing, nay, God is willing to open up these to the souls who are intently set upon allowing Him to have His way entirely, and who are willing in patience to wait for Him to make it known. When we come together praising God for all He has done and taught and given, we may at the same time be limiting Him by not expecting greater things. It was when God had given the water out of the rock that they did not trust Him for bread. It was when God had given Jericho into his hands that Joshua thought the victory over Ai was sure, and waited not for counsel from God. And so, while we think that we know and trust the power of God for what we may expect, we may be hindering Him by not giving time, and not definitely cultivating the habit of waiting for His counsel.

A minister has no more solemn duty than teaching people to wait upon God. Why was it that in the house of Cornelius, when "Peter spake these words, the Holy Ghost fell upon all that heard him"? They had said: "We are here *before* God to hear all things that are commanded thee *of God*." We may come together to give and to listen to the most earnest exposition of God's truth with little spiritual profit if there be no waiting for God's counsel.

And so in all our gatherings we need to believe in the Holy Spirit as the Guide and Teacher of God's saints when they wait to be led by Him into the things which God hath prepared, and which the heart cannot conceive.

More stillness of soul to realize God's presence; more consciousness of ignorance of what God's great plans may be; more faith in the certainty that God has greater things to show us; that He Himself will be revealed in new glory—these must be the marks of the assemblies of God's saints if they would avoid the reproach: "They waited not for his counsel."

My soul, wait thou only upon God!

Sixteenth Day

And His Light in the Heart

I wait for the Lord, my soul doth wait,
And in his word do I hope.
My soul waiteth for the Lord
More than they that watch for the morning:
I say, more than they that watch for the morning.
—Psalm 130:5, 6

With that intense longing the morning light is often waited for. By the mariners in a shipwrecked vessel; by a benighted traveller in a dangerous country; by an army that finds itself surrounded by an enemy. The morning light will show what hope of escape there may be. The morning may bring life and liberty. And so the saints of God in darkness have longed for the light of His countenance, more than watchmen for the morning. They have said: "More than watchmen for the morning, my soul waiteth for the Lord." Can we say that too? Our waiting on God can have no higher object than simply having His light shine on us, and in us, and through us, all the day.

God is light. God is a sun. Paul says: "God hath shined in our hearts to give the light." What light? "The light of the glory of God, in the face of Jesus Christ." Just as the sun shines its beautiful, life-giving light on and into our earth, so God shines into our hearts the light of His glory, of His love, in Christ His Son. Our heart is meant to have that light filling and gladdening it all the day. It can have it because God is our sun, and it is written, "Thy sun shall no more go down forever." God's love shines on us without ceasing.

But can we indeed enjoy it all the day? We can. And how can we? Let nature give us the answer. Those beautiful trees and flowers, with all this green grass, what do they do to keep the sun shining on them? They do nothing; they simply bask in the sunshine, when it comes. The sun is millions of miles away, but over all that distance it comes, its own light and joy; and the tiniest flower that lifts its little head upward is met by the same exuberance of light and blessing as flood the widest land-scape. We have not to care for the light we need for our day's work. The sun cares, and provides and shines the light around us all the day. We simply count upon it, and receive it, and enjoy it.

The only difference between nature and grace is this— that what the trees and the flowers do unconsciously, as they drink in the blessing of the light, is to be with us a voluntary and a loving acceptance. Faith, simple faith in God's Word and love, is to be the opening of the eyes, the opening of the heart, to receive and enjoy the unspeakable glory of His grace. And just as the trees, day by day, and month by month, stand and grow into beauty and fruit-fulness, just welcoming whatever sunshine the sun may give, so it is the very highest exercise of our Christian life just to abide in the light of God, and let it, and let Him, fill us with the life and the brightness it brings.

And if you ask, But can it really be, that just as naturally and heartily as I recognize and rejoice in the beauty of a bright sunny morning, I can rejoice in God's light all the day? It can, indeed. From my breakfast table I look out on a beautiful valley, with trees and vineyards and mountains. In our spring and autumn months the light in the morning is exquisite, and almost involuntarily we say, How beautiful! And the question comes, Is it only the light of the sun that is to bring such continual beauty and joy? And is there no provision for the light of God being just as much an unceasing source of joy and gladness? There is, indeed, if the soul will but be still and wait on Him, ONLY LET GOD SHINE.

Dear soul, learn to wait on the Lord, more than watchers for the morning! All within you may be very dark. But is that not the very best reason for waiting for the light of God? The first beginnings of light may be just enough to discover the darkness, and painfully to humble you on account of sin. Can you not trust the light to expel the darkness? Do believe it will. Just bow, even now, in stillness before God, and wait on Him to shine into you. Say, in humble faith, God is light, infinitely brighter and more beautiful than that of the sun. God is light—the Father. The eternal, inaccessible, and incomprehensible light—the Son. The light concentrated, and embodied, and manifested—the Spirit, the light entering and dwelling and shining in our hearts. God is light, and is here shining on my heart. I have been so occupied with the rushlights of my thoughts and efforts, I have never opened the shutters to let His light in. Unbelief has kept it out. I bow in faith—God, light, is shining into my heart. The God of whom Paul wrote: "God hath shined into our heart," is my God. What would I think of a sun that could not shine? What shall I think of a God who does not shine? No, God shines! God is light! I will take time, and just be still, and rest in the light of God. My eyes are feeble, and the windows are not clean, but I will wait on the Lord. The light does shine, the light will shine in me, and make me full of light. And I shall learn to walk all the day in the light and joy of God. My soul waiteth on the Lord, more than the watchers for the morning.

My soul, wait thou only upon God!

Seventeenth Day

In Times of Darkness

I will wait upon the LORD, that hideth his face from the house of Jacob, and I will look for him.

—Isaiah 8:17

Here we have a servant of God, waiting upon Him, not on behalf of himself, but of his people, from whom God was hiding His face. It suggests to us how our waiting upon God, though it commences with our personal needs, with the desire for the revelation of Himself, or of the answer to personal petitions, need not, may not, stop there. We may be walking in the full light of God's countenance, and yet God be hiding His face from His people around us; far from our being content to think that this is nothing but the just punishment of their sin, or the consequence of their indifference, we are called with tender hearts to think of their sad estate, and to wait on God on their behalf. The privilege of waiting upon God is one that brings great responsibility. Even as Christ, when He entered God's presence, at once used His place of privilege and honour as intercessor, so we, no less, if we know what it is really to enter in and wait upon God, must use our access for our less favoured brethren. "I will wait upon the LORD, who hideth his face from the house of Jacob."

You worship with a certain congregation. Possibly there is not the spiritual life or joy either in the preaching or in the fellowship that you could desire. You belong to a church with its many services. There is so much of error or worldliness, of seeking after human wisdom and culture, or trust in ordinances and observances, that you do not wonder that God hides His face in many cases, and that there is but little power for conversion or true edification. Then there are branches of Christian work with which you are connected—a Sunday school, a Gospel hall, a young men's association, a mission work abroad—in which the feebleness of the Spirit's working appears to indicate that God is hiding His face. You think too, you know the reason. There is too much trust in men and money; there is too much formality and self-indulgence; there is too little faith and prayer; too little love and humility; too little of the spirit of the crucified Jesus. At times you feel as if things are hopeless; nothing will help.

Do believe that God can help and will help. Let the spirit of the prophet come into you, as you value his words, and set yourself to wait on God, on behalf of His erring children. Instead of the tone of judgment or condemnation, of despondency or despair, realize your calling to wait upon God. If others fail in doing it, give yourself doubly to it. The deeper the darkness, the greater the need of appealing to the one only Deliverer. The greater the self-confidence around you, that knows not that it is poor and wretched and blind, the more urgent the call on you who profess to see the evil and to have access to Him who alone can help, to be at your post waiting upon God. Say on each new occasion, when you are tempted to speak or to sigh: "I will wait on the LORD, who hideth his face from the house of Jacob."

There is a still larger circle—the Christian Church throughout the world. Think of Greek, Roman Catholic, and Protestant churches, and the state of the millions that belong to them. Or think only of the Protestant churches with their open Bible and orthodox creeds. How much nominal profession and formality! How much of the rule of the flesh and of man in the very temple of God! And what abundant proof that God does hide His face!

What are those who see and mourn this to do? The first thing to be done is this: "I will wait on the LORD, who hideth his face from the house of Jacob." Let us wait on God, in the humble confession of the sins of His people. Let us take time and wait on Him in this exercise. Let us wait on God in tender, loving intercession for all saints, our beloved brethren, however wrong their lives or their teaching may appear. Let us wait on God in faith and expectation, until He shows us that He will hear. Let us wait on God, with the simple offering of ourselves to Himself, and the earnest prayer that He would send us to our brethren. Let us wait on God, and give Him no rest till He make Zion a joy in the earth. Yes, let us rest in the Lord, and wait patiently for Him who now hides His face from so many of His children. And let us say of the lifting up of the light of His countenance we long for for all His people, "I wait for the LORD, my soul doth wait, and my hope is in his word. My soul waiteth for the LORD, more than the watchers for the morning, the watchers for the morning."

My soul, wait thou only upon God!

Eighteenth Day

To Reveal Himself

And it shall be said in that day, Lo, this is our God; we have waited for him, and he will save us: this is the LORD; we have waited for him, we will be glad and rejoice in his salvation.

—Isaiah 25:9

In this passage we have two precious thoughts. The one, that it is the language of God's people who have been unitedly waiting on Him. The other, that the fruit of their waiting has been that God has so revealed Himself, that they could joyfully say: "Lo, this is our God.... this is the LORD." The power and the blessing of united waiting is what we need to learn.

Note the twice repeated, "We have waited for him." In some time of trouble the hearts of the people had been drawn together, and they had, ceasing from all human hope or help, with one heart set themselves to wait for their God. Is not this just what we need in our churches and conventions and prayer meetings? Is not the need of the Church and the world great enough to demand it? Are there not in the Church of Christ evils to which no human wisdom is equal? Have we not ritualism and rationalism, formalism and worldliness, robbing the Church of its

power? Have we not culture and money and pleasure threat-
ening its spiritual life? Are not the powers of the Church
utterly inadequate to cope with the powers of infidelity
and iniquity and wretchedness in Christian countries and
in heathendom? And is there not in the promise of God,
and in the power of the Holy Spirit, a provision made
that can meet the need, and give the Church the restful
assurance that she is doing all her God expects of her?
And would not united waiting upon God for the supply of
His Spirit most certainly seem the needed blessing? We
cannot doubt it.

The object of a more definite waiting upon God in our
gatherings would be very much the same as in personal
worship. It would mean a deeper conviction that God must
and will do all; a humbler and abiding entrance into our
deep helplessness, and the need of entire and unceasing
dependence upon Him; a more living consciousness that
the essential thing is to give God His place of honour
and of power; a confident expectation that to those who
wait on Him, God will, by His Spirit, give the secret of
His acceptance and presence, and then, in due time, the
revelation of His saving power. The great aim would be
to bring everyone in a praying and worshiping company
under a deep sense of God's presence, so that when they
part there will be the consciousness of having met God
Himself, of having left every request with Him, and of now
waiting in stillness while He works out His salvation.

It is this experience that is indicated in our text. The
fulfillment of the words may, at times, be in such striking
interpositions of God's power that all can join in the cry:
"Lo, this is our God... this is the LORD!" They may equally

become true in spiritual experience, when God's people in their waiting times become so conscious of His presence that in holy awe souls feel: "Lo, this is our God.... this is the LORD!" It is this, alas, that is too much missed in our meetings for worship. The godly minister has no more difficult, no more solemn, no more blessed task, than to lead his people out to meet God, and, before he preaches, to bring each one into contact with Him. "We are now here in the presence of God"—these words of Cornelius show the way in which Peter's audience was prepared for the coming of the Holy Spirit. Waiting before God, and waiting for God, and waiting on God, are the one condition of God showing His presence.

A company of believers gathered with the one purpose, helping each other by little intervals of silence, to wait on God alone, opening the heart for whatever God may have of new discoveries of evil, of His will, of new openings in work or methods of work, would soon have reason to say: "Lo, this is our God; we have waited for him, and he will save us: this is the LORD; we have waited for him, we will be glad and rejoice in his salvation."

My soul, wait thou only upon God!

Nineteenth Day

As a God of Judgment

Yea, in the way of thy judgments, O LORD, have we waited for thee... for when thy judgments are in the earth, the inhabitants of the world will learn righteousness.

—Isaiah 26:8, 9

The LORD is a God of judgment: blessed are all they that wait for him.

—Isaiah 30:18

God is a God of mercy and a God of Judgment. Mercy and judgment are ever together in His dealings. In the Flood, in the deliverance of Israel out of Egypt, in the overthrow of the Canaanites, we ever see mercy in the midst of judgment. In these, the inner circle of His own people, we see it too. The judgment punishes the sin, while mercy saves the sinner. Or, rather, mercy saves the sinner, not in spite of, but by means of, the very judgment that came upon his sin. In waiting on God, we must beware of forgetting this—as we wait we must expect Him as a God of Judgment.

"In the way of thy judgments, O LORD, have we waited for thee." That will prove true in our inner experience. If we are honest in our longing for holiness, in our prayer to be wholly the Lord's, His holy presence will stir up and discover hidden sin, and bring us very low in the bitter conviction of the evil of our nature, its opposition to God's law, its impotence to fulfil that law. The words will come true: "Who may abide the day of his coming, for he is like a refiner's fire." "O that thou wouldest come down, as when the melting fire burneth!" In great mercy God executes, within the soul, His judgments upon sin, as He makes it feel its wickedness and guilt. Many a one tries to flee from these judgments. The soul that longs for God, and for deliverance from sin, bows under them in humility and in hope. In silence of soul it says: "Arise, O LORD! and let thine enemies be scattered. In the way of thy judgments we have waited for thee."

Let no one, who seeks to learn the blessed art of waiting on God, wonder if at first the attempt to wait on Him only discovers more of his sin and darkness. Let no one despair because unconquered sins, or evil thoughts, or great darkness appear to hide God's face. Was not, in His own beloved Son, the gift and bearer of His mercy on Calvary, the mercy as hidden and lost in the judgment? Oh, submit and sink down deep under the judgment of your every sin. Judgment prepares the way, and breaks out in wonderful mercy. It is written: "Thou shalt be redeemed with judgment." Wait on God, in the faith that His tender mercy is working out His redemption in the midst of judgment. Wait for Him, He will be gracious to you.

There is another application still, one of unspeakable solemnity. We are expecting God, in the way of His judgments, to visit this earth: we are waiting for Him. What a thought! We know of these coming judgments;

we know that there are tens of thousands of professing Christians who live on in carelessness, and who, if no change come, must perish under God's hand. Oh, shall we not do our utmost to warn them, to plead with and for them, if God may have mercy on them! If we feel our want of boldness, want of zeal, want of power, shall we not begin to wait on God more definitely and persistently as a God of judgment, asking Him so to reveal Himself in the judgments that are coming on our very friends, that we may be inspired with a new fear of Him and them, and constrained to speak and pray as never yet. Verily, waiting on God is not meant to be a spiritual self-indulgence. Its object is to let God and His holiness, Christ and the love that died on Calvary, the Spirit and fire that burns in Heaven and came to earth, get possession of us, to warn and rouse men with the message that we are waiting for God in the way of His judgments. O Christian, prove that you really believe in the God of judgment!

My soul, wait thou only upon God!

Twentieth Day

Who Waits On Us

And therefore will the LORD wait, that he may be gracious unto you, and therefore will he be exalted, that he may have mercy upon you: for the LORD is a God of judgment: blessed are all they that wait for him.
—Isaiah 30:18

We must not only think of our waiting upon God, but also of what is more wonderful still, of God's waiting upon us. The vision of Him waiting on us will give new impulse and inspiration to our waiting upon Him. It will give an unspeakable confidence that our waiting cannot be in vain. If He waits for us, then we may be sure that we are more than welcome; that He rejoices to find those He has been seeking for. Let us seek even now, at this moment, in the spirit of lowly waiting on God, to find out something of what it means. "Therefore will the LORD wait, that he may be gracious unto you." We shall accept and echo back the message: "Blessed *are all they* that wait for him."

Look up and see the great God upon His throne. He is Love—an unceasing and inexpressible desire to communicate His own goodness and blessedness to all His creatures. He longs and delights to bless. He has inconceivably glorious purposes concerning every one of His children, by the power of His Holy Spirit, to reveal in them His love and power. He waits with all the longings of a father's heart. He waits that He may be gracious unto you. And each time you come to wait upon Him, or seek to maintain in daily life the holy habit of waiting, you may look up and see Him ready to meet you, waiting that He may be gracious unto you. Yes, connect every exercise, every breath of the life of waiting, with faith's vision of your God waiting for you.

And if you ask, How is it, if He waits to be gracious, that even after I come and wait upon Him, He does not give the help I seek, but waits on longer and longer? There is a double answer. The one is this. God is a wise husbandman, "who waiteth for the precious fruit of the earth, and hath long patience for it." He cannot gather the fruit till it is ripe. He knows when we are spiritually ready to receive the blessing to our profit and His glory. Waiting in the sunshine of His love is what will ripen the soul for His blessing. Waiting under the cloud of trial, that breaks in showers of blessing, is as needful. Be assured that if God waits longer than you could wish, it is only to make the blessing doubly precious. God waited four thousand years, till the fulness of time, ere He sent His Son; our times are in His hands; He will avenge His elect speedily; He will make haste for our help, and not delay one hour too long.

The other answer points to what has been said before. The giver is more than the gift; God is more than the blessing; and our being kept waiting on Him is the only way for our learning to find our life and joy *in Himself*.

Oh, if God's children only knew what a glorious God they have, and what a privilege it is to be linked in fellowship with Himself, then they would rejoice in Him! Even when He keeps them waiting they would learn to understand better than ever. "Therefore will the LORD wait, that he may be gracious unto you." His waiting will be the highest proof of His graciousness.

"Blessed are all they that wait for him." A queen has her ladies-in-waiting. The position is one of subordination and service, and yet it is considered one of the highest dignity and privilege, because a wise and gracious sovereign makes them companions and friends. What a dignity and blessedness to be attendants-in-waiting on the everlasting God, ever on the watch for every indication of His will or favour, ever conscious of His nearness, His goodness, and His grace! "The LORD is good to them that wait for him." "Blessed are all they that wait for him." Yes, it is blessed when a waiting soul and a waiting God meet each other. God cannot do His work without His and our waiting His time; let waiting be our work, as it is His. And if His waiting be nothing but goodness and graciousness, let ours be nothing but a rejoicing in that goodness, and a confident expectancy of that grace. And let every thought of waiting become to us simply the expression of unmingled and unutterable blessedness, because it brings us to a God who waits that He may make Himself known to us perfectly as the gracious One.

My soul, wait thou only upon God!

Twenty-first Day

The Almighty One

They that wait on the LORD shall renew their strength; they shall mount up with wings as eagles; they shall run, and not be weary; and they shall walk, and not faint.

—Isaiah 40:31

Waiting always partakes of the character of our thoughts of the one on whom we wait. Our waiting on God will depend greatly on our faith of what He is. In our text we have the close of a passage in which God reveals Himself as the everlasting and Almighty One. It is as that revelation enters our soul that the waiting will become the spontaneous expression of what we know Him to be—a God altogether most worthy to be waited upon.

Listen to the words: "Why sayest thou, Jacob, my way is hid from the LORD?" Why speakest thou as if God doth not hear or help?

"Hast thou not known, hast thou not heard, that the Everlasting One, the LORD, the Creator of the ends of the earth, *fainteth not, neither is weary?*" So far from it: "He giveth power to the faint, and to them that have no might he increaseth strength. Even the youths"—"the glory of young men is their strength"—"even the youths shall faint, and the young men shall utterly fall": all that is accounted strong with man shall come to nought. "*But* they that wait on the LORD," on the Everlasting One, who fainteth not, neither is weary, they "shall renew their strength; they shall mount up with wings as eagles; they shall run, and"—listen now, they shall be strong with the strength of God, even as He *shall "not be weary*; and they shall walk, and," even as He, "*not faint.*"

Yes, "they shall mount up with wings as eagles." You know what eagles' wings mean. The eagle is the king of birds, it soars the highest into the Heavens. Believers are to live a heavenly life, in the very presence and love and joy of God. They are to live where God lives; they need God's strength to rise there. To them that wait on Him it shall be given.

You know how the eagles' wings are obtained. Only in one way—by the eagle birth. You are born of God. You *have* the eagles' wings. You may not have known it; you may not have used them; but God can and will teach you to use them.

You know how the eagles are taught the use of their wings. See yonder cliff rising a thousand feet out of the sea. See high up a ledge on the rock, where there is an eagle's nest with its treasure of two young eaglets. See the mother bird come and stir up her nest, and with her beak push the timid birds over the precipice. See how they flutter and fall and sink toward the depth. See now how she "fluttereth over her young, spreadeth abroad her wings, taketh them, beareth them on her wings" (Deut. 32: 11), and so, as they ride upon her wings, brings them to a place of safety. And so she does once and again, each time casting them out over the precipice, and then again taking and carrying them. "So the LORD alone did lead him." Yes, the instinct of that eagle mother was God's gift, a single ray of that love in which the Almighty trains His people to mount as on eagles' wings.

He stirs up your nest. He disappoints your hopes. He brings down your confidence. He makes you fear and tremble, as all your strength fails, and you feel utterly weary and helpless. And all the while He is spreading His strong wings for you to rest your weakness on, and offering His everlasting Creator-strength to work in you. And all He asks is that you should sink down in your weariness and *wait on Him*; and allow Him in His Jehovah strength to carry as you ride upon the wings of His omnipotence.

Dear child of God, I pray you, lift up your eyes, and *behold your God!* Listen to Him who says that He "fainteth not, neither is weary," who promises that you too shall not faint or be weary, who asks nought but this one thing, that you should *wait on Him*. And let your answer be, With such a God, so mighty, so faithful, so tender,

My soul, wait thou only upon God!

Twenty-second Day

Its Certainty of Blessing

Thou shalt know that I am the LORD: for they shall not be ashamed that wait for me.

—Isaiah 49:23

Blessed are all they that wait for him.

—Isaiah 30:18

What promises! How God seeks to draw us to waiting on Him by the most positive assurance that it never can be in vain: "They shall not be ashamed that wait for me." How strange that, though we should so often have experienced it, we are yet so slow of learning that this blessed waiting must and can be as the very breath of our life, a continuous resting in God's presence and His love, an unceasing yielding of ourselves for Him to perfect His work in us. Let us once again listen and meditate, until our heart says with new conviction: *"Blessed are they* that wait for him!" In our sixth day's lesson we found in the prayer of Psalm 25: "Let none that wait on thee be ashamed." The very prayer shows how we fear lest it might be. Let us listen to God's answer, until every fear is banished, and we send back to Heaven the words God speaks, Yea, Lord, we believe what Thou sayest: *"All they* that wait for me shall *not* be ashamed." "Blessed are *all they* that wait for him."

The context of each of these two passages points us to times when God's Church was in great straits, and to human eye there were no possibilities of deliverance. But God interposes with His word of promise, and pledges His almighty power for the deliverance of His people. And it is as the God who has Himself undertaken the work of their redemption that He invites them to wait on Him, and assures them that disappointment is impossible. We too are living in days in which there is much in the state of the Church, with its profession and its formalism that is indescribably sad. Amid all we praise God for, there is, alas, much to mourn over! Were it not for God's promises we might well despair. But in His promises the living God has given, and bound Himself to us. He calls us to wait on Him. He assures us we shall not be put to shame. Oh, that our hearts might learn to wait before Him, until He Himself reveals to us what His promises mean, and in the promises reveals Himself in His hidden glory! We shall be irresistibly drawn to wait on Him alone. God increase the company of those who say: "Our soul waiteth for the LORD: he is our help and our shield."

This waiting upon God on behalf of His Church and people will depend greatly upon the place that waiting on Him has taken in our personal life. The mind may often have beautiful visions of what God has promised to do, and the lips may speak of them in stirring words, but these are not really the measure of our faith or power. No; it is what we really know of God in our personal experience, conquering the enemies within, reigning and ruling, revealing Himself in His holiness and power in our inmost being. It is this that will be the real measure of the spiritual blessing we expect from Him, and bring to our fellow men. It is as we know how blessed the waiting on God has become to our own souls, that we shall confidently hope in the blessing to come on the Church around us, and the keyword of all our expectations will be, He hath said: "All they that wait on me shall not be ashamed." From what He has done in us, we shall trust Him to do mighty things around us. "Blessed are all they that wait for him." Yes, blessed even now in the waiting. The promised blessings for ourselves, or for others, may tarry; the unutterable blessedness of knowing and having Him who has promised, the divine Blesser, the living Fountain of the coming blessings, is even now ours. Do let this truth get full possession of your souls, that waiting on God is itself the highest privilege of the creature, the highest blessedness of His redeemed child.

Even as the sunshine enters with its light and warmth, with its beauty and blessing, into every little blade of grass that rises upward out of the cold earth, so the everlasting God meets, in the greatness and the tenderness of His love, each waiting child, to shine in his heart "the light of the knowledge of the glory of God in the face of Jesus Christ." Read these words again, until your heart learns to know what God waits to do to you. Who can measure the difference between the great sun and that little blade of grass? And yet the grass has all of the sun it can need or hold. Do believe that in waiting on God, His greatness and your littleness suit and meet each other most wonderfully. Just bow in emptiness and poverty and utter impotence, in humility and meekness, and surrender to His will before

His great glory, and be still. As you wait on Him, God draws nigh. He will reveal Himself as the God who will fulfil mightily His every promise. And let your heart ever again take up the song: "Blessed are all they that wait for him."

My soul, wait thou only upon God!

Twenty-third Day

For Unlooked-for Things

For since the beginning of the world men have not heard, nor perceived by the ear, neither hath the eye seen, O God, beside thee, what he hath prepared for him that waiteth for him.

—Isaiah 64:4

The American Standard Version has: *"Neither hath the eye seen a God besides thee, who worketh for him that waiteth for him."* In the Authorized Version the thought is, that no eye hath seen *the thing* which God hath prepared. In the A.S.V. no eye hath seen a God, besides our God, who worketh for him that waiteth for Him. To both the two thoughts are common: that our place is to wait upon God, and that there will be revealed to us what the human heart cannot conceive—the difference is: in the A.S.V. it is *the God* who works, in the A.V. *the thing* He is to work. In 1 Corinthians 2:9 the citation is in regard to the things which the Holy Spirit is to reveal, as in the A.V., and in this meditation we keep to that.

The previous verses, specially from chapter 63:15, refer to the low state of God's people. The prayer has been poured out, "Look down from heaven" (v. 15). "Why hast thou hardened our heart from thy fear? Return for thy servants' sake" (v. 17). And 64:1, still more urgent, "Oh that thou wouldest rend the heavens, that thou wouldest come down... as when the melting fire burneth... to make thy name known to thy adversaries!" Then follows the plea from the past: "When thou didst terrible things which we looked not for, thou camest down, the mountains flowed down at thy presence." "For"—this is now the faith that has been awakened by the thought of things we looked not for, He is still the same God "neither hath the eye seen, O God, beside thee, what he hath prepared for him that waiteth for him." God alone knows what He can do for His waiting people. As Paul expounds and applies it: "The things of God knoweth no man, save the Spirit of God." "But God hath revealed them to us by his Spirit."

The need of God's people, and the call for God's interposition, is as urgent in our days as it was in the time of Isaiah. There is now, as there was then, as there has been at all times, a remnant that seek after God with their whole heart. But if we look at Christendom as a whole, at the state of the Church of Christ, there is infinite cause for beseeching God to rend the Heavens and come down. Nothing but a special interposition of almighty power will avail. I fear we have no right conception of what the so-called Christian world is in the sight of God. Unless God comes down "as when the melting fire burneth... to make known his name to his adversaries," our labours are comparatively fruitless. Look at the ministry—how much it is in the wisdom of man and of literary culture—how little in demonstration of the Spirit and of power. Think of the unity of the body—how little there is of the manifestation of the power of a heavenly love binding God's children into one. Think of holiness the holiness of Christ like humility and crucifixion to the world—how little the world sees that they have men among them who live in Christ in Heaven, in whom Christ and Heaven live.

What is to be done? There is but one thing. We must wait upon God. And what for? We must cry, with a cry that never rests, "Oh that thou wouldest rend the heavens ... come down, that the mountains might flow down at thy presence." We must desire and believe, we must ask and expect, that God will do unlooked-for things. We must set our faith on a God of whom men do not know what he has prepared for them that wait for Him. The wonder-doing God, who can surpass all our expectations, must be the God of our confidence.

Yes, let God's people enlarge their hearts to wait on a God able to do exceeding abundantly above what we can ask or think. Let us band ourselves together as His elect who cry day and night to Him for things men have not seen. He is able to arise and to make His people a name, and a praise in the earth. "He will wait, that he may be gracious unto you; blessed are all they that wait for him."

My soul, wait thou only upon God!

Twenty-fourth Day

To Know His Goodness

The Lord is good unto them that wait for him.
—Lamentations 3:25

There are none good but God." "His goodness is in the heavens." "Oh how great is thy goodness, which thou hast laid up for them that fear thee!" "O taste and see that the Lord is good!" And here is now the true way of entering into and rejoicing in this goodness of God—waiting upon Him. The Lord is good—even His children often do not know it, for they wait not in quietness for Him to reveal it. But to those who persevere in waiting, whose souls do wait, it will come true. One might think that it is just those who have to wait who might doubt it. But this is only when they do not wait, but grow impatient. The truly waiting ones will all have to say: "The Lord is good unto them that wait for him." Would you fully know the goodness of God, give yourself more than ever to a life of waiting on Him.

At our first entrance into the school of waiting upon God, the heart is chiefly set upon the blessings which we wait for. God graciously uses our need and desire for help to educate us for something higher than we were thinking of. We were seeking gifts; He, the Giver, longs to give Himself and to satisfy the soul with His goodness. It is just for this reason that He often withholds the gifts, and that the time of waiting is made so long. He is all the time seeking to win the heart of His child for Himself. He wishes that we should not only say, when He bestows the gift, How good is God! but that long ere it comes, and even if it never comes, we should all the time be experiencing: *It is good* that a man should quietly wait: "The LORD *is good* to them that wait for him."

What a blessed life the life of waiting then becomes, the continual worship of faith, adoring and trusting His goodness. As the soul learns its secret, every act or exercise of waiting just becomes a quiet entering into the goodness of God, to let it do its blessed work and satisfy our every need. And every experience of God's goodness gives the work of waiting new attractiveness, and instead of only taking refuge in time of need, there comes a great longing to wait continually and all the day. And however duties and engagements occupy the time and the mind, the soul gets more familiar with the secret art of always waiting. Waiting becomes the habit and disposition, the very second nature and breath of the soul.

Dear Christian, do you not begin to see that waiting is not one among a number of Christian virtues, to be thought of from time to time, but that it expresses that disposition which lies at the very root of the Christian life? It gives a higher value and a new power to our prayer and worship, to our faith and surrender, because it links us, in unalterable dependence, to God Himself. And it gives us the unbroken enjoyment of the goodness of God: "The

LORD is good unto them that wait for him."

Let me press upon you once again to take time and trouble to cultivate this much needed element of the Christian life. We get too much of religion at second hand from the teaching of men. That teaching has great value, even as the preaching of John the Baptist sent his disciples away from himself to the living Christ, if it leads us to God Himself. What our religion needs is—*more of God*. Many of us are too much occupied with our work. As with Martha, the very service we want to render the Master separates from Him; it is neither pleasing to Him nor profitable to ourselves. The more work, the more need of waiting upon God; the doing of God's will would then, instead of exhausting, be our meat and drink, nourishment and refreshment and strength. "The LORD is good unto them that wait for him." How good none can tell but those who prove it in waiting on Him. How good none can fully tell but those who have proved Him to the utmost.

My soul, wait thou only upon God!

Twenty-fifth Day

Quietly

It is good that a man should both hope and quietly wait for the salvation of the LORD.

—Lamentations 3:26

Take heed and be quiet: fear not, neither be faint-hearted." "In quietness and in confidence shall be your strength." Such words reveal to us the close connection between quietness and faith, and show us what a deep need there is of quietness, as an element of true waiting upon God. If we are to have our whole heart turned toward God, we must have it turned away from the creature, from all that occupies and interests, whether of joy or sorrow.

God is a being of such infinite greatness and glory, and our nature has become so estranged from Him, that it needs our whole heart and desires set upon Him, even in some little measure to know and receive Him. Everything that is not God, that excites our fears, or stirs our efforts, or awakens our hopes, or makes us glad, hinders us in our perfect waiting on Him. The message is one of deep meaning: "Take heed and be quiet"; "In quietness shall be your strength"; "It is good that a man should quietly wait."

How the very thought of God in His majesty and

holiness should silence us, Scripture abundantly testifies.

"The LORD is in his holy temple: let all the earth keep silence before him" (Hab. 2:20).

"Hold thy peace at the presence of the LORD God" (Zeph. 1:7).

"Be silent, O all flesh, before the LORD: for he is raised up out of his holy habitation" (Zech. 2:13).

As long as the waiting on God is chiefly regarded as an end toward more effectual prayer, and the obtaining of our petitions, this spirit of perfect quietness will not be obtained. But when it is seen that the waiting on God is itself an unspeakable blessedness, one of the highest forms of fellowship with the Holy One, the adoration of Him in His glory will of necessity humble the soul into a holy stillness, making way for God to speak and reveal Himself. Then it comes to the fulfillment of the precious promise, that all of self and self-effort shall be humbled: "The haughtiness of man shall be brought down, and the LORD alone shall be exalted in that day."

Let everyone who would learn the art of waiting on God remember the lesson: "Take heed, and be quiet"; "It is good that a man quietly wait." Take time to be separate from all friends and all duties, all cares and all joys; time to be still and quiet before God. Take time not only to secure stillness from man and the world, but from self and its energy. Let the Word and prayer be very precious; but remember, even these may hinder the quiet waiting. The activity of the mind in studying the Word, or giving expression to its thoughts in prayer, the activities of the heart, with its desires and hopes and fears, may so engage us that we do not come to the still waiting on the All-

Glorious One; our whole being is prostrate in silence before Him. Though at first it may appear difficult to know how thus quietly to wait, with the activities of mind and heart for a time subdued, every effort after it will be rewarded. We shall find that it grows upon us, and the little season of silent worship will bring a peace and a rest that give a blessing not only in prayer, but all the day.

"*It is good* that a man should... quietly wait for the salvation of the LORD." Yes, it is good. The quietness is the confession of our impotence. It will not be done with all our willing and running, with all our thinking and praying, we must receive it from God. It is the confession of our trust that our God will in His time come to our help—the quiet resting in Him alone. It is the confession of our desire to sink into our nothingness, and to let Him work and reveal Himself. Do let us wait quietly. In daily life let there be in the soul that is waiting for the great God to do His wondrous work, a quiet reverence, an abiding watching against too deep engrossment with the world, and the whole character will come to bear the beautiful stamp: Quietly waiting for the salvation of God.

My soul, wait thou only upon God!

Twenty-sixth Day

In Holy Expectancy

*Therefore will I look to the L*ORD*; I will wait for the God of my salvation: my God will hear me.*

—Micah 7:7

Have you ever read a little book, *Expectation Corners*? If not, get it; you will find in it one of the best sermons on our text. It tells of a king who prepared a city for some of his poor subjects. Not far from them were large storehouses, where everything they could need was supplied if they sent in their requests. But on one condition—that they should be on the outlook for the answer, so that when the king's messengers came with the answer to their petitions, they should always be found waiting and ready to receive them. The sad story is told of one desponding one who never expected to get what he asked, because he was too unworthy. One day he was taken to the king's storehouses, and there, to his amazement, he saw, with his address on them, all the packages that had been made up for him and sent. There was the garment of praise, and the oil of joy, and the eyesalve, and so much more. They had been to his door, but found it closed; he was not on the outlook. From that time on he learned the lesson Micah would teach us today. I will "look to the Lord; I will wait for the God of my salvation; my God will hear me."

We have more than once said: Waiting for the answer to prayer is not the whole of waiting, but only a part. Today we want to take in the blessed truth that it is a part, and a very important one. When we have special petitions, in connection with which we are waiting on God, our waiting must be very definitely in the confident assurance: "My God will hear me." A holy, joyful expectancy is of the very essence of true waiting. And this not only in reference to the many varied requests every believer has to make, but most especially to the one great petition which ought to be the chief thing every heart seeks for itself—that the life of God in the soul may have full sway. That Christ may be fully formed within, and that we may be filled to all the fullness of God. This is what God has promised. This is what God's people too little seek, very often because they do not believe it possible. This is what we ought to seek and dare to expect, because God is able and waiting to work it in us.

But God Himself must work it. And for this end our working must cease. We must see how entirely it is to be the faith of the operation of God who raised Jesus from the dead just as much as the resurrection, the perfecting of God's life in our souls is to be directly His work. And waiting has to become more than ever a tarrying before God in stillness of soul, counting upon Him who raises the dead, and calls the things that are not as though they were.

Just notice how the threefold use of the name of God in our text points us to Himself as the one from whom alone is our expectation. "I [will] look to the LORD; I will wait for the God of my salvation; my God will hear me." Everything that is salvation, everything that is good and holy, must be the direct mighty work of God Himself within us. Every moment of a life in the will of God there must be the immediate operation of God. And the one thing I have to do is this: to look to the Lord; to wait for the God of my salvation; to hold fast the confident assurance, "My God will hear me."

God says: "Be still, and know that I am God."

There is no stillness like that of the grave. In the grave of Jesus, in the fellowship of His death, in death to self with its own will and wisdom, its own strength and energy, there is rest. As we cease from self, and our soul becomes still to God, God will arise and show Himself. "Be still, and know," then you shall know "that I am God." There is no stillness like the stillness Jesus gives when He speaks, "Peace, be still." In Christ, in His death, and *in His life*, in His perfected redemption, the soul may be still, and God will come in, and take possession, and do His perfect work.

My soul, be thou still only unto God!

Twenty-seventh Day

For Redemption

Simeon... was just and devout, waiting for the consolation of Israel: and the Holy Ghost was upon him.... Anna, a prophetess.... spake of him to all them that looked for redemption in Jerusalem.

—Luke 2:25, 36, 38

Here we have the mark of a waiting believer. Just, righteous in all his conduct; devout, devoted to God, ever walking as in His presence; *waiting for the consolation of Israel*, looking for the fulfillment of God's promises: *and the Holy Ghost was on him*. In the devout waiting he had been prepared for the blessing. And Simeon was not the only one. Anna spoke to all that looked for redemption in Jerusalem. This was the one mark, amid surrounding formalism and worldliness, of a godly band of men and women in Jerusalem. They were waiting on God; looking for His promised redemption.

And now that the Consolation of Israel has come, and the redemption has been accomplished, do we still need to wait? We do indeed. But will not our waiting, who look back to it as come, differ greatly from those who looked forward to it as coming? It will, specially in two aspects. We now wait on God in the full power of the redemption;

and we wait for its full revelation.

Our waiting is now in the full power of the redemption. Christ spake: "In that day ye shall know that ye are *in me*. Abide in me." The Epistles teach us to present ourselves to God "as indeed dead to sin, and alive to God *in Christ Jesus*," "blessed with all spiritual blessings in heavenly places *in Christ Jesus*." Our waiting on God may now be in the wonderful consciousness, wrought and maintained by the Holy Spirit within us, that we are accepted in the Beloved, that the love that rests on Him rests on us, that we are living in that love, in the very nearness and presence and sight of God. The old saints took their stand on the Word of God, and waiting, hoping on that Word, we rest on the Word too—but, oh, under what exceeding greater privileges, as one with Christ Jesus! In our waiting on God, let this be our confidence: in Christ we have access to the Father; how sure, therefore, may we be that our waiting cannot be vain.

Our waiting differs too in this, that while they waited for a redemption to come, we see it accomplished, and now wait for its revelation *in us*. Christ not only said, Abide in Me, but also *I in you*. The Epistles not only speak of us *in Christ*, but of Christ *in us*, as the highest mystery of redeeming love. As we maintain our place in Christ day by day, God waits to reveal Christ in us, in such a way that He is formed in us, that His mind and disposition and likeness acquire form and substance in us, so that by each it can in truth be said, "Christ liveth in me."

My life in Christ up there in Heaven and Christ's life in me down here on earth—these two are the complement of each other. And the more my waiting on God is marked by the living faith *I in Christ*, the more the heart thirsts for and claims the Christ in me. And the waiting on God, which began with special needs and prayer, will increasingly be concentrated, as far as our personal life is concerned, on this one thing: Lord, reveal Thy redemption fully in me; let Christ live in me.

Our waiting differs from that of the old saints in the place we take, and the expectations we entertain. But at root it is the same: waiting on God, from whom alone is our expectation.

Learn one lesson from Simeon and Anna. How utterly impossible it was for them to do anything toward the great redemption—toward the birth of Christ or His death. *It was God's work. They could do nothing but wait.* Are we as absolutely helpless as regards the revelation of Christ in us? We are indeed. God did not work out the great redemption in Christ as a whole, and leave its application in detail to us.

The secret thought that it is so lies at the root of all our feebleness. The revelation of Christ in every individual believer, and in each one the daily revelation, step by step and moment by moment, is as much the work of God's omnipotence as the birth or resurrection of Christ. Until this truth enters and fills us, and we feel that we are just as dependent upon God for each moment of our life in the enjoyment of redemption as they were in their waiting for it, our waiting upon God will not bring its full blessing. The sense of utter and absolute helplessness, the confidence that God can and will do all—these must be the marks of our waiting as of theirs. As gloriously as God proved Himself to them the faithful and wonder-working God, He will to us too.

My soul, wait thou only upon God!

Twenty-eighth Day

For the Coming of His Son

Be... ye yourselves like unto men that wait for their Lord.

—Luke 12:36

Until the appearing of our Lord Jesus Christ: which in his own time he shall show, who is the blessed and only Potentate, the King of kings, and Lord of lords.

—1 Timothy 6:14, 15 (A.S.V.)

Turned to God from idols to serve the living and true God; and to wait for his Son from heaven.

—1 Thessalonians 1:9, 10

Waiting on God in Heaven, and waiting for His Son from Heaven, these two God hath joined together, and no man may put them asunder. The waiting on God for His presence and power in daily life will be the only true preparation for waiting for Christ in humility and true holiness. The waiting for Christ coming from Heaven to take us to Heaven will give the waiting on God its true tone of hopefulness and joy. The Father, who in His own time will reveal His Son from Heaven, is the God who, as we wait on Him, prepares us for the revelation of His Son. The present life and the coming glory are inseparably connected in God and in us.

There is sometimes a danger of separating them. It is always easier to be engaged with the religion of the past or the future than to be faithful in the religion of today. As we look to what God has done in the past, or will do in time to come, the personal claim of present duty and present submission to His working may be escaped. Waiting on God must ever lead to waiting for Christ as the glorious consummation of His work; and waiting for Christ, must ever remind us of the duty of waiting upon God as our only proof that the waiting for Christ is in spirit and in truth. There is such a danger of our being so occupied with the things that are coming more than *with Him* who is to come. There is such scope in the study of coming events for imagination and reason and human ingenuity, that nothing but deeply humble waiting on God can save us from mistaking the interest and pleasure of intellectual study for the true love of Him and His appearing. All you that say you wait for Christ's coming, *be sure that you wait on God now.* All you who seek to wait on God now to reveal His Son in you, see to it that you do so as men waiting for the revelation of His Son from Heaven. The hope of that glorious appearing will strengthen you in waiting upon God for what He is to do in you now. The same omnipotent love that is to reveal that glory is working in you even now to fit you for it.

"The blessed hope and appearing of the glory of the great God and our Saviour Jesus Christ" (Titus 2:13), is one of the great bonds of union given to God's Church throughout the ages. "He shall come to be glorified in his saints, and to be marveled at in all them that believe." Then we shall all meet, and the unity of the body of Christ be seen in its divine glory. It will be the meeting place and the triumph of divine love. Jesus receiving His own and presenting them to the Father. His own meeting Him and worshiping in speechless love that blessed face; His own meeting each other in the ecstasy of God's own love. Let us wait, long for, and love the appearing of our Lord and heavenly Bridegroom. Tender love to Him and tender love to each other is the true and only bridal spirit.

I fear greatly that this is sometimes forgotten. A beloved brother in Holland was speaking about the expectancy of faith being the true sign of the bride. I ventured to express a doubt. An unworthy bride, about to be married to a prince, might only be thinking of the position and the riches that she was to receive. The expectancy of faith might be strong, and true love utterly wanting. It is not when we are most occupied with prophetic subjects, but when in humility and love we are clinging close to our Lord and His brethren, that we are in the bride's place. Jesus refuses to accept our love except as it is love to His disciples. Waiting for His coming means waiting for the glorious coming manifestation of the unity of the body, while we seek here to maintain that unity in humility and love. Those who love most are the most ready for His coming. Love to each other is the life and beauty of His Bride, the Church.

And how is this to be brought about? Beloved child of God, if you would learn aright to wait for His Son from Heaven, live even now waiting on God in Heaven. Remember how Jesus lived ever waiting on God. He could do nothing of Himself. It was God who perfected His Son through suffering and then exalted Him. It is God alone who can give you the deep spiritual life of one who is really waiting for His Son: wait on God for it. Waiting for Christ Himself is so different from waiting for things that may come to pass! The latter any Christian can do; the former, God must work in you every day by His Holy Spirit. Therefore all you who wait on God, look to Him for grace to wait for His Son from Heaven in the Spirit which is from Heaven. And you who would wait for His Son, wait on God continually to reveal Christ in you.

The revelation of Christ in us as it is given to them who wait upon God is the true preparation for the full revelation of Christ in glory.

My soul, wait thou only upon God!

Twenty-ninth Day

For the Promise of the Father

He charged them not to depart from Jerusalem, but to wait for the promise of the Father.

—Acts 1:4 (A.S.V.)

In speaking of the saints in Jerusalem at Christ's birth, with Simeon and Anna, we saw how, though the redemption they waited for is come, the call to waiting is no less urgent now than it was then. We wait for the full revelation in us of what came to them, but what they could scarce comprehend. Even so it is with waiting for the promise of the Father. In one sense, the fulfillment can never come again as it came at Pentecost. In another sense, and that in as deep reality as with the first disciples, we daily need to wait for the Father to fulfil His promise in us.

The Holy Spirit is not a person distinct from the Father in the way two persons on earth are distinct. The Father and the Spirit are never without or separate from each other. The Father is always in the Spirit; the Spirit works nothing but as the Father works in Him. Each moment the same Spirit that is in us is in God too, and he who is most full of the Spirit will be the first to wait on God most earnestly, further to fulfil His promise, and still strengthen him mightily by His Spirit in the inner man. The Spirit in us is not a power at our disposal. Nor is the Spirit an independent power, acting apart from the Father and the Son. The Spirit is *the real living presence and the power of the Father* working in us. Therefore it is just he who knows that the Spirit is in him, who waits on the Father for the full revelation and experience of what the Spirit's indwelling is, for His increase and abounding more and more.

See this in the apostles. They were filled with the Spirit at Pentecost. When they, not long after, on returning from the Council, where they had been forbidden to preach, prayed afresh for boldness to speak in His name, a fresh coming down of the Holy Spirit was the Father's fresh fulfillment of His promise.

At Samaria, by the word and the Spirit, many had been converted, and the whole city filled with joy. At the apostles' prayer the Father once again fulfilled the promise. Even so to the waiting company—"We are all here before God"—in Cornelius' house. And so too in Acts 13. It was when men, filled with the Spirit, prayed and fasted, that the promise of the Father was afresh fulfilled, and the leading of the Spirit was given from Heaven: "Separate me Barnabas and Saul."

So also we find Paul in Ephesians, praying for those who have been sealed with the Spirit, that God would grant them the spirit of illumination. And later on, that He would grant them, according to the riches of His glory, to be strengthened with might by the Spirit in the inner man.

The Spirit given at Pentecost was not a something that God failed with in Heaven, and sent away out of Heaven to earth. God does not, cannot, give away anything in that way. When He gives grace, or strength, or life, He gives it by giving Himself to work it—it is all inseparable from Himself. [See note on Law, *The Power of the Spirit.*] Much more so the Holy Spirit. He is God, present and working in us. The true position in which we can count upon that working with an unceasing power is as we, praising for what we have, still unceasingly wait for the Father's promise to be still more mightily fulfilled.

What new meaning and promise does this give to our life of waiting! It teaches us ever to keep the place where the disciples tarried at the footstool of the Throne. It reminds us that, as helpless as they were to meet their enemies, or to preach to Christ's enemies, till they were endued with power, we too can only be strong in the life of faith, or the work of love, as we are in direct communication with God and Christ, and they maintain the life of the Spirit in us. It assures us that the omnipotent God will, through the glorified Christ, work in us a power that can bring to pass things unexpected, things impossible. Oh, what will not the Church be able to do when her individual members learn to live their lives waiting on God, and when together, with all of self and the world sacrificed in the fire of love, they unite in waiting with one accord for the promise of the Father, once so gloriously fulfilled, but still unexhausted!

Come and let each of us be still in presence of the inconceivable grandeur of this prospect: the Father waiting to fill the Church with the Holy Spirit. And willing to fill *me*, let each one say.

With this faith let there come over the soul a hush and

a holy fear, as it waits in stillness to take it all in. And let life increasingly become a deep joy in the hope of the ever fuller fulfillment of the Father's promise.

My soul, wait thou only upon God!

Thirtieth Day

Continually

Therefore turn thou to thy God: keep mercy and judgment and wait on thy God continually.

—Hosea 12:6

Continuity is one of the essential elements of life. Interrupt it for a single hour in a man, and it is lost; he is dead. Continuity, unbroken and ceaseless, is essential to a healthy Christian life. God wants me to be, and God waits to make me, I want to be, and I wait on Him to make me, every moment, what He expects of me, and what is well-pleasing in His sight. If waiting on God be of the essence of true religion, the maintenance of the spirit of entire dependence must be continuous. The call of God, "Wait on thy God continually," must be accepted and obeyed. There may be times of special waiting: the disposition and habit of soul must be there unchangeably and uninterrupted.

This waiting continually is indeed a necessity. To those who are content with a feeble Christian life, it appears a luxury something beyond what is essential to be a good Christian. But all who are praying the prayer, "Lord, make me as holy as a pardoned sinner can be made! Keep me as

near to Thee as it is possible for me to be! Fill me as full
of Thy love as Thou art willing to do!" feel at once that
it is something that must be had. They feel that there can
be no unbroken fellowship with God, no full abiding in
Christ, no maintaining of victory over sin and readiness
for service, without waiting continually on the Lord.

The waiting continually is a possibility. Many think
that with the duties of life it is out of the question. They
cannot be always thinking of it. Even when they wish to,
they forget.

They do not understand that it is a matter of the heart,
and that what the heart is full of, occupies it, even when
the thoughts are otherwise engaged. A father's heart may
be filled continuously with intense love and longing for
a sick wife or child at a distance, even though pressing
business requires all his thoughts. When *the heart* has
learned how entirely powerless it is for one moment to
keep itself or bring forth any good, when it has learned
how surely and truly God will keep it, when it has, in
despair of itself, accepted God's promise to do for it the
impossible, it learns to rest in God, and in the midst of
occupations and temptations it can wait continually.

This waiting is a promise. God's commands are
enablings; Gospel precepts are all promises, a revelation of
what our God will do for us. When first you begin waiting
on God, it is with frequent intermission and frequent
failure. But do believe God is watching over you in love
and secretly strengthening you in it. There are times when
waiting appears just losing time, but it is not so. Waiting,
even in darkness, is unconscious advance, because it is
God you have to do with, and He is working in you. God

who calls you to wait on Him, sees your feeble efforts, and works it in you. Your spiritual life is in no respect your own work; as little as you begin it, can you continue it. It is God's Spirit who has begun the work in you of waiting upon God; He will enable you to wait continually.

Waiting continually will be met and rewarded by God Himself working continually. We are coming to the end of our meditations. Would that you and I might learn one lesson: God must, God will work continually. He ever does work continually, but the experience of it is hindered by unbelief. But He, who by His Spirit teaches you to wait continually, will bring you to experience also how, as the Everlasting One, His work is never-ceasing. In the love and the life and the work of God there can be no break, no interruption.

Do not limit God in this by your thoughts of what may be expected. Do fix your eyes upon this one truth: in His very nature, God, as the only Giver of life, *cannot do otherwise than every moment work in His child*. Do not look only at the one side: "If I wait continually, God will work continually." No, look at the other side. Place God first and say, *"God works continually; every moment I may wait on Him continually."* Take time until the vision of your God working continually, without one moment's intermission, fill your being. Your waiting continually will then come of itself. Full of trust and joy the holy habit of the soul will be: "On thee do I wait *all the day*." The Holy Spirit will keep you ever waiting.

My soul, wait thou only upon God!

Moment by Moment

I the Lord do keep it: I will water it every moment.

Dying with Jesus, by death reckoned mine;
Living with Jesus, a new life divine;
Looking to Jesus till glory doth shine,
Moment by moment, O Lord, I am Thine.

Moment by moment I'm kept in His love;
Moment by moment I've life from above;
Looking to Jesus till glory doth shine;
Moment by moment, O Lord, I am Thine.

Never a battle with wrong for the right,
Never a contest that He doth not fight;
Lifting above us His banner so white,
Moment by moment I'm kept in His sight.

Never a trial that He is not there,
Never a burden that He doth not bear,
Never a sorrow that He doth not share,
Moment by moment I'm under His care;

Never a heartache, and never a groan,
Never a teardrop and never a moan;
Never a danger but there on the throne,
Moment by moment He thinks of His own.

Never a weakness that He doth not feel,
Never a sickness that He cannot heal;
Moment by moment, in woe or in weal,
Jesus, my Saviour, abides with me still.

Thirty-first Day

Only

My soul, wait thou only upon God;
For my expectation is from him.
He only is my rock and my salvation.

—Psalm 62:5, 6

It is possible to be waiting continually on God, but not *only* upon Him. There may be other secret confidences intervening, and preventing the blessing that was expected. And so the word *only* must come to throw its light on the path to the fulness and certainty of blessing. "My soul, wait thou *only* upon God.... He *only* is my rock."

Yes, "My soul, wait thou only upon God." There is but one God, but one source of life and happiness for the heart; "He *only* is my rock"; "my soul, wait thou *only* upon [God]." You desire to be good. "There is none good but God," and there is no possible goodness but what is received directly from Him. You have sought to be holy: "There is none holy but the LORD," and there is no holiness but what He by His Spirit of holiness every moment breathes in you. You would fain live and work for God and His kingdom, for men and their salvation. Hear how He says: "The Everlasting God, the Creator of the ends of the earth. He alone fainteth not, neither is weary. He giveth power to the faint, and to them that have no might he increaseth strength. They that wait upon the LORD shall renew their strength." He only is God; He only is your Rock: "My soul, wait thou only upon God."

"My soul, wait *thou* only upon God." You will not find many who can help you in this. Enough there will be of your brethren to draw you to put trust in churches and doctrines, in schemes and plans and human appliances, in means of grace and divine appointments. But "my soul, wait thou only upon God" Himself. His most sacred appointments become a snare when trusted in. The brazen serpent becomes Nehushtan; the ark and the temple a vain confidence. Let the living God alone, none and nothing but He, be your hope.

"*My soul*, wait thou only upon God." Eyes and hands and feet, mind and thought, may have to be intently engaged in the duties of this life; "*My soul*, wait thou only upon God." You are an immortal spirit, created not for this world but for eternity and for God. O my soul, realize your destiny. Know your privilege, and "wait thou *only upon God.*" Let not the interest of religious thoughts and exercises deceive you; they very often take the place of waiting upon God. "My soul, wait *thou*," your very self, your inmost being, with all its power, "wait thou only upon God." God is for you, you are for God; wait only upon Him.

Yes, "my soul, wait thou *only* upon God." Beware of two great enemies—the world and self. Beware lest any earthly satisfaction or enjoyment, however innocent it appears, keep you back from saying, "I will go to God, my exceeding joy." Remember and study what Jesus says about denying self, "Let a man deny himself." Tersteegen says: "The saints deny themselves in everything." Pleasing self in little things may be strengthening it to assert itself in greater things. "My soul, wait thou *only* upon God"; let Him be all your salvation and all your desire. Say continually and with an undivided heart: "From him cometh my expectation. He only is my Rock; I shall not be moved." Whatever be your spiritual or temporal need, whatever the desire or prayer of your heart, whatever your interest in connection with God's work in the Church or the world—in solitude or in the rush of the world, in public worship or other gatherings of the saints, "My soul, wait thou *only* upon God." Let your expectations be from Him alone. "He only is my [thy] rock."

"My soul, wait thou only upon God." Never forget the two foundation truths on which this blessed waiting rests. If ever you are inclined to think this "waiting only" too hard or too high, they will recall you at once. They are: your absolute helplessness; the absolute sufficiency of your God. Oh, enter deep into the entire sinfulness of all that is of self, and think not of letting self have aught to say one single moment. Enter deep into your utter and unceasing impotence ever to change what is evil in you, or to bring forth anything that is spiritually good. Enter deep into your relation of dependence as creature on God, to receive from Him every moment what He gives. Enter deeper still into His covenant of redemption, with His promise to restore more gloriously than ever what you have lost, and by His Son and Spirit to give within you unceasingly, His actual divine presence and power. And thus wait upon your God continually and only.

"My soul, wait thou only upon God." No words can tell, no heart conceive, the riches of the glory of this mystery of the Father and of Christ. Our God, in the infinite tenderness and omnipotence of His love, waits to be our life and joy. Oh, my soul, let it be no longer needed that I repeat the words, "Wait upon God," but let all that is in me rise and sing: "Truly my soul waiteth upon God. On thee do I wait all the day."

My soul, wait thou only upon God!

Note

My publishers issued a work of William Law on the Holy
Spirit.[1] I have said how much I owe to the book. What this
author puts more clearly than I have anywhere else found
are these cardinal truths:

1. That the very Nature and Being of a God, as the only
Possessor and Dispenser of any life there is in the universe,
imply that He must every moment communicate to every
creature the power by which it exists, and therefore also
much more the power by which it can do that which is
good.

2. That the very Nature and Being of a creature, as owing
its existence to God alone, and equally owing to Him
each moment the continuation of that existence, imply
that its happiness can only be found in absolute unceasing
momentary dependence upon God.

3. That the great value and blessing of the gift of the
Spirit at Pentecost, as the fruit of Christ's Redemption,
is that it is now possible for God to take possession of
His redeemed children and work in them as He did before
the fall in Adam. We need to know the Holy Spirit as the
Presence and Power of God in us restored to their true
place.

4. That in the spiritual life our great need is the knowledge
of two great lessons. The one our entire sinfulness and
helplessness—our utter impotence by any effort of
our own to do anything toward the maintenance and

1. *The Power of the Spirit*: A humble, earnest, and affectionate
address to the clergy. Out of print; may be difficult to locate.

increase of our inner spiritual life. The other, the infinite willingness of God's love, which is nothing but a desire to communicate Himself and His blessedness to us to meet our every need, and every moment to work in us by His Son and Spirit what we need.

5. That, therefore, the very essence of true religion, whether in Heaven or upon earth, consists in an unalterable dependence upon God, because we can give God no other glory, than yielding ourselves to His love, which created us to show forth in us its glory, that it may now perfect its work in us.

I need not point out how deep down these truths go to the very root of the spiritual life, and specially the life of waiting upon God. I am confident that those who are willing to take the trouble of studying this thoughtful writer will thank me for the introduction to his book.

"Wait Thou Only Upon God"

My soul, wait thou only upon God.
—Psalm 62:5

A God... who worketh for him that waiteth for him.
—Isaiah 64:4 (A.S.V.)

"Wait only upon God"; my soul, be still,
And let thy God unfold His perfect will,
Thou fain would'st follow Him throughout this year,
Thou fain with listening heart His voice would'st hear.
Thou fain would'st be a passive instrument
Possessed by God, and ever Spirit-sent
Upon His service sweet—then be thou still,
For only thus can He in thee fulfil
His heart's desire. Oh, hinder not His hand
From fashioning the vessel He hath planned.
"Be silent unto God," and thou shalt know
The quiet, holy calm He doth bestow
On those who wait on Him; so shalt thou bear
His presence, and His life and light e'en where
The night is darkest, and thine earthly days
Shall show His love, and sound His glorious praise.
And He will work with hand unfettered, free,
His high and holy purposes through thee.
First *on* thee must that hand of power be turned,
Till in His love's strong fire thy dross is burned,
And thou come forth a vessel for thy Lord,
So frail and empty, yet, since He hath poured
Into thine emptiness His life, His love,
Henceforth through thee the power of God shall move

And He will work *for* thee. Stand still and see
The victories thy God will gain for thee;
So silent, yet so irresistible,
Thy God shall do the thing impossible.
Oh, question not henceforth what thou canst do;
Thou canst do *nought*. But He will carry through
The work where human energy had failed
Where all thy best endeavors had availed
Thee nothing. Then, my soul, wait and be still;
Thy God shall work for thee His perfect will.
If thou wilt take no less, *His best* shall be
Thy portion now and through eternity.

Freda Hanbury

For Elma Johnston, Ishbel McBoyle,
and Ewen and Jean Macdonald,
and in memory of Jenny Sim,
great teachers

Contents

Acknowledgements

Many people assisted me in the course of writing this book. I am especially grateful to those who read the draft: my parents, Maggi Brown, Martin Ceadel, Roger Cotes, David Creed, Emma Furniss, Philip Giddings, Chris Hanretty, David Ireland, Scot Peterson, Maria Pretzler, Sarah Taylor-Rozyk and Richard Wood. All offered invaluable comments that improved the text greatly. I had very helpful conversations on varied issues with Adrian Blau, Michael Lamb, Paul Martin and Paul Swaddle, while John Curtice, Ron Johnston, Michael Lamb, Gemma Rosenblatt and Andy White assisted in finding, confirming or analysing data. Again, I am deeply grateful to them all. The team at Biteback, especially Iain Dale, Sam Carter and Hollie Teague, have been fantastic throughout. All errors and other shortcomings remain my own.

Introduction

The rules that govern elections to the Westminster Parliament are up for grabs. We, as citizens, are going to have more influence over the form these rules will take than ever before. The new coalition government are committed to having a referendum on one set of reforms. Others will be decided in Parliament – but not without a great deal of public debate and argument. These debates are crucial to the future character of our democracy, but are not always easy for everyone to follow. This book is here to help.

Elections matter. They decide who governs. They provide our best means of influencing what those in power do: though we can scream and shout in the streets, it is only the fear of our votes in the ballot box that is likely to make politicians listen. They are the most concrete expression of our democratic society. They are our most widely shared ritual: eight or nine million of us now attend a religious service at least once a month; ten million voted in the 2009 *X Factor* final; and twenty million watched the 2010 World Cup final; but very nearly thirty million of us voted in the most recent general election.

The rules by which these elections are conducted make a big difference. They have a major impact on who gets elected. In the 2005 general election, Labour won just 35 per cent of the UK-wide vote, but secured fully 55 per cent of the seats in the House of Commons, allowing the party to govern alone for the following five years. The electoral rules currently in place in most of the world's democracies would have denied Labour an overall majority of seats and forced it to seek out coalition allies. In Germany in 1983, for example, the conservative Christian Democrats won 48.8 per cent support – more than any British party has obtained since the

1950s. Yet still it was short of a majority in the German Parliament and had to rely on a coalition with the liberal Free Democrats.

Beyond who gets elected, the electoral rules shape the whole character of politics. They can have a big impact on whether the parties cluster towards the centre of the political spectrum or offer a more varied set of options. They influence the relationship between MPs and their constituents: whether MPs have deep roots in a local constituency or looser ties to a bigger region, and whether voters choose between individual candidates or between parties. Many electoral reformers argue that our current electoral system was partly to blame for the abuses of the MPs' expenses system that were uncovered in 2009: MPs in safe seats, they say, can grow complacent and exploit the perks of office too freely.

The debate over electoral reform matters for all these reasons. But this is a debate that is especially worth following because its outcome lies in our hands. The government plans a referendum on whether we should retain our current 'first past the post' electoral system or move towards another system known as the 'alternative vote'. The other reforms that they propose – including giving citizens the right to recall MPs without having to wait for a general election – will be enacted through votes in Parliament, but here too there will be ample opportunity for public debate to influence outcomes. For the House of Lords, the government is planning even more radical reform, with most members to be elected by some form of proportional representation. Many – including the Liberal Democrats and some senior figures within the Labour Party – argue that this radical option should be pursued for the House of Commons too.

So we can expect vigorous debate over the electoral system in the coming months and years, and we are going to be asked to play our own direct part in choosing between alternatives. But the subject of electoral reform is one that most voters find incredibly arcane. Whenever these issues are aired, we are plunged immediately into an alphabet soup of AV, AMS, STV and MMP. Mysterious terms such as d'Hondt and Sainte Laguë are bandied about. Even the political hacks often seem only dimly aware of what such words might mean or what implications they might have for the character of our politics.

This book aims to cut through all these obscurities and help you grasp what is at stake when the electoral system is discussed. The chapters that follow will look in turn at the various options that are likely to figure significantly in the coming debates. They will outline each system and give you the information you need in order to judge what reforms – if any – you think should be adopted. I will not be arguing in favour of any particular option myself. The choices are yours; my goal is simply to help you make them.

1. What is an electoral system?

Many people, I suspect, are a bit embarrassed to ask the most basic question of all – what actually *is* an electoral system? They think that this, at least, is a question they should be able to answer. Yet there is no shame in being unable to define what an electoral system is or in not knowing how electoral systems differ from each other. In fact, even the experts disagree about it. There are two main approaches that we can take when thinking about electoral systems. I'll call one of these the narrow approach, the other the wide approach.

The narrow approach: the electoral system's core

The narrow approach focuses on election day itself. It sees the electoral system as comprising two elements: the rules that determine the kind of vote that we can cast, and the mechanisms by which the votes cast are translated into seats in Parliament.

In elections to the House of Commons at present, the vote that we can cast is a very simple one: all we can do (assuming we don't want to spoil our ballot paper) is vote for a single local candidate. Voters in some other countries – such as the United States, Canada and India – are asked to make a similar choice. But voters in most countries cast some different kind of vote. Some systems, such as the electoral systems in Australia and Ireland, allow voters to rank the candidates in order of preference. In others, and in elections to the European Parliament in Great Britain, voters cast their ballot not for a single candidate, but for a list of candidates put up by a party or other group. In still other systems, voters can indicate separately their preferences among parties and among candidates. In Sweden, for example, voters choose a party and then, if they wish, also select one of the candidates who this party has nominated. In Germany, New Zealand, Scotland and Wales, voters cast two separate votes: one for a local candidate and one for a regional or national party slate, making it possible to support one party's candidate locally, but another party nationally.

In terms of the translation of votes into seats, meanwhile, the system used for Commons elections is again straightforward. The country is divided into constituencies; within each constituency, the candidate who wins most votes is elected as its MP. Here too, many alternatives exist. Some systems, such as those used in France and Australia, require the winning candidate to get not just more votes than any other candidate, but, rather, more votes than all the other candidates combined – an *absolute* rather than a *relative* majority. Others dispense with constituencies or divide the country into large constituencies, each of which elects several MPs; they then distribute the seats across the parties in proportion (at least roughly) to the votes those parties have won. These are systems of proportional representation (PR), and variants are used across much of Europe, Latin America and elsewhere.

These two features – the nature of votes and the translation of votes into seats – sum up what most experts and enthusiasts focus on when they think about the electoral system. They define the core of the system. The UK system that I have just described is what is generally known as 'first past the post'. The coming referendum will offer a choice between this system and another, namely the alternative vote, which can be defined in terms of the same two features.

Because most of the debate concentrates on this narrow conception of the electoral system, that's where most of this book will focus too. Given the choice we're being offered in the referendum, our top priority is to compare first past the post and the alternative vote. We also need to bear in mind the various forms of proportional representation. Though we won't be given the opportunity to opt for a proportional system in the referendum, many people will argue we should be, and the government wants to introduce such a system for the House of Lords.

It would be wrong, however, to limit the focus to the narrow understanding of the electoral system alone. Many other rules influence the conduct and the outcomes of elections, and changes to some of these are currently under discussion. So it is time now to turn to the wide view of electoral systems.

The wide approach: the electoral system broadly understood

According to the wide approach, the electoral system is best understood as including all the rules that govern the process of electing Parliament. Whereas the narrow approach focuses just upon what happens at the polling station and the election count, the wide approach recognises that elections are about much more than that. Before any votes can be cast, the date of the election needs to be set, and there are many rules governing when this can happen and who can do it. Then we need rules governing who can be a candidate and how they are selected and formally nominated. Elections are always preceded by campaigns, so there are rules shaping how these campaigns are conducted and financed. Come election day, it needs to be clear not just what kinds of vote can be cast, but also who can cast them, so rules on who is eligible to vote – and whether they are required to vote – also matter. And we might pay attention to the mechanics of voting: whether, for example, voting is computerised or involves marking an old-fashioned ballot paper. Finally, even after election day, the electoral process is not necessarily over. In particular, the idea that we should be able to recall a miscreant MP without having to wait for another general election has built up extraordinary momentum in the UK in the last couple of years.

Rules on when elections take place

All democracies define a maximum period within which fresh elections must take place. In the UK, this is currently five years. (Strictly speaking, Parliament must be dissolved not more than five years after it first met. Allowing for the election campaign and the interlude between election day and the first session of the new parliament, this means that the time between elections can in fact be a little more than five years.) Among stable democracies, such a lengthy term is actually quite unusual. Most European countries have a four-year limit. In Australia and New Zealand it is three years. In the United States just two years elapse between elections to the House of Representatives.

A related issue much debated in the UK recently concerns who can call an election and in what circumstances. Until 2010, there were two possible routes to an election before the maximum five-year term was up. First, the prime minister could ask the monarch to call an election just about any time under the powers of the royal prerogative. Second, an election was called if the government lost a vote of confidence in Parliament and no alternative government could be formed. The coalition government is changing this. Henceforth, the prime minister has no power to seek a dissolution of Parliament on his own; instead, so long as the government retains the support of the parliamentary majority, a two-thirds vote in the House of Commons will be needed to call an early election. It will still be possible – contrary to much misleading media comment – to remove the government by simple majority in a vote of no confidence, and this will still lead to fresh elections if no new government can be formed. But a fourteen-day delay on dissolution is now introduced, presumably in order to dissuade prime ministers from engineering their own defeat in a confidence vote so as to trigger an early election. These changes bring the UK closer to the practice in most other democracies, where early elections are the exception rather than the rule.

A final aspect of timing concerns the day on which elections are held. Elections in the UK are conventionally held on Thursdays (though there is nothing in law saying this must be so, and the convention emerged only in the mid twentieth century). The United States holds elections on Tuesdays. In most democracies, however, elections take place at the weekend, and many people advocate a move to weekend voting in the UK in the hope that it would boost turnout.

Rules on who can be a candidate and how candidates are selected and nominated

Almost any citizen over the age of eighteen in the UK can be a candidate in parliamentary elections. The rules on this changed for the elections in 2010: before that, candidates had to be at least twenty-one. To get on to the ballot paper, a budding candidate must secure ten signatures and deposit £500 with the local electoral authorities – the money is returned if she or he wins at least 5 per cent of the constituency vote on election day. Many countries share similar provisions, though others dispense with the deposit requirement, often instead demanding a far greater number of signatures.

Though just about anyone can become a candidate, in the UK it's almost always only the candidates of the major parties who stand any chance of winning election. The rules by which the big parties select their candidates are therefore very important. They have changed significantly in the last few years, and further reform is planned. So this is a matter that we will explore in more detail later in the book.

Rules on how election campaigns are conducted and financed

The rules governing campaigns have also seen big changes in the UK recently. The most visible innovation has been the introduction of televised leaders' debates, which famously transformed the 2010 election campaign, triggering a fleeting Lib Dem surge and requiring the parties to rewrite their campaign strategies. There have also been big changes to the regulation of campaign spending: before 2001, spending by candidates in their own constituencies was capped, but the parties could spend as much as they liked at the national level; now, there are limits at both levels. The most contentious issue concerns how the parties raise funds – particularly whether they are allowed to accept large donations. Everyone agrees that further reforms are needed here, but it has so far been impossible to find consensus on what those changes should be. This is another subject that we'll look into in more detail later.

Rules on who can and who must vote

The UK, like the other older democracies, saw a step-by-step expansion of the right to vote in the nineteenth and early twentieth centuries. By 1928, almost all men and women over the age of twenty-one had the right to vote, and in 1970 this age threshold was reduced to eighteen. There has been much discussion of late over whether the voting age should be further reduced to sixteen. A few countries – including Austria and Brazil, as well as Guernsey, Jersey, and the Isle of Man – have made this move already, and Labour and the Liberal Democrats both supported such a change in their 2010 election manifestos.

Another debate revolves around whether those with the *right* to vote should also have a *duty* to vote. Compulsory voting has rarely been seriously advocated in the UK. Yet it is enforced in fifteen countries around the world, including Belgium, Australia, and much of Latin America. Its supporters say that it encourages people to engage with politics and overcomes problems of low turnout among society's more marginalised groups. Its opponents, meanwhile, argue that it infringes upon our civil liberties and that it addresses only the symptoms of voters' disillusionment with politics, not the underlying causes.

Rules governing the mechanics of voting
Even among those of us who find electoral systems strangely fascinating, the mechanics of how we cast our vote were traditionally regarded as pretty indigestible fare. All that changed, however, with the hanging chads of Florida in the American presidential election of 2000. The confusion they caused showed that whether we vote using traditional pencil and paper or by cranking levers and punching holes or through flashy new touch-screen technology can really make a difference to the outcome of a closely fought election. The debates on this issue have continued in the US because of concerns that some of the computerised voting systems introduced in the wake of Bush v. Gore are open to hacking and abuse.

In the UK, we have stuck with our trusted method of marking a cross on a slip of paper. But major change has nevertheless occurred in the form of a rapid expansion in the use of postal voting. Before 2001, voters wanting to cast their ballot by post had to state a reason for wishing to do so; now, requests for a postal vote are automatically granted. As a result, the number of postal votes has ballooned: from 4 per cent of the total in 2001 to 19 per cent in 2010.

Rules on the recall of MPs

The traditional pattern, in the UK as in most democracies, has been that MPs, once lawfully elected, cannot be removed from office until the next general election. There have long been exceptions to this in some US states, however, where voters have been able to recall their representatives if dissatisfied with their performance, and a smattering of similar provisions can be found elsewhere around the world. The idea of recall elections had never been an issue of debate in the UK. But it has burst on to the scene since the MPs' expenses scandal, and all three major parties promised it in their 2010 election manifestos. This will be a significant change to our political system that we'll need to discuss in depth later.

The preceding paragraphs give a whirlwind tour of the sorts of issue that are up for grabs in debates over the electoral system. We're not going to have space to investigate all of them in depth in this book, but there is still much to get our teeth into.

2. How can we judge the options?

Many possible reforms to the electoral system will be discussed in the coming months and years. Before we start to look at these in detail, we need to get some sense of how to judge between them. What is it that we want from our electoral system? What aspects of our democracy and our political system might our choices affect?

Supporters of particular reforms will spend much of the debate engaged in a battle of criteria. They will lay out what they claim an electoral system should achieve. Then they will show – hey presto! – that their preferred system ticks all the boxes perfectly. In reality, however, there are many possible factors to take into account, and no one system performs best on all of them. We shouldn't concentrate on just one or two criteria and ignore all the others.

I'll start with what is surely the most basic democratic criterion: the electoral system should reward popularity.

Rewarding popularity

The basic principle of any democratic election is that popular support should translate into political influence: winning more support among voters should mean winning greater influence in the corridors of power. This is so fundamental that it might hardly seem worth mentioning; surely any electoral system that is worth taking seriously would satisfy this criterion. Yet that's not the case. In fact, all of the electoral systems that are likely to be discussed in the UK can fail this test under some circumstances.

Rewarding popularity has several aspects. For one thing, if a party's share of the vote goes up from one election to the next, it would be reasonable to expect its share of the seats to go up as well (or, at least, not go down). Yet that doesn't always happen. In the UK general election of 2010, the Liberal Democrats' share of the vote was 23 per cent, up a percentage point on 2005. Yet their share of the seats fell: they won sixty-two seats in 2005 (after allowing for boundary changes), but only fifty-seven in 2010. Conversely, while the Green Party's share of the vote fell slightly in 2010, they gained a seat in the House of Commons for the first time ever. Such outcomes are less likely in countries using proportional electoral systems, but they can still happen: in the 2007 election in Ireland, for example, the largest party, Fianna Fáil, lost four seats, even though its share of the vote slightly increased.

Inconsistent results from one election to the next may be troubling. Of much greater concern, however, are anomalies within the same election, where one party is ahead of another in votes but behind in seats. As was widely reported during the 2010 general election campaign, patterns in the distribution of votes across seats made it entirely possible that, even if the Liberal Democrats had gained more votes than any other party, still they would have come a distant third in terms of seats won in the House of Commons. When this happens we can say that, in an entirely objective sense, the wrong party has won the election. In the end, this didn't happen in the UK in 2010. But it has happened before here and elsewhere – most famously in the United States in 2000, when George Bush won the presidency even though more people voted for Al Gore. Such outcomes are in themselves indefensible – though, of course, we might still defend the systems that can produce them if they score well on other grounds.

An even stranger result arises if, within a single constituency, an increase in support reduces a candidate's chances of winning. This seems very odd indeed: under our current first past the post system, winning more votes can't possibly do you any harm. Yet some experts worry that some electoral systems do generate scenarios in which a candidate would be better off winning fewer votes. I'll explore this further as we get into the details of particular systems.

A final type of anomaly is the possibility that one candidate is elected even though another is preferred by more voters. Of the

650 MPs elected in the UK in 2010, 210 won the support of an absolute majority of the voters in their constituency. But the remaining 440 were elected on less than 50 per cent of the vote. In some of these constituencies, a majority of voters might well have preferred one of the losing candidates over the candidate who was elected: the winner was able to secure victory only because support for his or her opponents was divided. We will need to think about how likely such results are under the various alternative electoral systems.

Fair representation in Parliament and government

We can all agree it's bad if – as we've just seen can happen – the wrong party wins an election. The principle underlying this judgement is the idea that the electoral system should translate votes fairly into positions of power. Many electoral reformers argue we should take the principle of fairness much further.

The most common argument concerning fairness in the electoral system is that parties should win seats in Parliament in proportion to their share of the votes: a party that receives, say, 20 per cent of the votes should win about 20 per cent of the seats. Elections in the UK frequently deviate far from that ideal. In the general election of 2010, though the Lib Dems, as we have seen, secured 23 per cent of the vote, they won fewer than 9 per cent of the seats, whereas the Conservatives, on 36 per cent of the vote, won 47 per cent of the seats. Even greater deviations from proportionality have occurred in the past: in 2005, Labour won 55 per cent of the seats on the basis of just 35 per cent of the vote; in 1983, Labour was just 2 percentage points ahead of the SDP/Liberal Alliance in terms of votes, yet won nine times as many seats. Looked at from another point of view, the Conservatives won a seat in 2010 for every 35,000 votes cast for them and Labour won a seat for every 33,000 votes, but the Lib Dems needed 120,000 votes for each seat they won. The 286,000 voters who supported the Green Party, meanwhile, captured just one seat, and the 920,000 UKIP voters gained no representation at all.

Such patterns look pretty unfair. They arise because the votes for parties like the Lib Dems and (even more) UKIP are thinly spread across the country, and there are rarely enough of them in any one constituency to elect an MP. If these votes were concentrated in fewer constituencies, such parties could elect more MPs. That can be seen from the success of smaller parties that do have concentrated votes. For example, the Democratic Unionist Party won fewer than a fifth of the votes of UKIP, but because these votes were concentrated in a small number of seats in Northern Ireland it was able to capture eight parliamentary seats – one seat for every 21,000 votes. So a viewpoint that happens to gain support only in small parts of the country can be well represented, while a position where the supporters are just as numerous but more spread out can go completely unrepresented. For most electoral reformers, this is entirely perverse.

Another argument focused on fair representation concentrates on the representation not of parties, but of social groups – above all women and ethnic minorities. Of the 650 MPs elected in the UK in 2010, 143 are women – 22 per cent of the total. Though that is a record high, it is still clearly far short of parity with men, and there has been only slow progress since 1997, when 18 per cent of MPs were women. There were no MPs at all from ethnic minorities between 1945 and 1987. Now there are twenty-seven, but that is still just half the number we would expect if ethnic minorities were represented in proportion to their share of the UK population. Some people are not greatly worried by such disparities: they point out that a person can represent your views or interests even if they don't look like you. For others, however, it is vital that Parliament should reflect the make-up of society. Thus, an important criterion for many people who think about electoral systems is the likelihood that a system will produce such a socially representative Parliament.

So far we have been talking about fair representation in Parliament. But general elections in this country have two functions: they determine the composition of the House of Commons and they determine who can form the government. All parliamentary democracies share this feature, in contrast to presidential systems such as the United States, where the executive and the legislature are elected separately.

Many people would say that what matters more is not fairness in the translation of votes into seats in Parliament, but rather fairness in the translation of votes into real power in government: after all, it is in government that most of the important decisions are taken. And it may well be that fairness in the distribution of seats leads to an *unfair* distribution of government power: small parties, it is often said, can hold the larger parties to ransom, extracting huge concessions in return for their support. Germany's Free Democrats, for example, held office continuously as part of the governing coalition between 1969 and 1998, even though their vote barely ever exceeded 10 per cent. They were able to exert considerable influence over government policy throughout that period. If this problem of 'the tail wagging the dog' is serious, it will greatly undermine the claim that proportional representation is the fairest system.

Effective, accountable government

No one would seriously deny that fairness matters when we judge electoral systems. But many people would say that it is not what matters most. As we have just seen, elections are not just about ensuring we are represented in Parliament, they are also about choosing a government. When we think about electoral systems, therefore, we also need to think about how far they allow our governing structures to operate effectively and accountably.

It is here that supporters of first past the post often place much emphasis. The coalition governments produced by proportional representation, they argue, lead to instability and indecision. Just look at countries such as Italy (before it moved away from PR in the 1990s) and Israel. First past the post, by contrast, most often generates single-party governments, which are free from endless coalition bargaining and bickering and free from the threat of coalition collapse. In addition, advocates of the status quo point out that first past the post allows voters to hold governments clearly to account: if we are dissatisfied with a government's performance, we can 'throw the rascals out' and install another party in their place. Under proportional representation, by contrast, losing parties can prop themselves up in government through new coalition deals.

Yet defenders of proportional representation have responses to all these points. They question whether single-party governments are such a good thing, as they can concentrate power in the hands of a few, allowing ill-considered decisions to be nodded through without proper deliberation. Italy's dysfunctional pattern of stable instability – forty-nine governments between 1946 and 1994, but the same party clinging on to power as the cornerstone of every one of those administrations – is the exception, not the rule. Try looking instead at Sweden or Spain, where governments have been stable and clear alternations in power have occurred. And even in Italy, it's not obvious that its messy government history has been all that damaging: Italy's economic growth since the Second World War has been far higher than Britain's.

So there are strong arguments on both sides here, and they will require careful weighing.

Voter choice and turnout

So far I've been looking at arguments about how proportional the electoral system should be: some people see high proportionality as essential; others think effective, accountable government requires clear majorities. This choice traditionally lies at the heart of the debate among electoral system experts and activists, as well as politicians.

There is plenty of evidence, however, that this debate doesn't much matter to ordinary voters. Most of us are not tribal supporters of one or other party, so we don't follow closely whether the party we vote for is over- or under-represented. In past elections where one party has won most votes but another has come top in terms of seats – in 1951 and in the first of the two elections in 1974 – hardly anyone noticed the anomaly; it just didn't seem to matter to many people.

Wherever voters have been asked in detail about what they want from the electoral system, what comes up again and again is a desire for choice. Whether we look at focus group research conducted here in the UK or at citizens' assemblies set up to deliberate on electoral systems in parts of Canada, a demand for 'voter choice' repeatedly comes to the fore. When a review of the voting system used for Westminster elections was set up in the late 1990s under the chairmanship of Lord Jenkins, extending 'voter choice' was one of the goals it was required to pursue.

But what is 'voter choice'? This is actually often not clear: it could mean a number of different things. One relates to a point we have already discussed: the accountability of governments. The choice of government should be made by voters, not by post-election deal-making among politicians behind closed doors. So it should be clear to voters before polling day what possible governments they are choosing between – whether those are single-party governments or coalitions of parties that voters know will work together if they win enough seats. And voters should be able to make a clear choice, voting out a government if they judge its performance to be inadequate.

Another aspect of choice concerns the range of options available to us. First past the post can be criticised for limiting the options available to citizens: few constituencies have more than two candidates with any serious chance of winning, and the majority of constituencies are in fact 'safe seats' where there is almost no chance that the incumbent will be defeated. That leaves us as voters with little choosing to do. Furthermore, it is often said that first past the post pressurises all the significant parties to cluster around the political centre ground: only there can they secure sufficient votes to win seats. As a result, all the parties sound the same, and the differences of vision between them can appear more manufactured than real.

Choice relates also to the degree to which we can express our preferences. In first past the post, all we can do is express support for one candidate over all the others. But other systems allow us to say much more than that: to separate out our support for a candidate and for a party, or to rank the candidates from most to least preferred. Given that far fewer voters today have rigid preferences for one party over all others than was true in past decades, it can be frustrating that all we can do is express a single, black-and-white yes/no choice.

Finally, choice may refer to the frequency with which we are able to make our voices heard through the ballot box. At present, five years can go by from one general election to the next, and only politicians can decide that an early election should be held. Among the reform proposals planned for the coming months, one – the power to recall MPs – will give voters the capacity for the first time to demand an early election in their constituency if their MP has engaged in wrongdoing. Many reformers also contend that the maximum period between elections should be reduced, particularly if the norm is now to be that parliaments run their full term.

These aspects of choice can matter to people just because, as modern citizens used to controlling our own lives, many of us find it frustrating that our ability to express our wishes at the ballot box is so very limited. Beyond this, expanding voter choice is said by many to be a good way of tackling voters' disillusionment with politics and of boosting turnout at elections: if we had more to choose from and if outcomes in many places were not such foregone conclusions, more of us might bother to turn up at the polling station. For example, the Power Inquiry, an independent report published in 2006 that advocated wide-ranging political reforms, argued for changes in the electoral system partly in order to encourage more citizens to see voting as worthwhile. Though turnout has risen slightly at each of the last two elections, it remains lower than in any post-war election before 2001, and if electoral reform could spur a revival of turnout, that would certainly be a strong argument in its favour.

But increased voter choice is not necessarily an unalloyed good. Expanding the range of options sounds attractive. But if that means empowering extremists, many of us might have second thoughts. The British National Party secured two seats in the European Parliament in 2009 as a result of the proportional electoral system that is used there. Under first past the post, they would have had no chance, just as they came nowhere near to winning a Westminster seat in 2010. It is also sometimes said that the opportunity to express multiple preferences would be confusing or burdensome: for example, when the Jenkins Commission reviewed electoral reform options in the late 1990s, it concluded that too much choice could become 'oppressive rather than liberating'. And if we are worried about turnout, asking people to take time out to vote more often is hardly likely to help: where elections are held most often – in Switzerland and the United States – turnout is typically far lower than here.

So the call to expand voter choice is immediately appealing. But we need to think carefully about what it means. We should not take for granted that it is an entirely good thing.

The constituency link

There are few principles of electoral system design that are voiced more often in the UK than that of the 'constituency link'. The terms of reference for the Jenkins Commission required 'the maintenance of a link between MPs and geographical constituencies'. Even many prominent supporters of electoral reform insist that the 'constituency link' must not be lost.

So what exactly is meant by the constituency link? Supporters of the status quo say it is the principle that every MP should be linked to a particular constituency and, correspondingly, that every voter should have a local MP to whom they can turn for advice or help and whom they can hold accountable at election time. This allows a strong bond to build up between voters and their unique MP. But some advocates of change take a slightly different view. They suggest that it could be better if each constituency had several MPs: that way, when we wish to contact our MP, we could choose the MP whose views are closest to our own or who has special expertise in a particular policy area.

What all supporters of some kind of constituency link share is the view that we should be able to choose the individuals who represent us, not just the parties. Elections to the European Parliament in Great Britain since 1999 have been held using a form of proportional representation that allows us to vote only for a party: we have no say over who the party's candidates are. I am aware of no one who thinks that would be a good system for electing the House of Commons. By contrast, under first past the post, we are choosing not just a party, but also an individual. Some forms of proportional representation go further, allowing voters to choose among their preferred party's candidates or even to build up their own slate of candidates across several parties.

Support for the constituency link is partly a reflection of British tradition. In addition, it stems from widespread disillusionment with political parties. In the past, parties were champions of fundamental beliefs about how the world should be. Today, however, most of us see them as machines that turn MPs into zombies and manage political debate so tightly that nothing interesting or meaningful is ever said. We yearn for a system that could deliver thoughtful and principled MPs who fight for their core beliefs. For the House of Lords, most of us want a democratic system, but we do not want a clone of the House of Commons in which members become lobby fodder for the party whips. So there would be strong support for an electoral system that weakened political parties and strengthened the independence of our individual representatives.

But I'd like to urge some caution here. Few of us have much time for political parties. But, actually, they are fundamental to the effective operation of our democracy. As I said above, we choose the government in this country not directly, but by voting for MPs in Parliament. We can influence the formation of the government only because the local candidates we vote for in elections are members of teams: in choosing between candidates, we are also expressing our preference for which team should make up the government. Without these teams – without cohesive political parties – the processes of deciding the government and devising policies would be determined much more by post-election deal-making, and so accountability to us, as voters, would be greatly weakened.

What's more, while maintaining MPs' focus on their local constituency is good for keeping them rooted in realities away from the Westminster bubble, it can have its disadvantages too. MPs need to strike a balance between what is good for the country as a whole and what is best for their local patch. A survey conducted after the 2005 election found that one (unnamed) MP was spending a staggering 97 per cent of his or her time on constituency business, which hardly suggests that s/he was giving much attention to the major national policy decisions regularly to be voted on at Westminster.

So while there are good reasons for seeking an electoral system that encourages independence among our MPs and among members of the upper house, we should not get carried away. Though political parties often seem to sap the lifeblood from the body politic, we do need them. An electoral system that focuses attention on local candidates can be a good thing, but we should be wary of going too far.

Keeping MPs in check

Electoral reform has become a significant issue in public debate since the eruption of a scandal over MPs' expenses in May 2009. The claim advanced by advocates of refom has been that, because our current system produces hundreds of 'safe seats', incumbents get complacent and start to take the perks of office too much for granted. Reform that eliminated these safe seats would therefore reduce the likelihood of such misbehaviour in the future.

Yet misbehaviour comes in many forms. The political scientists Benjamin Nyblade and Steven Reed distinguish two basic types of corruption: looting, where politicians extract private gain from public office, and cheating, where politicians use corrupt means in order to win office in the first place. Most of the behaviour revealed by the expenses scandal was not corrupt in any criminal sense, but some of it nevertheless fell into the category of looting. Using evidence from Japan, Nyblade and Reed find that such behaviour is more likely where MPs face little competition for their seats, just as Britain's electoral reformers argue. But cheating, they find, is more likely in highly competitive seats, where politicians are tempted to use any means available to capture the few extra votes they need to secure election.

Thus, even if the safe seats argument correctly diagnoses the best response to the expenses scandal, the reforms it implies might end up, in the long run, encouraging other forms of misbehaviour instead. We need to be wary of leaping for solutions to the problems that happen to be most obvious to us today while ignoring their knock-on effects.

Summing up

I've discussed many possible criteria for judging electoral systems: many factors that we might want to take into account when deciding which reforms, if any, to support. Coming to conclusions is going to require that we examine all the electoral system options in detail in relation to these criteria. Then, at the end, we will consider how we can go about adding together all these many pieces of the jigsaw puzzle.

3. The current system: first past the post

The electoral system currently used to elect members of the House of Commons doesn't take long to explain. The country is divided into constituencies (650 at the last election), each of which elects one MP. Voters in each constituency are presented with a set of candidates to choose from and are able to vote for one of those candidates by placing an X by that candidate's name on the ballot paper. Whichever candidate wins most votes is elected. The national result is obtained simply by adding up all of these local outcomes.

This system is generally known as 'first past the post'. That's actually quite a misleading title. There's no 'post' – no fixed number of votes that a candidate has to win in order to secure election. In fact, if there are many candidates and the field is divided, it's possible to be elected on quite a small share of the vote. Simon Wright, for example, was elected on just 29 per cent of the vote in Norwich South in 2010 and (in the all-time record) Russell Johnston secured election on just 26 per cent of the vote in Inverness in 1992. For this reason, political scientists generally prefer to refer to this system by a different name: 'single member plurality' ('single member' because each constituency elects just one MP; 'plurality' because winning requires a candidate to win a plurality of the votes – that is, more votes than anyone else – not necessarily an absolute majority). I'll stick with the more familiar 'first past the post' here. But it's important to bear the inaccuracy in mind, as we will see shortly when we investigate how the system operates in practice.

First past the post is sometimes presented as though it has been an immutable bedrock of the British political system since time immemorial. The *Daily Express*, for example, recently referred to it as 'the centuries-old first past the post system'. The Conservative

MP Bernard Jenkin says it 'has served our democracy for 300 years', while his colleague David Davis thinks it has been 'very effective throughout history'. Such statements are not entirely accurate. In fact, first past the post has been used to elect all MPs in the UK only since 1950. Before that, there were always some constituencies that each elected more than one MP (indeed, before 1885, this was the norm), and a variety of methods were used to choose these MPs. In addition, first past the post is now the exception for elections in the UK, rather than the rule: different systems are used to elect the devolved assemblies in Scotland, Wales, Northern Ireland, and London, the directly elected mayors in London and other towns and cities, the UK members of the European Parliament, and local councillors in Scotland and Northern Ireland. In fact, beyond the House of Commons, the only other elections conducted under first past the post are for local councils in England and Wales.

Nevertheless, it is true that, in classic British fashion, the electoral system for Westminster has evolved gradually over several centuries. We have seen no sudden redesign of the system's underlying logic, as has occurred in many other countries.

First past the post is used to elect the main national legislative chamber in forty-eight countries around the world today, making it the second most frequently used system. These countries range from the two largest democracies in the world – India and the United States – to tiny island states such as Grenada and St Lucia. But the UK is the only European country that uses it. Most of the countries that use first past the post have been doing so for some decades: it's not a system that many countries have chosen to adopt in recent years. But there are a few exceptions to this: Sierra Leone, for example, moved to first past the post in 2007, and Bhutan followed suit in 2008.

Having established what first past the post is and how widely it is used, let's see how it measures up against our criteria.

Rewarding popularity

There is one very clear sense in which first past the post does reward popularity: victory in any constituency always goes to the candidate who has won most votes. There is no danger that winning more votes might do a candidate's chances of election any harm. The relationship between votes and outcome within a constituency is entirely unambiguous.

Nevertheless, two major doubts about first past the post in relation to this criterion need to be investigated. First, while victory at constituency level always goes to the candidate with most votes, it is not clear that it always goes to the candidate with the greatest popularity. Second, while local constituency results under first past the post might seem straightforward, once those local results are added up across the country as a whole, they can produce some very odd national outcomes.

At the constituency level, the important question concerns whether the candidate with most votes is necessarily also the most popular candidate. Most MPs these days – in 2010, 440 out of 650 – are elected on less than half the vote. In each of these cases, it is possible – at least in theory – that another candidate could have defeated the winner in a head-to-head contest. Suppose a constituency is divided 60/40 between left-wing voters and right-wing voters, but that, while there is only one right-wing candidate, there are two left-wing candidates. It's then quite possible that the right-wing candidate could win because the left-wing vote splits, even though the majority of voters would have preferred either of the left-wing candidates. Given that Lib Dem voters tend (or at least tended until the 2010 coalition government was formed) to lean to the left, this scenario might describe fairly accurately the situation in a constituency like Northampton North, which the Conservatives won on 34 per cent of the vote in 2010, even though Labour and the Lib Dems between them had 57 per cent.

An even more serious difficulty with first past the post arises when we add up all the constituency results and look at the national outcome. As became clear to many people during the 2010 election campaign, it is quite possible for first past the post to produce an outcome where one party wins the most votes nationwide while another party wins most seats. For example, the best poll for the Lib Dems during the campaign, conducted by YouGov shortly after the first leaders' debate and published in *The*

Sun on 20 April, gave the Lib Dems 34 per cent of the vote, the Conservatives 31 per cent, and Labour 26 per cent. The model used by the BBC and other media organisations estimated that this would have given the Lib Dems just 153 seats, while Labour would have come out on top with 241 seats and the Conservatives would have been just behind on 227. So the leading party in terms of votes would have trailed a distant third in seats, while the third-placed party on the basis of votes would have secured more seats than anyone else.

There is surely no way to justify such results, and they are a clear distortion of the popular will. They arise because of what is known as electoral system *bias*. Bias can of course mean many things, but here it's being used to refer to something quite specific: a situation in which two parties can get different shares of the seats even if they secure identical shares of the votes. At present, the bias in the UK electoral system is huge: the BBC's pre-election model suggested that, had all three big parties secured exactly 31 per cent of the vote, Labour would have won about 314 seats, the Conservatives about 207, and the Lib Dems about 100.

There are several reasons for this bias. One relates to the geographical spread of the parties' votes. The Lib Dems' votes are spread fairly evenly across the country. As a result, they come second in many constituencies: they did so in 243 constituencies in 2010, considerably more than any other party. Under first past the post, however, you win a seat only if you come first. The Lib Dems therefore won many votes without capturing a seat in return. Support for Labour and the Conservatives, by contrast, is lumpier: it is high in the party heartlands but often low elsewhere. So fewer of those parties' votes are wasted in areas where they have no chance of capturing a seat. Another source of bias lies in the structure of the constituencies: as the Conservatives point out, Labour-held constituencies tend at present to be smaller than Conservative-held constituencies, so that fewer votes are needed for Labour to win a seat. The Conservatives argue that the procedures for redrawing constituency boundaries need to be changed to address this. Towards the end of the chapter, we'll investigate to what extent their proposals would solve the problem.

Supporters of first past the post acknowledge that results in which, in effect, the wrong party wins the election are unsettling. But they argue that such outcomes are very rare and that they are more than compensated for by the benefits that first past the post brings on other criteria. It's useful, therefore, to see just how often these 'wrong winner' outcomes occur. Looking at Westminster, there have been three elections since the beginning of the twentieth century in which the party that came first in votes was not the party that won most seats: in 1929, 1951, and the first of the two elections in 1974. That's three elections out of a total of twenty-nine – or a fraction over 10 per cent. Looking more broadly at first past the post elections across eleven countries (I'll say a bit more shortly about which countries these are and why I've chosen them), we find that eighteen out of 177 have produced the wrong winner – again, a fraction over 10 per cent. So about one election in ten under first past the post produces the wrong winner. On such an important issue, this is surely a worrying error rate.

Fair representation in Parliament and government

Bias, where parties on the same share of the votes get different shares of the seats, is a subset of the wider phenomenon of *disproportionality*, which exists wherever there's a difference between a party's vote share and its seat share. To see the difference between bias and disproportionality, we can imagine an electoral system in which the largest party is automatically awarded three quarters of the seats. This system contains no bias: it works in exactly the same way whichever party is largest. But it is also very disproportional: the largest party is greatly over-represented, while all other parties are left to share the meagre leftovers.

The UK's first past the post system is often criticised for its disproportionality as well as its bias. Specifically, it tends to give the largest party a significant bonus of seats relative to its vote share, while under-representing the smaller parties.

We have already seen a few examples of this disproportionality. In the 2010 election, the Conservatives captured 47 per cent of the seats on 36 per cent of the vote, Labour won 40 per cent of the seats on 29 per cent of the vote, while the Lib Dems won just 9 per cent of the seats for their 23 per cent of the vote, and UKIP, on 3 per cent of the vote, secured no seats at all. In order to be able to compare disproportionality across elections and electoral systems, it is useful to work out a single figure for the overall level of disproportionality in each election. Various ways of doing this have been used, but a method proposed by the Irish political scientist Michael Gallagher is now the most widely accepted. Those of you who like maths can look up the details of Gallagher's index of disproportionality in the Appendix (p. 167). The rest of us can be content that it puts a number on the total amount of disproportionality in an election result. The higher this number, the greater the divergence between the parties' vote and seat shares, and the greater, therefore, the overall disproportionality.

The value of Gallagher's index for the UK general election of 2010 was 15.1. What does that mean? Well, actually, we don't know what it means unless we compare it with the results of other elections elsewhere; without doing this, we have no sense of whether this is a high number or a low number. Figure 1 therefore compares the average level of disproportionality in elections in the UK with disproportionality in thirty-five other democracies. I have chosen this set of countries for comparison because it has a great pedigree: it was used by the political scientist Arend Lijphart in his celebrated study of democratic systems, *Patterns of Democracy*, published in 1999. Wherever possible, I'll keep to this set of countries over a variety of comparisons, which will allow some careful analysis of how the various electoral systems work in practice.

Of Lijphart's thirty-six democracies, nine use first past the post, while two more – New Zealand and Papua New Guinea – used it until recently. These were the eleven countries that I picked out when looking at wrong winner elections in the last section. For now, Figure 1 compares these cases with all the remaining countries as a block.

The pattern that emerges from Figure 1 is very clear: first past the post is the most disproportional electoral system in widespread use among democratic countries today. Most other systems translate the popular votes into seats much more accurately. Mauritius might look like an exception, but actually its electoral system is very similar to first past the post, so it too fits the general pattern.

Figure 1. Disproportionality of election results, 1945–2010: first past the post compared

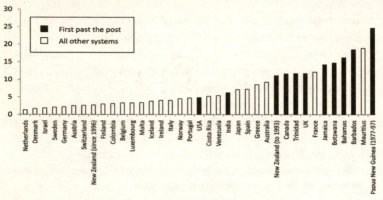

Note: The bars show averages across all elections since 1945 or since democratisation where that is later. See the Appendix for details of sources and calculations.

The idea of disproportionality focuses on the representation of political parties. But representation of women and minorities is also a matter of widespread concern. Is the under-representation of these groups in the House of Commons the fault of the electoral system?

There is strong reason to think that – at least in part – it is. Under first past the post, parties seek the strongest possible candidates for their most winnable constituencies, so they will tend to choose someone whom they can imagine as an MP. And most people's image of an MP is shaped by the MPs they are used to – who are, on the whole, white, middle-class, and male. In proportional systems, by contrast, each party has to put up a slate of candidates in each of the multi-member constituencies and has a strong incentive to seek diversity among those candidates in order to attract votes from a broad range of voters. Figure 2 presents evidence on this, showing the percentage of MPs who are women in the main legislative chamber in those of our thirty-six democracies for which the current numbers are available. As we can see, the countries that use first past the post tend to cluster towards the bottom end of the range.

Figure 2. Percentage of MPs who are women, 2010: first past the post compared

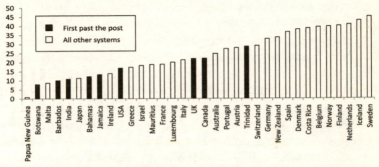

Note: Figures correct as of 30 September 2010. Source: Inter-Parliamentary Union (www.ipu.org). Data are unavailable for Columbia and Venezuela.

We can also see, however, that the relationship between the electoral system and the election of women isn't absolute: some of the countries that use first past the post do better than quite a few countries with other systems. Indeed, when we turn to the representation of ethnic minorities, some cross-national comparisons actually find very little evidence that the electoral system makes much of a difference. If we think about it, this perhaps makes sense: the argument that the strongest candidate is a white male holds true only if people's attitudes towards the representation of women and minorities remain prejudiced or shaped by outmoded stereotypes. As these attitudes dwindle, so too should the ill effects of first past the post. Still, it is clear that the legacy of past prejudices has not disappeared yet, and many would say that, given the scale of the current inequality, we should not just sit about waiting for it to do so.

At least for the time being, then, first past the post performs pretty badly in terms of representing the make-up of society in Parliament and even worse in terms of parliamentary representation of parties. But representation in Parliament is not all that matters: we also need to look at representation in government. Here, according to supporters of first past the post, supposedly proportional systems in fact produce highly disproportional outcomes. First past the post, they say, generally gives one party an overall majority of the seats in Parliament – hung parliaments such as the current one are rare. This makes it automatic that the largest party holds power. Under proportional systems, however, situations in which no party wins an overall majority become much more common. When that happens, a small party that holds the balance of power between two larger parties – such as the Lib Dems in the UK today – can extract huge concessions during coalition negotiations, allowing 'the tail to wag the dog'.

What should we make of this argument? It is true that Nick Clegg has won big policy concessions from David Cameron on major issues such as taxation and political reform. Indeed, the very fact that electoral reform is now so high on the British political agenda testifies to the Lib Dems' power within the current government. Writing in the *Daily Express* just after the coalition deal was sealed, the former Conservative MP Ann Widdecombe argued that the Lib Dems had been able to wield unacceptable influence. 'It is utter madness,' she said, 'that the party with the least share of the vote and which actually lost seats should dictate the terms of government.' She continued, 'If anybody wants to see why we should never agree to a system of proportional representation then that person has only to look at the ludicrous machinations which have followed this election because that is what would become the norm.'

But the picture is mixed. The Lib Dems hold five of the twenty-three full positions in the coalition cabinet – 22 per cent of the total. That is more than twice their 9 per cent share of the seats in the Commons, but very close to their 23 per cent share of the popular vote at the election. In fact, of all the votes won by Conservatives and Lib Dems at the election, Conservatives won three fifths and Lib Dems two fifths. So it is far from clear that the Lib Dems are over-represented in government at all. Looking across the period from 1945 to 2010, we see that the Conservatives, who averaged 41 per cent of the vote at general elections, were in government for 53 per cent of the time, while Labour, averaging 40 per cent of the vote, held government office for 47 per cent of the time. Other parties averaged 19 per cent of the vote, but (until the formation of the current coalition) held not a single ministerial post.

How does this compare with patterns seen elsewhere? Figure 3 summarises the evidence. Just as Figure 1 showed disproportion-alities between parties' vote shares and their seat shares, so Figure 3 is based on discrepancies between the time each party has spent in government since 1945 and that party's average share of the vote. Ideally, we want to know not just how much time a party has spent in government, but also how much power it has had while in government: in coalitions comprising several parties, we can expect some parties to exert more influence than others. I have weighted the numbers in Figure 3 to allow for such differences, but these are no more than approximations. Should you be interested, you'll find further details and discussion at p. 168 of the Appendix.

Figure 3. Disproportionality of governing power since 1945: first past the post compared

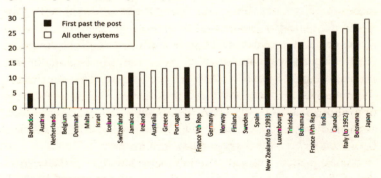

Note: The figures cover the period from 1945 (or democratisation if later) until the most recent election. See the Appendix for details of sources and how the numbers are calculated. Presidential countries (Columbia, Costa Rica, the United States, and Venezuela) are not included. Data are not available for Mauritius or Papua New Guinea.

Most of the countries using first past the post cluster towards the upper end of the graph: the idea that this electoral system leads to a close relationship between a party's support and its share of real governing power is just not correct. Still, there are exceptions: the UK is located around the middle of the range, while Jamaica and, especially, Barbados, are in the bottom half. In the UK, disproportionality of power-holding is significant, but there are many countries where it is higher. Whether it would be increased or decreased by a move to a different electoral system is something that we will need to investigate further.

Effective, accountable government

Our next criterion focuses not on the fairness of election outcomes, but on the effectiveness and accountability of government. Much of the case made by supporters of first past the post concentrates here. Their starting point is that first past the post makes it more likely than any of the other systems under consideration that one party will win a majority of the seats in the House of Commons. On this basis, they make three further arguments: first, that first past the post promotes government stability; second, that it enhances accountability; and, third, that these features and others combine to produce effective government.

It's certainly correct that under first past the post it is more likely that one party will win a majority of the seats in Parliament than under any of the other electoral systems discussed here. That's so for two reasons. First, the disproportionality that we saw in the previous section favours large parties: only they can accumulate sufficient votes to win large numbers of constituency contests. In consequence, the largest party almost always secures a large premium in seats compared to its share of the vote. Second, voters know that first past the post has this effect, and they tend therefore to concentrate their votes on the few parties that have a serious chance of winning. As a result, one party is often able to win an absolute majority of seats. In fact, of the eighteen Westminster elections since 1945, one or other of the main two parties has secured a majority over all other parties in sixteen. Before 2010, the only election where that did not happen was that of February 1974.

Still, we should not exaggerate this effect. Whenever the great majority of votes go to two parties – as they did in the early post-war decades – one of these parties is likely, under first past the post, to win a majority of seats. But when the vote is spread more widely across parties – as it is today – that becomes much less likely. In the election of 1951, the Conservatives and Labour between them won 97 per cent of the vote and almost 99 per cent of the seats. In 2010, their combined vote share was just 65 per cent, while their seat share was 87 per cent. It was therefore no accident that the 2010 election delivered a hung parliament: the more seats the Lib Dems and other smaller parties win, the harder it is for either of the big two parties to build an overall majority.

If this pattern continues, we can expect many more hung parliaments in the future. It's useful to look across the Atlantic – not to the United States, but to Canada. Canada has had twenty-one elections since 1945, of which ten failed to produce a majority for one party. The reason is simply that Canada has a multi-party system, with different parties doing well in different parts of the country. The same could apply here: if the Lib Dems maintain their popularity, hung parliaments could become commonplace, and first past the post will no longer reliably deliver single-party governments. Nevertheless, it will remain true that first past the post makes such governments more likely than any other system.

The next claim about first past the post is that it encourages stable government. The record of government stability in the UK since 1945 is certainly impressive. Almost all parliaments have lasted for four or five years. Only once – in 1979 – has a government collapsed mid-term, and even it was already well into its fifth year. Short parliaments – in 1950–51, 1964–6, and 1974 – have followed very close election results, but in each case stability was more or less restored after the following election. This stability arises, of course, because of the tendency towards single-party majorities. In contrast to this, it's easy to find countries that use proportional representation where the business of government has been much less stable. Italy is the most famous example: on one definition, it has had sixty separate governments in the sixty-five years since 1946.

We should be cautious of handpicked examples such as these: they will tell the story that those who come up with them want us to hear, but they won't necessarily tell the whole truth. Not all countries using proportional representation are like Italy: there are also stable cases, such as Germany and Spain, where governments routinely serve out their full four-year terms. Similarly, not all countries with first past the post have a brilliant record of stability: Canada's minority governments often stick around only for a year or two before a fresh election is called. Still, the overall evidence is that governments do tend to last longer under first past the post than with other electoral systems. This is clear from Figure 4, which reproduces Arend Lijphart's findings for the average duration of governments across our thirty-six democracies between 1945 and 1996. Even Canada is comfortably in the upper half of the range. If we think stability matters, we should notch up a point in favour of first past the post.

Figure 4. Average duration of governments in years, 1945–1996

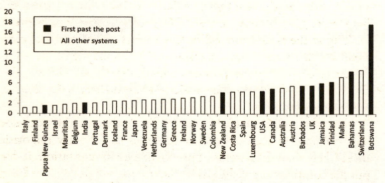

Source: Arend Lijphart, *Patterns of Democracy*, pp. 132–3. Note: There is much disagreement over what needs to happen for us to say that a government has ended. Lijphart gets round this by providing the average of two measures. One sees the government as changing only when there is a change in which parties form the government. The other says the government also changes when the prime minister does or there is an election or a change in whether the government holds a majority in Parliament.

The next argument is that first past the post is the system that best enables voters to determine the composition of government and hold it to account. If a party wins a parliamentary majority, the argument goes, it automatically forms the government: the outcome stems directly from how voters cast their ballots, not from post-election dealing among party leaders behind closed doors. And if we don't like the current government, we can vote it out and elect an alternative: there's no opportunity for a losing party to stay in power by attracting new coalition allies. As Ann Widdecombe puts it, 'One of the virtues of first past the post is that the nation can comprehensively dismiss an unsatisfactory government as Labour found in 1979 and the Conservatives in 1997. Coalitions, however, are all but impossible to get rid of: they just break up and re-form.'

As ever, there are counter-arguments to this line of reasoning. As I've mentioned, occasionally it's the wrong party that wins a majority – hardly a sign that voters are in charge. As we've just seen, first past the post makes single-party majorities more likely, but it doesn't guarantee them. Indeed, the rise of third parties means that the chances of hung parliaments are much higher today than they were in the past. For these reasons, the well-known elections expert John Curtice argues that first past the post 'cannot be relied upon to help make governments accountable to their voters'. Furthermore, looking at the issue from a different angle, the criticisms of coalitions are also sometimes exaggerated. Coalitions aren't always the products of mysterious post-election deal-making: parties often signal ahead of election day which of the other parties they are willing to work with.

Nevertheless, most analysts agree that first past the post does enhance accountability: because it makes single-party majorities more likely than do systems of proportional representation, it does put the composition of the government more squarely in the hands of voters. Indeed, some say that the choice of electoral system is fundamentally about choosing whether you think proportionality or accountability is more important. There are analysts who question this line. But the balance of argument and evidence supports the view that first past the post scores high marks on the accountability criterion.

The final point for discussion in this section is effectiveness: the proponents of first past the post argue that it is the system most likely to produce effective government. The tendency towards single-party government means that ministers can pursue a clear vision, rather than a hodge-podge of coalition compromises. Stability means that governments can get the job done and plan over the medium term. Accountability means that ineffective governments can be got rid of easily. The hung parliaments and coalition governments commonly produced by other electoral systems, by contrast, are said to leave the economy rudderless. Scare stories abounded in the run-up to the 2010 election that a hung parliament would take us towards Greek-style economic collapse. The *Daily Mail* quoted a financial adviser saying, 'A hung parliament will be the worst possible result for our economy.' He continued, 'The pound will suffer the most and could depreciate 10 per cent or 15 per cent. It could trigger a similar situation to the 1970s, when the government was eventually forced to go to the International Monetary Fund for a loan.' A poll by the Chartered Institute for Securities and Investment found that City types thought a hung parliament would be the worst possible election outcome for the economy.

Figure 5. Average annual inflation rate under first past the post and other electoral systems, 1997–2007

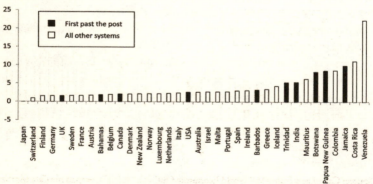

Source: Calculated from IMF World Economic Outlook (2010).

The fact that the 2010 election delivered a hung parliament (unusually for first past the post) without triggering so much as the earliest hint of a financial meltdown might lead us to doubt these worries. We might also note that Greece faces genuine economic crisis even though it has had single-party majority governments for almost all of its democratic history. Still, it would be good to gather some more systematic evidence.

Evaluating arguments about effectiveness isn't straightforward: what counts as effective depends on what you want government to do, and that's a highly subjective matter. But there are some objectives that we can all agree on. Governments, as we know all too well at present, should be able to keep the budget deficit under control. They should also limit inflation and they should keep unemployment as low as possible. Figures 5 to 7 summarise evidence in relation to these three indicators. Good quality, comparable data are available for all of our thirty-six countries for inflation; evidence is a bit more limited in the cases of unemployment and the budget deficit – and unfortunately the best data don't yet cover the economic crisis of the last few years. Nevertheless, one message comes through loud and clear from all three figures: the countries using first past the post do not cluster in any one part of the chart;

Figure 6. Average unemployment rate under first past the post and other electoral systems, 1997–2007

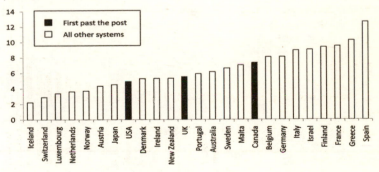

Source: Calculated from IMF World Economic Outlook (2010). Comparable data for the remaining countries are not available.

the electoral system therefore seems not to have a big impact on a country's economic performance.

When it comes to economic matters, however, even a small impact can be important. A persistent difference of just one or

two percentage points in the inflation or unemployment rate or in
the budget deficit can have a major effect on the long-term health
of the economy and its people. Such small differences cannot be
picked up by the sort of rough-and-ready procedure used in Figures
5 to 7. But political scientists and economists have investigated
possible links between electoral systems and economic performance
in great depth. Their research points to some clear conclusions, but
the effects they find don't all point in the same direction. On the
one hand, Torsten Persson finds that countries with proportional
electoral systems are more likely to adopt economic policies that
promote growth, such as open trade regimes. On the other hand,
Persson and his colleague Guido Tabellini find that budget deficits
are lower by 2 per cent of national income in countries with first
past the post and other similar systems. More ambiguously, several
studies find that government spending in general and welfare
spending in particular are higher under PR than under first past
the post – suggesting that what we think of electoral systems should
depend in part on whether we want a bigger or a smaller state.

Figure 7. Average government budget surplus or deficit as a percentage of GDP under
first past the post and other electoral systems, 1997–2007

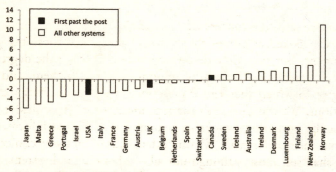

Source: Calculated from IMF World Economic Outlook (2010). Comparable data for the
remaining countries are not available.

All of this suggests that the effectiveness of economic policy-
making should not be at the heart of the debate over electoral
reform. Doom-mongers will no doubt argue that even a midge's

shuffle in the direction of greater proportionality will take us down the road to economic ruin, but there is no evidence to support that at all. Countries with proportional electoral systems seem to be capable of governing themselves perfectly well, despite the increased instability that hung parliaments and coalition governments can bring.

Putting all these various points together, what can we conclude? First past the post does make single-party majorities more likely than other systems and does promote stability – though the degree to which it has done so in the UK in recent decades might not be sustained in the future. Single-party majorities and stability don't matter greatly in themselves – but they are valuable if they promote accountability and effectiveness. In general, it seems that first past the post does indeed allow voters to hold governments to account more effectively than proportional systems, though its success rate should not be exaggerated. By contrast, there is very little evidence for the claim that first past the post leads to a government that is more effective in delivering what most of us want.

Voter choice and turnout

As we've seen, the concept of 'voter choice' has many facets. We've already looked at one of them: voters' ability to choose the government. But two more deserve our attention here: the degree to which voters have a range of options available to them, and the degree to which they can express their preferences among those options. We can deal with the second of these very quickly: first past the post allows voters to give only very limited information about their preferences. We can in fact express only one choice. As we shall see, most – though not all – other electoral systems give voters the chance to say much more about their preferences among parties and candidates than this.

What, then, about the range of options available to us? 4,133 candidates ran in the general election of 2010 – an average of more than six per constituency. That was a record high and it might suggest that the choice available to voters is very healthy indeed.

Yet most of those candidates were not serious options at all, at least for any voter wanting to influence who got elected. Opponents of first past the post, indeed, argue that the range of options it offers to voters is very limited. They argue that most constituencies are safe seats, such that it is entirely obvious before even a single vote has been cast who is going to win. They also argue that first past the post encourages parties and candidates to crowd around the political centre ground, such that all the significant candidates are much of a muchness anyway. What should we make of these arguments?

First, what counts as a safe seat? At one extreme, we could say that there are almost no safe seats. In the 2010 general election, the largest swing in any constituency – the largest shift in votes from one party to another – was 23 per cent, in Belfast East, where Northern Ireland's First Minister Peter Robinson was defeated in the wake of the scandals that assailed his wife, Iris. Across the whole country, there are just ten seats in which the incumbent party could absorb such a big swing against it and still hold on. So if our criterion for safety is that a seat is truly impregnable, the claim that there are large numbers of safe seats must be rejected. But that clearly sets the bar too high: swings of that scale are quite exceptional. In fact, even in years of major flux in the House of Commons, most constituencies do not change hands. In 2010, 115 seats switched from one party to another, while 535 stuck with the same party. In 1997, which saw the largest seat change of any post-war election, 475 of 659 constituencies returned the same party as before. Just twenty-nine seats – fewer than one in twenty – changed hands in 2001 and sixty-two in 2005. So worries about safe seats are well founded.

The claim that first past the post generates a mind-numbing battle between Tweedledum and Tweedledee also has considerable merit. In order to get anywhere under first past the post, a party needs to accumulate a large number of votes. It is much more likely to achieve that if it eschews radical terrain and fixes its message upon the centre ground. Labour mysteriously forgot that under the leadership of Michael Foot in 1983, when it campaigned under a left-wing manifesto famously dubbed 'the longest suicide note in history'. And it paid the price with its lowest vote share since 1918. Under proportional systems, the large parties face similar pressures: they want to maximise their votes just as much as their counterparts under first past the post. The difference is that smaller parties have much greater chances of success in these systems, and they can carve out niches for themselves away from the centre of the political spectrum.

So choice is limited under first past the post: often the outcome is all but guaranteed by polling day, and even where that is not the case the range of options can be highly constrained. As I've suggested, however, while choice sounds like a wonderful thing in the abstract, we are not always so sure that we like it when it confronts us directly. If greater choice means greater power for extremists, we might prefer the limits that first past the post imposes. Many voters might value a system that encourages candidates towards the centre ground of politics: after all, that's where most voters place themselves.

Voter choice matters partly because it's valuable in itself – without choice, we do not have democracy. It also matters if it promotes turnout: we might be more likely to bother to vote if there is a serious choice to be made. The last three elections in the UK have yielded lower turnout than at any other time in the post-war era. Many supporters of electoral reform have argued that a shift to proportional representation, by reducing the number of

Figure 8. Average turnout at elections since 1980

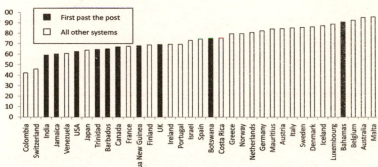

Note: New Zealand is excluded because it changed its electoral system halfway through the period. The figure for Papua New Guinea excludes the most recent election, held under the alternative vote. Source: International Institute for Democracy and Electoral Assistance (www.idea.int).

safe seats, making every vote count, and enhancing the range of options available, would help reverse that turnout decline.

Are they right? Figure 8 shows turnout across our thirty-six democracies at the most recent election. Countries using first past the post are mostly found in the bottom half of the range, suggesting that this electoral system indeed suppresses turnout. This fits with what most analysts have found. But it isn't an open-and-shut case: some of the more sophisticated statistical analyses in fact find very little relationship between the electoral system and turnout, and there's no evidence to suggest that electoral reform would radically alter levels of voter engagement. The goal of increasing turnout certainly can't be used on its own to justify a move to proportional representation.

The constituency link

The 'constituency link' is one of the most cherished parts of the British political system. It's seen as helping to keep MPs in touch with realities on the ground. It forces those MPs to engage with a full range of voters, rather than just their own natural supporters. It also gives voters a point of ready access into the political system. Even proponents of radical change in our electoral system agree that whatever new system might be introduced would have to maintain or enhance the constituency link.

I suggested before that we shouldn't get carried away with the constituency link: if MPs are too focused upon constituency case work they may have to neglect the important national issues that are the responsibility of the House of Commons to resolve. I won't pursue that point further here. But it's important to ask how effective the constituency link really is under first past the post. It can usefully be broken down into two parts: MPs' connection to their constituency and individual voters' connection to their MP.

There's no doubt that first past the post does strengthen MPs' ties to their constituency and does force MPs to engage with a broad spectrum of the population. An interesting case study of this (and, indeed, of the importance of electoral systems in general) is provided by the British representatives in the European Parliament.

Before 1999, British MEPs were elected by first past the post and, just like their Westminster colleagues, most of them maintained constituency offices and held regular constituency surgeries. Since 1999, a form of proportional representation has been used. While the constituency offices still exist in some form or other, a detailed study by David Farrell and Roger Scully has found that the volume of MEPs' constituency work has fallen sharply and MEPs' sense of connection to their constituents has greatly diminished. As we'll see, different forms of proportional representation could have produced a different outcome here. But first past the post clearly comes out well from the comparison. In a world where the position of politician is increasingly professionalised, first past the post does confront MPs with the realities of ordinary lives at their surgeries and in their mailboxes.

But how much does the constituency link matter for us as citizens? For some it matters a great deal: all politicians proudly tell of the cases in which they have helped someone with their application for housing or put pressure on the local bus companies to sort out their timetables. But for many voters, the constituency link is largely meaningless. Fewer than 10 per cent of us say we have contacted our MP over the last three or so years. Indeed, fewer than half of us can even correctly name our MP. If the constituency link, at least from voters' perspective, is largely a myth, we might wonder just how much weight should be placed upon it.

Keeping MPs in check

Our final criterion stems directly from the previous two. Supporters of first past the post argue that that system allows voters to get to know their MP and make a judgement on him or her come election day. If voters conclude that their MP is not up to scratch or does not have their interests at heart, they can vote him or her out. As a result, MPs have a strong incentive to keep on their toes and to work hard in their constituents' interests. Opponents, meanwhile, argue that the preponderance of safe seats under first past the post means that, in fact, most MPs are entirely secure. If so inclined, they can concentrate on feathering their own beds without risk of reprisals. The MPs' expenses scandal of 2009 highlighted the importance of this debate.

This scandal also offers an opportunity to test out the arguments. If the advocates of reform are right, we should expect MPs in safe seats to have been more deeply implicated in the scandal than those whose position was more precarious. Following the scandal, a review of expenses paid between 2004 and 2009 was conducted by a retired civil servant, Sir Thomas Legg. He recommended that 327 MPs repay at least some money. Figure 9 shows the average repayment per MP, categorised according to the size of their majority at the 2005 election. There isn't much evidence of a connection. There are some problems with these numbers – for example, they don't take account of the 'flipping' of second home designations – so they might not tell the whole story. Nevertheless, it seems pretty clear that what matters more is transparency rather than the electoral system: once the expenses claims were exposed, all miscreant MPs suffered. Many of the worst offenders were forced to stand down, no matter the size of their majority.

Figure 9. Average expenses repayment required per MP

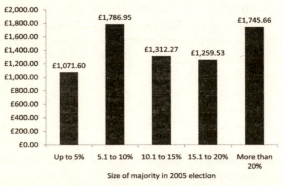

Note: Based on the final figures reported by Sir Thomas Legg on 4 February 2010. Source: 'Full list of MPs' expenses repayments', BBC News Online.

Those advocating electoral reform since the expenses scandal broke have placed heavy weight on the argument that safe seats under first past the post encourage complacency and misbehaviour.

They have done so because this has been the issue of greatest concern to voters. But it's not actually the strongest argument for electoral reform: the evidence on it is weak. If we are going to change the electoral system, we should do so for some of the reasons already discussed, not because we think it will turn our MPs into saints.

Reforming first past the post without getting rid of it

Let's take stock for a moment. We have looked at a range of criteria, and the evidence presented so far suggests a mixed picture. First past the post performs well on some grounds: it promotes stable and accountable government and it keeps MPs in touch with realities on the ground. On other criteria, it performs badly: it does not accurately translate votes into seats in the House of Commons and in extreme cases it can produce election outcomes that clearly contradict what the people voted for; it also limits the choices available to voters.

Before turning to other electoral systems, we should think about whether we can tweak the operation of first past the post in ways that address its drawbacks. Many supporters of first past the post say it scores well in almost all respects: they don't object to its disproportionality, because that is the flipside of a system that produces stable, accountable, single-party government. The only point on which they acknowledge the current system is seriously lacking is bias: there is no way anyone can argue it is healthy that the system can give more seats to one party even when another party has won more votes. The Conservatives therefore want to keep first past the post while addressing the problem of bias. They argue that they can do so by changing the mechanisms by which constituency boundaries are drawn.

The issue here is that, under the current rules, constituencies vary quite widely in the number of electors they contain. At the extremes, the Western Isles constituency (Na h-Eilean an Iar) had 21,780 eligible voters at the 2010 election, while the constituency covering the Isle of Wight had 109,902. These cases are exceptional for geographical reasons. But it's not unusual even for neighbouring constituencies to differ in terms of electorate by fifteen or twenty thousand voters: within London, for example, East Ham had 90,674 voters, whereas neighbouring Leyton and Wanstead had 63,540. There are three main reasons for these differences. First, different parts of the country have different levels of representation: Wales, Northern Ireland, and the Scottish Highlands and Islands are over-represented compared to the rest of Scotland and England. Second, the boundary commissions that draw up the constituencies cannot (for the most part) cross local government divisions such as counties or Scottish council areas, so they can't borrow a chunk of a neighbouring county in order to give a constituency the right number of voters. Third, people move over time: even new boundaries, such as those used in 2010, are out of date by the time they come into force, because they're based on population when the review process began.

The reason these differences generate bias is that they affect the parties in different ways. Labour does well from the over-representation of Wales. And because people like to move into affluent areas, which generally vote Conservative, Conservative seats tend over time to grow compared to Labour seats. In the 2010 election – despite the fact that new boundaries were being used for the first time – the seats won by Labour contained an average of 68,366 eligible voters, while the Conservative-held seats had 72,218. This meant that it took fewer votes to elect a Labour than a Conservative MP.

The coalition government is therefore proposing three changes. First, they want to abolish the over-representation of Wales and Northern Ireland: from now on, all parts of the UK except the sparsely populated Scottish Highlands and Islands will have the same ratio of population to seats. Second, they will prioritise the equality of constituency electorates over the integrity of local authority areas. Again with the exception of the Scottish Highlands and Islands, constituencies will be allowed to deviate from the national average by no more than 5 per cent, which will be achievable only by allowing some constituencies to cross county boundaries. Third, they want to speed up the review process. Reviews are currently held every eight to twelve years and have lately taken up to seven years to complete. As a result, the boundaries used in 2005 were based on the electoral registers in 1991 and, if the rules remained as now, the current boundaries, based on registers between 2000 and 2003, would still be used for the election in 2015. The plan is that, from now on, reviews should be completed every five years, so that the boundaries in 2015 will be based on electoral registers in early 2011.

How much difference will this make? Some seem to think that it will solve the problem of bias in the electoral system. But it will not. As I mentioned, there are several sources of bias in the current system. Inequality in constituency electorates is only one of these, and it's not the most important. A group of political scientists based at Bristol and Plymouth universities have estimated the total amount of bias in recent general elections and have also worked out how much of this bias is attributable to different causes. Their figures for bias between the two main parties at the last two elections are shown in Table 1. The total bias between the two main parties in 2005 was 112 seats. This means that, had both Labour and the Conservatives won exactly the same number of votes as each other (strictly speaking, had they both won 34.7 per cent of the vote, which is halfway between the vote shares that they actually got), Labour would have won 112 seats more than the Conservatives. This bias was far lower in 2010, at fifty-four seats.

Table 1. Consevative–Labour bias in the 2005 and 2010 elections

	2005	2010
Total bias	112	54
Bias attributable to:		
☐ differences in average constituency electorates between countries	6	9
☐ differences between constituency electorates within countries	20	9
☐ differences in turnout between constituencies	38	31
☐ differences in support for and seats won by other parties	9	4
☐ the efficiency with which a party's votes are spread across the country	35	0

Source: Ron Johnston, 'Reducing the Size of the House of Commons and Equalising Its Constituencies', paper given at The Constitution Unit, UCL, 23 July 2010.

We can see that, in each election, the largest chunk of the overall bias was produced by differences in turnout. Turnout tends to be substantially lower in Labour-held seats than it is in Conservative-held seats. This means that, even if the number of eligible voters is exactly the same between constituencies, the number of votes actually needed to win a Labour seat is lower. The second largest component of bias in 2005 was the efficiency with which each party's votes were spread across the country. A party can translate its votes into seats most efficiently if it 'wins small and loses big' – if it just wins the seats that it wins, while it loses by big margins the seats that it loses. That way it doesn't waste too many votes. Labour's votes were much more efficiently distributed than the Conservatives' in 2005. By 2010, however, this gap had entirely vanished: the Conservatives caught up with Labour in targeting their campaign resources on key marginal seats; as a result, their votes were spread much more efficiently than before.

These two sources of bias are beyond the control of electoral system engineers: tweaking constituency boundaries does not affect them. The same applies to the small part of bias that arises from the pattern of support for smaller parties. Changing boundary review procedures has scope to change only the two parts of bias that derive from differences in the size of constituency electorates, which came in total to twenty-six seats in 2005 and eighteen in 2010. Even if these sources of bias can be tackled, all the others will remain untouched.

Achieving perfect equality of constituency sizes is almost impossible. But eliminating the over-representation of Wales and Northern Ireland will remove most of the bias that arises from differences in the size of constituency electorates among the component countries of the United Kingdom. Increasing the frequency of reviews and requiring deviations between constituencies to be much smaller, meanwhile, will remove much of the bias coming from within-country differences.

It's important to ask whether these changes are worth while given the relatively small gains that they entail. Most people will agree that it makes sense to end the over-representation of Wales and Northern Ireland: now that they have their own assemblies, the old rationale for this over-representation has gone. Scotland's former over-representation has already been eliminated (allowing, as ever, for the exception of the Highlands and Islands) for this reason. The plan to increase the frequency and speed of boundary reviews is causing some concern – the boundary commissions will need increased budgets to cope with these changes and opportunities for local consultation will be curtailed. But these are fairly minor worries: certainly, Labour's claims that the proposals are tantamount to 'the most blatant gerrymander of parliamentary constituency boundaries since the days of rotten boroughs' are entirely without foundation. Nevertheless, it can legitimately be said that the coalition parties are addressing only those iniquities in the current system that harm Conservative and Lib Dem interests while retaining those that do not. In particular, the government has said little about the problem that some groups – particularly the young and the disadvantaged – are badly represented on the electoral registers that are used to calculate population numbers. Yet there is no easy solution to this problem, despite what some Labour politicians (having failed to tackle it themselves during thirteen years in government) would have us believe.

The aspect of the changes that is causing widest unease is the plan to prioritise the equalisation of constituencies over the preservation of local community ties. A petition against hiving off part of the Isle of Wight to a mainland constituency was presented to Parliament in September having gathered over 16,000 signatures. A vigorous campaign has also been launched in Cornwall, part of which, if the government's plans are implemented, will need to be in a constituency that includes part of Devon. People in areas such as these are concerned that their distinct identities will be eroded and their particular local interests inadequately represented. Some MPs also have qualms about having to deal with multiple local councils. All of this disruption will be introduced to remove just a small component of overall bias amounting to only a handful of seats.

So the planned changes to boundary review procedures are well motivated: no one can condone bias in the electoral system. But they will leave most of that bias untouched and some of the proposed changes will create new problems of their own. Whether the gains they will bring justify the disruption they will cause is debatable. More broadly, almost none of the disadvantages of first past the post can be tackled through such tinkering alone.

We've seen, then, that first past the post, despite its significant strengths, is far from perfect. But no electoral system is. The question we need to tackle is whether an alternative system can be devised that does any better.

4. The alternative vote

The coming referendum will give us a choice between two electoral systems: either the first past the post system that we already have or the system known as the alternative vote. So what exactly is the alternative vote? How does it differ from first past the post? What are the arguments for and against its introduction?

How the alternative vote works

In many ways, the alternative vote system – AV for short – looks very similar to first past the post. Just as under the current system, the country is divided into constituencies, each electing one MP. On election day, voters are given a ballot paper listing candidates. The object of the election is to choose the candidate who is most popular.

But the alternative vote differs from first past the post in two key ways. The first concerns what voters write on the ballot paper. Under first past the post, you are allowed to vote for only one candidate, by placing a cross next to her or his name. Under the alternative vote, by contrast, you can rank the candidates in order of preference: you place a '1' next to the candidate you favour most, a '2' next to your second preference, and so on. In the version of the alternative vote that is proposed for the UK, voters will be able to rank as many of the candidates as they wish: you'll be able, if you want, to express just your first preference, or to rank some of the candidates but not all, or to work your way through the whole list, from first preference to last.

The second difference concerns how the votes are counted and the result of the election decided. As we've seen, it's often the case under first past the post that a candidate is elected with less than half the vote in their constituency. Table 2 shows some extreme examples from the 2010 election. We might well question whether it's fair or legitimate that a candidate can be elected even when more than two voters in three supported someone else.

Table 2. MPs elected on low vote share

Norwich South		Brighton Pavilion	
	Votes (%)		Votes (%)
Simon Wright, LD	29.4	Caroline Lucas, Green	31.3
Charles Clarke, Lab	28.7	Nancy Platts, Lab	28.9
Antony Little, Con	22.9	Charlotte Vere, Con	23.7
Adrian Ramsey, Green	14.9	Bernadette Millam, LD	13.8
Steve Emmens, UKIP	2.4	Nigel Carter, UKIP	1.8
Leonard Heather, BNP	1.5	Ian Fyvie, Socialist LP	0.3
Gabriel Polley, WRP	0.2	Soraya Kara, CURE	0.1
		Leo Atreides, Ind.	0.0
Oldham East and Saddleworth		Northampton North	
	Votes (%)		Votes (%)
Phil Woolas, Lab	31.9	Michael Ellis, Con	34.1
Elwyn Watkins, LD	31.6	Sally Keeble, Lab	29.3
Kashif Ali, Con	26.4	Andrew Simpson, LD	27.9
Alwyn Stott, BNP	5.7	Ray Beasley, BNP	3.3
David Bentley, UKIP	3.9	Jim MacArthur, UKIP	3.1
Gulzar Nazir, Christian P.	0.5	Tony Lochmuller, Green	1.1
		Eamonn Fitzpatrick, Ind.	0.8
		Timothy Webb, Christian P.	0.2
		Malcolm Mildren, Ind.	0.1

The main objective of the alternative vote is to avoid scenarios like this. At the first stage of the counting process, the first preferences of all the voters are added up. If a candidate has secured more than half of all these first preferences, he or she is declared the winner: there's no debate about the fact that this is clearly the most popular candidate. But if no candidate has won more than half of the first preferences, the alternative vote system probes beyond these first preferences to see which of the candidates has broader support. It does this by progressively eliminating the lowest placed candidates and 'redistributing' their votes until a majority winner is found. Looking at Table 2 again, in Norwich South, for example, it's clear that Gabriel Polley, who won 102 votes for the Workers'

Revolutionary Party, stands no chance of election. So we would eliminate him from the count, look at his supporters' second preferences, and redistribute his votes accordingly. These 102 votes would clearly not be enough to push any candidate over the 50 per cent threshold, so we would then have to eliminate the next candidate, the BNP's Leonard Heather. This process would continue until one of the leading candidates got over 50 per cent. If some voters expressed only their first preference or their first few preferences, we could whittle the field down to two candidates and find that neither has passed 50 per cent, as some voters have not said which of these two candidates they prefer. In that case, whichever of these last two candidates ended up with more votes would be declared the winner.

Table 3. Election result in Banks constituency, Australia, 2010

	1st count	Elimination of Parsons	2nd count	Elimination of Spight	3rd count
Melham, Daryl (Labor)	36,034	+436	36,470	+6,680	43,150
Delezio, Ron (Liberal)	38,178	+583	38,761	+1,958	40,719
Spight, Paul (Green)	8,062	+576	8,638	Excluded	
Parson, Michael (One Nation)	1,595	Excluded			

It will be helpful to look at a real-world example. The most prominent country that uses the alternative vote to choose its MPs is Australia. Table 3 gives the breakdown of the counting process from the Banks constituency in New South Wales at the 2010 election. Ron Delezio, the candidate of the Liberal Party (which is Australia's equivalent of the Conservatives) had a fairly clear lead in terms of first preferences over his Labor Party rival. But his share of the vote was less than 46 per cent – too little for outright victory. The process of excluding the bottom candidates therefore began. Michael Parsons, having come last, was eliminated first. The counting officials looked at the ballots cast for him and redistributed them to the remaining candidates according to the second preferences marked on them. Still, however, no one had a majority: the votes from Michael Parsons were insufficient to push any of the remaining candidates over the 50 per cent mark. So the next step was to exclude the third-placed Green candidate. He did have a substantial chunk of the vote. When he was eliminated and his supporters' next preferences were counted, the great majority – over three quarters – went to Labor's Daryl Melham. This transfer lifted Melham ahead of Delezio, securing his election to the Australian Parliament.

Australia's Labor and Green parties both occupy the left of the political spectrum. The alternative vote system allows the two parties to maintain their separate identities and run candidates against each other without the risk that by splitting the left-wing vote they will allow a candidate from the right to win. The same applies equally to parties on the right that don't want to give an advantage to the left.

AV's cousins

Australia is the only country with a long history of using AV to elect its Parliament. This system has also been introduced more recently in Fiji (which has used the alternative vote since 1999) and Papua New Guinea (which switched from first past the post to the alternative vote before the elections of 2007). One of the arguments sometimes offered against AV is that it is little used: if it were such a good system, surely more countries would have adopted it.

In fact, that's slightly misleading. First, several more countries do use the alternative vote in some way: Ireland, for example, uses this system to elect its president; and it's also used for some local elections in the United States. Second, the alternative vote has some close cousins that bulk up the family numbers. The most familiar of these cousins, at least for some British voters, is the 'supplementary vote' system used to choose directly elected mayors in London and some other towns and cities. The supplementary vote is a truncated version of AV: voters can express just two preferences and all but the top two candidates are eliminated after the first round of counting. Another set of cousins are the 'multiple round' voting systems, under which voters go to the polls more than once. France, for example, has two-round elections. The first round looks just like first past the post, except that a candidate can be elected only if she or he wins more than half the votes cast. If no candidate reaches that threshold, a second round is held one or two weeks later, which only the leading candidates can enter. The precise rules are different for presidential and for parliamentary elections, but, in either case, whoever wins most votes in the second round is declared the winner.

Because AV is so similar to these run-off systems, it is often referred to – particularly in the United States – as the system of 'instant run-off'. In a multiple round system, one or more candidates are eliminated after each round and voters have to return to the polls to say whom they support from the candidates who remain. A similar run-off takes place under AV, but without the need for voters to go back to the polling station: in giving their second preference, voters have in effect said, 'if my first preference is eliminated at the first round, this is the candidate who I vote for at the second round'. Once we add in multiple round systems, AV and its cousins are used by twenty-two countries to elect their national Parliament and by most countries with a directly elected president.

It's also worth noting that AV and other related systems are used to determine the winners of many other sorts of contest. The most recent high profile example is September 2010's Labour leadership election, which Ed Miliband won through an alternative vote system. Ed's brother David gained most first preferences; as the sole Blairite in the race, he could unite those committed to a centrist strategy, whereas voters leaning further left were divided among several candidates. But the majority of those eligible to vote preferred Ed as leader over David. David might have won under first past the post by slipping through a divided field. But AV revealed Ed's wider support and allowed this to determine the result.

In fact, all three main parties use the alternative vote or (in the Conservatives' case) a very close cousin to choose their party leader. It will be interesting to ask politicians who oppose AV for Westminster elections whether they also oppose it for party elections. AV is also used within the House of Commons for choosing the Speaker and the chairs of select committees, and the government plans to use it in the elections for police commissioners that are scheduled for 2012. Beyond the world of politics, AV is used now to decide the winner of the Oscar for best picture and in many elections to students' unions, professional associations, and other such bodies. AV's multiple round cousins are used gradually to whittle down the field of contestants in both *Big Brother* and *The X Factor*.

On the other hand, we should be careful to distinguish AV from systems that look quite similar but are actually significantly different. The voting system used at the Eurovision Song Contest, for example, looks at first glance quite like the alternative vote: each country ranks the performers in order of preference; the winner is determined by adding up the votes across the countries. But there's a crucial difference. At Eurovision, each preference is given a number of points: the first preference gets twelve points, the second preference ten, and so on. All of these preferences count towards the final result. If the alternative vote were used, by contrast, only the first preferences – only the twelves – would be counted at first. Only if no one got more than half of these would you start to look at the tens, eights and lower preferences. Points-based systems like this are used elsewhere too – for example, in Formula One racing. But these are not alternative vote systems. Rather, they are versions of what's called the 'Borda count', named after the eighteenth-century French mathematician who invented them. It will be useful to bear this difference in mind when we consider how the alternative vote performs against our various criteria.

Election results under the alternative vote

Before we get to our criteria, however, we should take a quick look at the overall impact of the alternative vote upon elections in the UK. How would recent elections have turned out had the alternative vote been used rather than first past the post?

That is by no means an easy question to answer. We could try to estimate results under the alternative vote on the basis of the actual election results. But the actual results give us no information about voters' second and lower preferences, as voters under first past the post express only one preference. Indeed, we can't even assume that the one preference that voters express under first past the post would be their first preference under the alternative vote; as we'll see later, some voters who vote tactically under first past the post might not do so under AV. Some voters might express themselves quite differently if elections were held using AV.

Analysts have used two main methods to try to get round these problems. One is to ask people for their second preference as well as their first when conducting opinion polls and to use this information in order to make estimates. The other is to give poll respondents a brief description of how AV works and then ask them to fill out an AV ballot paper. Figure 10 reports estimates using both of these techniques (those using the first technique are labelled '1', those using the second '2') and compares them to the actual results under first past the post.

Figure 10. Estimated election results under the alternative vote, compared to actual results

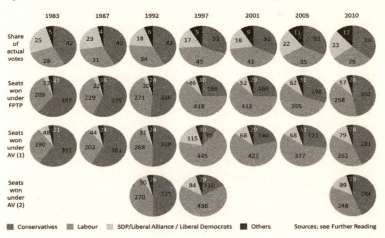

There's a lot of information in Figure 10, so it will be useful to take a moment to digest it. Looking at the first two elections covered – in 1983 and 1987 – we see that AV would have made very little difference. The Conservatives and Labour would both have lost some seats to the advantage of the SDP/Liberal Alliance. But the Conservatives would have retained healthy majorities while the smaller parties would have remained significantly under-represented. The changes in the distribution of seats would again have been small in 1992, but this time they would have had more political significance: they would have left the Conservatives winning pretty much exactly half of all the seats, thereby depriving them of their working majority. The Conservatives could still have entered office on their own – helped when necessary by the Ulster Unionists. But John Major's government would have been even more fragile than it was in reality.

It's in 1997, however, that things get really interesting. The first set of estimates reported in Figure 10, made by the respected political scientist John Curtice, suggest that the Conservatives would have been reduced to just 70 seats in this election had AV been in place. Indeed, they would have come well behind the Lib Dems in terms of seats even though they scored significantly more votes. The second set of estimates, produced by another top-notch team led by Patrick Dunleavy, suggests that the Conservatives' losses would have been less dramatic. Still, the Conservatives' share of the seats would have been little more than half their entitlement under strict proportionality.

Why would AV have produced such an extreme result in 1997? The basic reason is that most Labour voters would have given their second preferences to the Lib Dems while most Lib Dems would have transferred their vote to Labour – voters for these two parties formed an anti-Conservative bloc. Under first past the post, the Conservatives could win many seats where this bloc was in the majority because anti-Conservative voters were divided between two candidates. Under AV, however, these votes would have coalesced at second and subsequent rounds of counting and many Conservatives would have been defeated. This effect gradually unwound over subsequent elections as Lib Dems became disillusioned with Labour. Nevertheless, AV would still have increased Labour's majority in both 2001 and 2005 while leaving the Conservatives under-represented.

By 2010, we get back roughly to where we started. The impact of AV on seats won would have been fairly small, with the Conservatives and Labour both losing some seats and the Lib Dems gaining. As in 1992, however, these slight changes would have significantly altered the post-election landscape. Whereas under the actual result the Lib Dems could form a majority coalition only with the Conservatives, had AV been used, it appears that the Lib Dems could easily have entered government with either the Conservatives or Labour. That would have increased the Lib Dems' bargaining power and made the post-election negotiations much less predictable.

Rewarding popularity

Having taken a quick look at the overall impact of the alternative vote upon election outcomes, it's now time to think about how AV measures up against our various criteria. Let's start again with the issue of whether AV rewards popularity. There's one issue here that we can dispose of quickly – namely the question of whether AV can deliver victory to the wrong party at the national level. We might hope that AV would avoid the problems that first past the post can lead to here – after all, it prevents minority winners at the local level. In fact, however, it does not. As we have just seen, at most elections, the national result under AV is unlikely to be much different from the result under first past the post. That's especially the case in close elections – which are precisely the elections in which a wrong winner is most likely. A number of Australian elections – including three out of the last six state elections in South Australia – have delivered wrong winners, despite the use of AV. On this score, therefore, AV offers little improvement on first past the post.

But the main debate surrounding the alternative vote focuses on the local level. AV's supporters argue that it ensures victory in each constituency for the most popular candidate. AV's opponents argue precisely the opposite: that it steals victory from the rightful winner. We need to untangle what is going on in this dispute.

Beginning with the case for the alternative vote, imagine a very simple constituency contest in which just two candidates run – Labour and Conservative. In a two-candidate race, first past the post and the alternative vote are identical. One candidate will get more than 50 per cent of the vote (unless there's a tie) and is therefore the winner. There's no doubt that this is the most popular candidate. Let's say that, in our constituency, the Conservative candidate scores a narrow victory, beating her opponent by 52 per cent to 48 per cent.

Now suppose that, at the next election, another candidate enters, representing UKIP. The voters' preferences haven't changed at all. It's still the case that 52 per cent of them prefer the Conservative candidate over the Labour candidate. But they now have a third candidate to choose from. Suppose that 10 per cent of them prefer the UKIP candidate over either of the alternatives and therefore vote for him. As in the rest of the country, the Eurosceptic UKIP takes most of its votes from the Conservatives – say that four in every five of UKIP's votes come from previous Conservative supporters while one in five comes from previous Labour voters. That means that Labour's candidate secures 46 per cent of the vote, the Conservative 44 per cent, and UKIP 10 per cent, so the Labour candidate wins. But the voters' preferences haven't changed: it's still the case that more of them want the Conservative candidate than the Labour candidate (or the UKIP candidate) to be their MP. In that sense, the Conservative remains most popular.

That's the core of the case for AV. If there is a candidate who would defeat every other candidate in a head-to-head contest, then that must be the most popular candidate. In scenarios such as the one I've just described, first past the post fails to elect such candidates, but AV succeeds. Wherever AV elects a different candidate from first past the post, we can expect to find the same scenario. Two or more candidates occupy similar political ground – Conservative and UKIP in recent elections in the UK, or Labour and the Lib Dems between 1997 and 2005. Under first past the post, but not AV, this split allows a candidate from another part of the political spectrum to steal the election.

As we've seen, in most constituencies the alternative vote wouldn't actually change the election result. In some, the leading candidate will secure more than 50 per cent of first preferences. Even where that isn't the case, most of the candidates who lead after the first count will pick up sufficient lower preferences to pass that threshold later on. In these cases, the effect of the alternative vote would be to legitimise the result: to make it clear that the MP commands majority support among constituents. But in those constituencies where the result does change, the alternative vote, according to its supporters, saves us from an unjust outcome.

How, then, do AV's opponents respond? The main issue concerns whether we should accept the claim that the most popular candidate is the one who would win a series of hypothetical head-to-head contests against all the other candidates. Surely, in the view of the defenders of the status quo, these imaginary contests are missing the point. What matters is the contest that actually takes place, and the most popular candidate in that contest is simply the one who wins most votes – the one who is the first choice of most voters.

But this is to treat our first preferences as much more absolute and concrete than they really are. In the example just given, some voters' first preference is for the Conservative candidate when there are only two candidates, but for UKIP when there are three candidates: their first preference is not something fixed and sacrosanct. Just because UKIP have entered the race doesn't change in any way these voters' clear preference for the Conservatives over Labour. Their main preference is for a candidate from the right; within that, they then have varying enthusiasm for different candidates of the right. First past the post fails to capture this structure in our preferences, whereas the alternative vote, in this respect, performs better.

Some people's preference structures are well suited to first past the post: these are the people who are committed to a particular ideology, represented by one candidate and party, and care little for the rest. But others are better suited to the alternative vote: these are the voters for whom no party is perfect but several have varying degrees of merit. Given the collapse in party membership and in feelings of partisan loyalty in the UK in recent decades, it seems safe to assume that the second sort of voter is more common today than the first.

AV's opponents might accept that first past the post offers a crude way of gauging voters' preferences but still argue that AV is fatally flawed. Under AV, close contests could sometimes be decided by very low preferences indeed: there were some constituencies in the 2010 Australian election where ninth or tenth preferences may have made a difference to the outcome. It needs to be asked whether such low preferences are meaningful and whether election results should be determined by them. Voters might have some clear preferences among parties and candidates, but do we really have seven or eight or even more? As Winston Churchill put it during a debate on the introduction of AV in 1931, 'The decision ... is to be determined by the most worthless votes given for the most worthless candidates.'

Churchill and his modern heirs do have a point here: many of us haven't even heard of some of the candidates whom we find on the ballot paper on polling day, never mind have any clear preferences among them. But it's not clear that this provides a strong argument against the alternative vote. The candidates we haven't heard of and don't have views on are generally going to be the no-hopers who are never going to win the election anyway; that we can't decide how to rank them is very unlikely to make a difference to the election outcome.

In addition, ambiguities in the order of our preferences can occur at the top of that ordering as well as at the bottom. Some voters, for example, might find it difficult to distinguish between the three main parties but still clearly prefer them to the remaining candidates, whom they (rightly or wrongly) view as a mix of extremists and nutters. Election outcomes are sometimes determined by voters who could easily have swung the other way, but that is just as true under first past the post as it is under the alternative vote.

AV's opponents may still come back and say that it promotes not the most popular candidate, but the least unpopular, and that it therefore favours the bland and the equivocating over the distinctive and decisive. Given the graduated nature of preferences that we have already seen, the conceptual difference between most popular and least unpopular is a bit like the difference between a glass half full and a glass half empty. Nevertheless, the more concrete point has genuine substance: centrists tend to do well from AV, because they can act as compromise candidates when neither left nor right can secure a majority on its own. In some circumstances, that is a considerable virtue. In Papua New Guinea, the alternative vote was adopted for the 2007 election precisely in order to force candidates to appeal beyond their own tribe, in the hope that this would reduce inter-tribal tensions. But it may be argued that the needs of British politics lie elsewhere: that we need more conflict and contrast rather than less. Voters are increasingly turned off by a political class that they view as 'all the same'. We are frustrated by politicians who refuse to give a straight answer to any question for fear of offending some body of voters. These tendencies are already apparent under first past the post, but if the alternative vote increased them further that might harm our democracy.

A quick glance at the discourse of Australian politics will cast doubt on the idea that politics under the alternative vote is all about sucking up to each other. But AV, even more than first past the post, does require politicians to appeal beyond their own party's support base. If you think we have too much compromise already, you are likely to have doubts about the merits of the alternative vote. On the other hand, if you dislike political tribalism, you might notch this up as a point in AV's favour.

It's time to take stock for a moment. Our goal is to elect the most popular candidate in each constituency. According to AV's supporters, it makes sense to think of the most popular candidate as being the one who could win a head-to-head contest with every other candidate. Sometimes there is no such candidate, but if there is, he or she should certainly win the election. AV's opponents offer several arguments against this view, but we have found that none of them holds much water. In fact, this way of thinking about popularity has a long pedigree – it's often called the Condorcet criterion, after the eighteenth-century French mathematician the Marquis de Condorcet, who explored it in depth. So far, then, AV is doing pretty well.

A problem for AV's supporters, however, is that AV itself sometimes fails to satisfy the Condorcet criterion. Look back again at the 2010 election result from Oldham East and Saddleworth in Table 2. It seems very likely that the Lib Dem candidate, Elwyn Watkins, was the Condorcet winner in this constituency – given what we know about the second preferences of Conservative and Labour voters, he would probably have defeated every other candidate in a head-to-head contest. But would he have been elected under the alternative vote? The first candidates to be eliminated – those of the

Christian Party, UKIP, and the BNP – all come from the political right. Had they transferred their support to the Conservatives, the Conservative candidate could have leapfrogged the Lib Dem and entered a final head-to-head with Labour. The Lib Dem would thus have been unable to show the breadth of his popularity.

Results such as these arise because of the way in which the alternative vote counts a voter's second and lower preferences: it takes account of these only after the candidates whom the voter placed higher have been eliminated from the race. As a result, the order in which the candidates happen to be eliminated can sometimes make a difference to who ultimately comes out on top. At least in theory, this can yield some very strange results indeed. In particular, it can lead to something that elections wonks call 'non-monotonicity' – the condition in which a candidate loses an election as a result of gaining support. I provide an example of non-monotonicity under the alternative vote in the Appendix (p. 169). But the reason I consign that example to the Appendix is that non-monotonic outcomes are probably little more than mathematical possibilities: you need to imagine a pretty unlikely distribution of preferences in order to generate them. Similarly, though the alternative vote can fail to choose the most popular candidate (the Condorcet winner), it does so much less often than does first past the post. This point demonstrates – again – that no electoral system is perfect, but it doesn't provide an argument in favour of the status quo.

Before summing up this discussion of popularity and moving on to our other criteria, we need to consider one further argument against AV. The Conservative backbench MP Daniel Kawczynski, who co-chairs the All-Party Group for the Promotion of First Past the Post, says the alternative vote creates 'two classes of voter': some are given a second vote, in that their second (indeed, sometimes their third, fourth, fifth) preferences are counted, while others have only one. Kawczynski offers some powerful arguments in defence of the status quo, but this isn't one of them: his claim just doesn't stand up. Under the alternative vote, only one of a voter's preferences counts towards the final result: each voter's ballot has the same weight as every other. If your second preference is counted, that's because the candidate to whom you gave your first preference has already been eliminated from the race. So no one has two votes.

Kawczynski also offers a more nuanced version of the argument: AV, he says, discriminates against those voters who take a principled stand and vote for just one candidate, while favouring voters who are willing to prostitute themselves across a range of parties. Again, this argument doesn't stack up. Why would a voter decide to express just one preference? One reason might be that you don't want your lower preferences to harm your favourite candidate's chances of election. But this is based on a straightforward misunderstanding of how AV works. Expressing your lower preferences under the alternative vote can never harm your first preference: to repeat, your lower preferences won't even be counted unless the candidate you placed first has already been eliminated from the contest. Remember the difference between the alternative vote and Eurovision. In the latter, all of the preferences expressed by each country count. The ten points that the UK gives to, say, Serbia, might allow Serbia to defeat whichever country – say, Ireland – we give our twelve points to. But the alternative vote isn't like that: so long as our top preference is in the race, no one is even going to look at which country we gave the second spot to. Higher preferences under the alternative vote can never be harmed by lower preferences.

So the only reasons for marking only your first preference would be either that you want to make a personal statement – 'I'm Labour/Tory through and through' – or that you don't care which candidate is elected if your top pick can't win. It's your free choice to vote this way if you want, but it doesn't give you any grounds for complaint if the result happens not to go the way you wanted.

In terms of our criterion of rewarding popularity, then, the alternative vote clearly comes out ahead of first past the post. It is not perfect: it does not address the problem that the wrong party will sometimes win the election at the national level; nor does it always choose the most popular candidate – the Condorcet winner – at the local level. But it does make it more likely than first past the post that the candidate who is elected is the candidate with most support among voters. That is presumably why

AV or one of its cousins is used for internal elections in all the major political parties.

Fair representation in Parliament and government

As we saw in Figure 10, the alternative vote generally makes some difference to the overall distribution of seats compared to first past the post, but not very much. That means that AV does not overcome the problems of disproportional representation that first past the post suffers. Like first past the post, it gives seats only to local winners, making no attempt to distribute seats in proportion to votes. If we look back to Figure 1 on p. 30, we can find two countries that use the alternative vote or one of its cousins: Australia and France. Both are located towards the disproportional end of the spectrum.

Figure 11 adds further evidence by mapping disproportionality in actual elections in the UK since 1983 against disproportionality in the AV simulations shown in Figure 10. The average level of disproportionality across these elections remains almost identical whichever system is used: it is 17.2 for first past the post and 17.3 for the alternative vote. Up to 1992 and then again in 2010, AV would have been slightly more proportional than first past the

Figure 11. Disproportionality under first past the post and the alternative vote in the UK since 1983

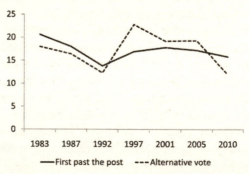

Source: Calculated from the data in Figure 10. Only the first set of simulations for alternative vote is used.

post: it would have reduced slightly the over-representation of the two big parties and the under-representation of the Lib Dems. In 1997, 2001 and 2005, however, AV would actually have increased disproportionality: though it would still have helped to address the under-representation of the Lib Dems, it would have increased the under-representation of the Conservatives and given Labour even more of an over-sized majority than they had already.

We can draw out three main points from this. First, in terms of the overall proportionality of representation in Parliament, the alternative vote performs just as badly as first past the post. Stemming from this, AV also does badly in terms of the representation of women and minorities. Figure 2 on p. 31 suggests that the proportion of female MPs would not be significantly changed by the adoption of AV: Australia and France are both located close to the UK on the graph.

Second, however, adopting AV would go some way towards reducing the under-representation of the Liberal Democrats. With 23 per cent of the vote in 2010, the Lib Dems won fewer than 9 per cent of the seats. Under AV, if the estimate used here is correct, they would have won 12 per cent. AV is good for the Lib Dems because the party is large enough to be in the running in many constituencies and because its centrist position means it would pick up many voters' second preferences. So the alternative vote does go some way to reduce this aspect of disproportionality, though it would do nothing to address the under-representation of parties like UKIP and the Greens.

Finally, AV increases disproportionality whenever one of the two main parties is well ahead: it tends to exaggerate landslide victories. That's because a party that scores very well in first preferences is likely also to do well in second preferences, allowing it to pick up still more seats than under first past the post. This is a really serious issue. Had AV been used in 1997, it would have given Labour an even bigger majority than the party won anyway: Labour would have gained extra seats from the Conservatives by picking up the lion's share of vote transfers from the Lib Dems. According to the estimates used here, Labour, on 43 per cent of the vote, would have captured 68 per cent of the seats, while the Conservatives, on 31 per cent of the vote, would have held on to only 11 per cent of the seats. It should be said that these numbers are debatable: the other set of estimates that I reported in Figure 10 produce a less extreme result, with the Conservatives on 17 per cent of the seats. Even so, the Conservatives would still have been badly under-represented. The value of an electoral system that is capable of producing such huge distortions must be seriously questioned. Results such as these would have called the legitimacy of the system into grave doubt. They would also have made it very difficult for an effective parliamentary opposition to the Labour government to function.

In terms of proportionality, therefore, the alternative vote never performs much better than first past the post and sometimes performs significantly worse. This offers a powerful argument for opposing a switch to AV in the UK.

Effective, accountable government

The fact that the alternative vote generally doesn't produce hugely different results from first past the post in terms of the overall distribution of seats in Parliament means that it doesn't greatly alter the effectiveness or accountability of government either. Some Conservatives seem to think (or, at least, want voters to believe) that the alternative vote would prevent them ever again from forming a majority government, but that's just not true. The Conservatives would have secured comfortable majorities in 1983 and 1987 (and presumably in earlier elections too). They might even have squeaked home with a majority in the closely fought election of 1992.

Nevertheless, the particular effects upon proportionality that we have just seen do have implications: the increased strength of the Liberal Democrats would make hung parliaments more likely than at present; the exaggeration of landslides, meanwhile, would make excessive majorities more likely. As we saw in the last chapter, while there is little evidence that coalitions are less effective than single-party governments, there is good reason to think they weaken voters' ability to determine what the composition of government will be. And at the other end of the scale there is no doubt that very large majorities are undesirable, allowing government to run roughshod over Parliament and making it very difficult for opposition parties to fulfil their important functions. They permit excessive concentration of power, increasing the likelihood that decisions will be ill-considered or will fail to reflect the interests of the broader public. If you are a fan of single-party governments with moderately sized majorities, therefore, you are likely, on this criterion, to prefer first past the post over the alternative vote.

Voter choice and turnout

The introduction of the alternative vote would expand voter choice in three important ways. First, it would allow voters to say much more about the structure of their preferences. Those voters who genuinely have a preference for only one candidate would be able to express that, just as now. But those who don't see politics in such black-and-white terms would be able to record the full range of their preferences across all the candidates.

Second, voters would be able to express their genuine preferences, rather than sometimes having to vote tactically for a candidate with a chance of winning. A Green Party supporter in a Conservative–Labour marginal, for example, could confidently vote for the Green candidate, but still, in their second preference, indicate whether they would prefer to be represented by a Conservative or a Labour MP. It would not be right to say that incentives for tactical voting are entirely eliminated by AV: the mathematicians can devise scenarios in which casting a tactical vote does make sense. But these possibilities are fairly marginal and, in general, the alternative vote allows voters to say exactly what they think without fear of letting the wrong candidate in.

Third, more voters under AV would be able to see that their votes have contributed to the outcome of the election: no longer would it be possible for two-thirds of the ballot papers cast in a constituency to be effectively wasted.

On the other hand, the alternative vote would do little to diminish the preponderance of safe seats. The safest seats, where one candidate regularly secures over 50 per cent of the vote, would be entirely untouched by the introduction of AV. Such seats – which amounted to almost a third of the total in 2010 – would be won, just as now, on the basis of first preferences. Some safe seats – in which the incumbent faces a significant but divided opposition – might no longer be safe. But, as we have seen, the number of constituencies producing a different result under AV than under first past the post would not be large, and almost all of these would be marginal anyway. Indeed, a few seats – in which the incumbent would benefit from transfers of second preferences – would become safer under AV than they are at present.

Finally, the effects of AV upon the range of options available to voters are intriguing. On the one hand, if the claim is correct that AV further encourages all significant parties to compete in the same middle ground of politics in order to secure election, then it should diminish the range of options that voters can choose from. On the other hand, because a vote cast in the first instance for a candidate from a minor party would no longer be a wasted vote, we would expect AV to give fringe parties a boost. In order to reconcile these competing tendencies, we need to remember the distinction between votes and seats. AV would make it easier for a broad range of candidates to win votes. But it would make it harder for parties located too far from the centre ground to pick up seats, because these candidates would struggle to win over second preferences. So AV would tend to increase the spread of votes across candidates, but reduce the range of candidates with a chance of winning. As we have seen already, whether you think this desirable or not depends on your viewpoint. On the one hand, you might think politics would be better off if a few more mavericks won election, and therefore regret the tendency of AV to make this less likely. On the other hand, you might be glad that AV would make it harder for parties like the BNP to slip through a divided field of moderates, and you might value a system that encourages candidates to appeal beyond their core support base.

Overall, the alternative vote does in many ways allow greater voter choice than does first past the post, but the impact should not be exaggerated. Would the introduction of AV boost turnout? Certainly, we might imagine that third-party supporters, who today must choose between expressing their true preferences and casting a vote that counts, might be more inclined to turn out if a system were introduced that allows them to do both of these things. But how many voters this would affect isn't very clear. We don't have much direct evidence of the effects of AV on turnout: Australia has compulsory voting, so doesn't provide a useful point of comparison. Evidence discussed later suggests that no electoral system will dramatically change the number of people who vote. Even if AV does have an effect, therefore, it's probably pretty small.

The constituency link

The alternative vote would leave the constituency link largely unchanged: each MP would still be elected in a single-member constituency, and each voter would still have one MP to turn to if they wanted assistance on some matter. If you think this traditional form of the constituency link should be retained, AV should cause you no qualms.

Indeed, to some degree, AV would enhance the constituency link. The requirement for the winning candidate, if possible, to pass a 50 per cent threshold would leave more voters feeling that their MP was someone they had helped to choose. MPs would have the added legitimacy of winning the backing of more than half their participating electorate. Still, the difference here would not be enormous: the connection created by giving a candidate your third or fourth preference is presumably not going to be very great; and once an election is over, the outcome is generally accepted as legitimate already.

Keeping MPs in check

Given that moving to the alternative vote wouldn't have much impact on the number of safe seats or on the constituency link, we can also conclude that it would do little to change voters' ability to keep their MP in check. The voters in a constituency would still be able to throw their MP out of office if they felt she or he was not doing an adequate job. Equally, however, they would face the problem that, in many constituencies, one or other party has a near-impregnable majority, such that deposing its candidate will be possible only in fairly extreme circumstances. The alternative vote would not have prevented the abuse of MPs' expenses and, in this respect, is no different from first past the post. Some AV supporters will try to tell you that voting for this system in the referendum is the best way to express your anger with the political class. They will claim, as at least one Lib Dem MP has done, that 'AV would end safe seats'. But this claim is just plain wrong, and anyone trying to link AV with preventing a repeat of the expenses scandal is playing fairly loose with the facts.

Summing up

Overall, the most important point to note is that the alternative vote and first past the post are in most respects not very different from each other: the reform that we are being offered in the coming referendum is not very radical. AV is not a proportional system that distributes mandates across the parties. Rather, like first past the post, it's a 'majoritarian' system: it rewards only the single most popular candidate in each constituency; and at the national level it tends (though somewhat less reliably than first past the post) to produce single-party governments that command a majority of the seats in Parliament. Both systems are good if you value strong government and the current constituency link. On the other hand, both systems are bad if you think that opinion in society should be accurately represented in the chamber of the Commons.

The alternative vote differs from first past the post in two principal respects. First, it is more likely to secure the election of the candidate who has broadest support in the constituency. In terms of the local result, there is no doubt that AV is superior. Second, however, it can produce some undesirable effects in the national result. In particular, it can exaggerate landslides, which is clearly unhealthy both for representation and for the effectiveness of government. It could have produced a result in 1997 so distorted as to lead to serious questioning of the legitimacy of our political system.

So, as ever with electoral systems, there are advantages and disadvantages. Which system you think best will depend on how you weight the various criteria.

One final point about the alternative vote should be made. Most electoral reform activists don't really like this system, but will nevertheless campaign for it in the referendum. They'll do so partly because they see it as a slight improvement on first past the post, but also partly because they think it would open the way towards further, more radical reform at a later date. It would strengthen the Liberal Democrats – the only major party that backs a proportional system. It might also accustom voters to the idea that our existing electoral rules are not sacrosanct. Similarly, many opponents of reform recognise that the alternative vote in itself would not radically alter our political system, but want to avoid giving the reform movement a foot in the door. They know that a 'no' vote in this referendum would put any further talk of electoral reform off the agenda for many years to come. So in deciding how to vote in the coming referendum, we should be thinking in part about whether we support more radical change to the electoral system further down the line.

5. Simple proportional representation

If we want to shift radically away from first past the post, we have to look not to the alternative vote, but to some form of proportional representation. The introduction of PR would transform the composition of Parliament and give the government a very different complexion. It's not an option that we'll be able to vote for in the coming referendum, but most reform supporters hold it as their long-term goal, and the government plans to introduce it for the House of Lords. So what would a proportional system look like in practice? And would the changes it would usher in be welcome or unwelcome?

Whenever newspapers report on elections that are held in other countries using proportional voting systems, they almost inevitably resort to the cliché of 'a complex form of proportional representation'. That makes the subject of proportional representation seem terribly forbidding. In fact, some forms of proportional representation are incredibly simple. The complexity comes not so much in the intrinsic nature of most proportional systems, but in the diversity of these systems. There's no single electoral system called 'proportional representation'. Rather, there's a whole family of systems. And it's a pretty extended family with multiple branches and half-blood relations.

We'll therefore introduce the basics of proportional representation (PR for short) by looking at some of the simpler systems that fall within this family. Such systems are in fact not very likely to be introduced for elections to Westminster: they are generally thought not to fit well with Britain's tradition of local representation. But they provide us with a good way of getting into the subject matter.

The simplest form of all

The primary objective of a proportional electoral system is to ensure that the distribution of people's preferences across political parties is accurately reflected in the composition of Parliament. If a party has the support of 40 per cent of voters, it should win about 40 per cent of the seats in Parliament; if it has 10 per cent support, it should win 10 per cent of the seats; and so on. Such an outcome can be achieved very simply. Voters vote not for a single candidate, but rather for a party with a list of candidates. These votes are tallied up across the whole country, and the seats are then distributed across the parties in proportion to them. Thus, if, as in the UK at the moment, the parliamentary chamber had 650 members, just a tiny fraction of the national vote would be needed in order to secure a seat. A party like the Liberal Democrats, on 23 per cent of the vote, would win about 150 seats. A party like the British National Party, with just under 2 per cent of the vote, would secure around 12 seats.

In fact, no country in the world uses quite such a simple system to elect its national Parliament, though some, such as Israel and South Africa, come close. The main problems with such a system are probably pretty clear. First, it generally leads to extreme fragmentation of Parliament, with many parties often needed to build a governing coalition. Second, it may grant considerable power to extremists, who may hold the balance of power and thus have the ability to hold the larger parties to ransom. Third, it allows for no constituency link at all: there are no constituencies, so no MP has the job of looking out for the interests of any particular locale, and voters have no obvious point of contact in the political system.

Wherever proportional representation is used in practice, therefore, some modifications are introduced either to limit fragmentation of the party system or to introduce some element of candidate focus (or both).

Limiting fragmentation in Parliament

Though proportional electoral systems are designed to deliver the proportional representation of popular opinion in Parliament, even their advocates generally agree that the idea of proportionality should not be taken too far. Politics should not be reduced simply to endless bargaining among numerous special interests: it should be necessary to build up a reasonably broad movement of support before you should have a significant influence over national decision-making. There are three main ways in which proportionality can be limited within (still!) simple systems of proportional representation: through the introduction of legal thresholds; through the use of constituencies; and through the precise formula that is used for translating votes into seats.

A legal threshold can be used to set a lower limit on the share of the vote that a party must win before it is granted any seats in Parliament. Some countries have low thresholds: in the Netherlands a party needs 0.67 per cent of the national vote in order to obtain a seat. Others have higher thresholds: Germany and New Zealand both have thresholds of 5 per cent. The effects of such thresholds are entirely straightforward: a party whose share of the vote falls below the threshold gets no seats, while any party that passes the threshold wins seats in proportion to its votes.

The second method of limiting fragmentation is to introduce constituencies. As we saw above, if you elect a chamber of 650 members by proportional representation with no legal threshold and no constituencies, then parties on only a fraction of 1 per cent of the vote will be able to secure representation. But you could, alternatively, divide the country into, say, 130 constituencies, each electing five members in proportion to local vote shares. Then the barrier for entry into Parliament would be much higher: in order to capture one of the five seats in a constituency, a party would need a substantial chunk of the local vote. The fewer the seats allocated within any constituency, the greater the share of the votes required to capture one of those seats.

We can see this from the results of the European Parliament elections in 2009. The MEPs from Great Britain (but not Northern Ireland) are elected using precisely the simple form of proportional representation that we're looking at here: voters vote for a party rather than a candidate; seats are allocated to parties according to their share of the vote within eleven regions across the country. These regions vary in size: the North East region has the smallest population and therefore gets only three seats, while the largest region is the South East, which elects ten seats. In the North East, because there were so few seats available for allocation, the small parties necessarily went without representation. Each of the three largest parties in the region – Labour, the Conservatives, and the Lib Dems – captured one of the seats. But UKIP, in fourth place, could not win a seat, even though it secured over 15 per cent of the regional vote. In the South East, by contrast, the share of the vote needed to win one of the ten seats was much less: Labour held on to a seat even though its vote in the region fell to just 8 per cent.

In fact, more than anything else, it is the size of the constituencies – measured in terms of the number of seats that are allocated within them – that determines just how proportional a system of proportional representation is. Given its importance, political scientists generally refer to this aspect of the size of a constituency as constituency *magnitude*, to distinguish it from the size of the electorate or the size of the geographical area covered by the constituency. If constituency magnitude is very high, then the outcome (assuming there are no legal thresholds) can be very proportional indeed. If the constituency magnitude is low, the degree of proportionality is limited and only the largest parties will gain representation. Indeed, if you reduce the constituency magnitude as far as it will go – such that each constituency elects just one member – then you end up back where we started in Chapter 3, with the system of first past the post.

So far I've been suggesting that proportional electoral systems are not as complex as some of their opponents like to suggest: in many ways, they are really quite straightforward. Even I have to admit, however, that the third aspect of the system that can affect proportionality – the exact formula that is used for translating votes into seats – is a bit arcane. It is here that much of the most obscure language of electoral systems – d'Hondt, Sainte-Laguë, Droop quota, etc. – is relevant. In fact, for most of us, the precise details of these formulas don't matter much, and the important point is that some mechanism is used for working out the proportional allocation of seats across parties. Still, different formulas do have slightly different effects. So I'll give a quick introduction here, and I'll provide some further details in the Appendix (starting at p. 171) for those of you who are interested.

Take a look at the vote shares of the various parties in the South East region in the European Parliament elections of 2009:

Conservative	UKIP	Liberal Democrat	Green	Labour	BNP	Other
34.8%	18.8%	14.1%	11.6%	8.2%	4.4%	8.0%

As I mentioned, there were ten seats available for allocation among these various parties. So how many seats should each party get? We might start off by saying that, if there are ten seats available, each party definitely deserves one seat for every 10 per cent of the vote that it wins. So that means that we can give three seats to the Conservatives, and one each to UKIP, the Lib Dems, and the Greens. But that means that we have allocated only six seats: who should get the four seats that remain? The obvious answer is that these seats should go to the parties that come closest to securing (another) 10 per cent of the votes. UKIP got a seat for its first 10 per cent share, but has not yet got another seat despite winning an additional 8.8 per cent, so we allocate the next seat to UKIP. Still we have three seats left, so the next one goes to Labour, on 8.2 per cent, followed by the Conservatives, who have a 'remainder' of 4.8 per cent, followed by the BNP, on 4.4 per cent. Overall, then, using this method of allocating the seats, the Conservatives get four seats, UKIP two, and the Lib Dems, the Greens, Labour, and the BNP one each.

This method of allocation is actually used in some countries. It's known as the method of largest remainders with the Hare quota (or LR–Hare), and it looks very sensible on paper. But most advanced democracies with proportional electoral systems in fact avoid it, because it's capable of producing some weird outcomes. Even if we look just at the figures above from the South East region, the result produced by this method looks rather inequitable. After the initial allocation of seats on the 10 per cent principle, the Conservatives had three seats and the Lib Dems one. This meant that the Conservatives had one seat for every 11.6 per cent of their vote, while the Lib Dems had one seat for their 14.1 per cent share. Surely it is odd, given these numbers, that it was to the Conservatives that we gave another seat, rather than the Lib Dems: the Conservatives already had more seats per vote than the Lib Dems did. Similarly, it seems unfair that the Lib Dems and the BNP should have ended up with one seat each, even though the Lib Dems had more than three times as many votes. Had the second seat gone to the Lib Dems rather than the BNP, the Lib Dems would have had a seat for every 7.05 per cent of their vote – still a larger share than the BNP got in total.

When we make these comparisons, we're appealing to an alternative logic for working out the proportional allocation of seats to parties: the logic of looking at the average number of votes per seat for each party, and allocating the seats according to whose average is highest. This logic is the basis for a second method of allocating seats. Unsurprisingly, this is often referred to as the 'highest averages' method, though it also goes by the name of the d'Hondt method, after a Belgian mathematician who was one of its inventors. The d'Hondt method is used in many countries, and this is the formula actually used for the allocation of British seats in the European Parliament too. The Appendix works through the details of how d'Hondt operates in practice. But it follows the logic that we appealed to in the previous paragraph, successively giving out seats to the party with the highest ratio of votes to seats until all the seats have been allocated. It thereby overcomes some of the anomalies that we saw: it strips the BNP of its seat, allocating it instead to the Lib Dems. Thus, the actual outcome of the election was that the Conservatives got four seats, UKIP and the Lib Dems got two each, and Labour and the Greens got one each.

As I said, those of you who are interested in the details of these

Table 4. 2010 election results under different proportional systems

	Actual result		Nationwide PR				PR in constituencies			
			No threshold		5% threshold		No threshold		5% threshold	
	Votes (%)	Seats (no.)	LR–Hare	D'Hondt	LR–Hare	D'Hondt	LR–Hare	D'Hondt	LR–Hare	D'Hondt
Conservative	36.1	307	235	241	266	266	239	254	242	254
Labour	29.0	258	189	193	214	214	203	213	207	213
Lib Dems	23.0	57	150	153	170	170	154	149	157	149
UKIP	3.1	0	20	20			7	0	3	0
BNP	1.9	0	12	12			8	0	2	0
SNP	1.7	6	11	11			13	13	13	13
Green	1.0	1	6	6			1	0	1	0
Sinn Féin	0.6	5	4	3			4	6	4	6
Democratic Unionist	0.6	8	4	3			4	5	4	5
Plaid Cymru	0.6	3	4	3			6	3	6	3
SDLP	0.4	3	3	2			3	3	3	3
Ulster Conservatives and Unionists	0.3	0	2	2			3	3	3	3
English Democrats	0.2	0	2	1			0	0	0	0
Alliance	0.1	1	1	0			0	1	0	1
Respect	0.1	0	1	0			0	0	1	0
Traditional Unionist Voice	0.1	0	1	0			1	0	0	1
Speaker (John Bercow)	0.1	1	1	0			1	0	1	0
Christian Party	0.1	0	1	0			0	0	0	0
Indep. Community and Health Concern	0.1	0	1	0			0	0	0	0
Independent	0.1	1	2	0			2	0	2	0
Level of disproportionality (Gallagher index)	15.1		0.2	1.0	5.8	5.8	2.4	4.3	3.3	4.3

formulas can turn to the Appendix (p. 171) for more information. For now, the important point is that different formulas have somewhat different effects upon the overall outcome. In general, the system using largest remainders and the Hare quota is more favourable to small parties than d'Hondt, which tends slightly to over-represent the larger parties – as we have seen in the fact that the BNP gained a seat under the former system but not the latter. A range of other systems are possible, though these two are by far the most common.

These various effects are illustrated for the 2010 general election in Table 4, which simulates the results under different versions of simple PR. As with the AV simulations that we looked at in the previous chapter, a health warning is required here. Table 4 uses the votes that were actually cast in the 2010 election (under first past the post) and plugs these into various PR systems. In reality, however, had PR actually been used, the distribution of votes would have been different: the smaller parties would have picked up more support, as such votes would no longer have been 'wasted'. So Table 4 doesn't predict what the result would actually have been under these systems. What it does allow is a comparison among the forms of proportional representation.

Table 4 looks first at proportional representation applied nationwide with no threshold. As you can see, even with the existing vote distribution, this system leads to considerable fragmentation, giving significant chunks of representation to UKIP and the BNP and at least some representation to many even smaller groups. As expected, the d'Hondt method for allocating seats generates a slightly less diffused result than does the system using largest remainders and the Hare quota, but the difference isn't dramatic. The bottom row of the table shows the overall level of disproportionality for each system using the index that I introduced in Chapter 3. A score of zero on this index means perfect proportionality. You can see that either proportional formula comes very close to that when applied nationwide. But the introduction of a 5 per cent threshold reduces proportionality quite significantly: at a stroke, all parties but the big three are eliminated. In reality, some of the smaller parties could probably pass a 5 per cent threshold: as I said, they would win more votes if PR were used than they actually did in 2010. But others would not: Northern Ireland's parties, for example, would go entirely unrepresented, as Northern Ireland contains fewer than 5 per cent of all UK voters.

Given the UK's tradition of local representation, no simple PR system could ever be introduced here without constituencies. These would most probably be based where possible on counties and other established units. The right-hand side of Table 4 simulates the election results for a variety of such systems. These use eighty constituencies containing, on average, just over eight seats each. The first thing to note is that the introduction of constituencies reduces fragmentation: the very smallest parties no longer win seats. Nevertheless, proportionality is still much higher than under first past the post: these systems still deserve the name of proportional representation. As expected, proportionality is greater under the largest remainders system than under d'Hondt: notably, d'Hondt in constituencies gives no representation to UKIP or the BNP. Introducing a requirement that parties win 5 per cent of the constituency vote before they can win any seats makes no difference under d'Hondt, which gives no seats to such small parties anyway. But it does reduce the seat shares of some small parties when it's combined with largest remainders.

There are various other patterns to be found in the numbers presented in Table 4: I'll leave you to explore these as you wish. You will also find a few more details of the calculations and the results at p. 178 of the Appendix.

Introducing a focus on candidates

The second problem that we saw with the very simplest form of proportional representation was that it focuses attention entirely on national political parties rather than on candidates and localities. MPs represent the country as a whole, so there are no local representatives who will speak up for the interests of a particular area. Voters can choose only among parties, not among candidates. Often, voters will have no knowledge of who most of their representatives are: many will be anonymous party hacks who have little impact in the wider community and no incentive to build up a personal reputation with constituents.

These problems can partly be overcome through the introduction of constituencies. For the House of Commons for example, a county like Lincolnshire could form its own constituency. As now, this would elect seven MPs. But whereas, now, these MPs are elected in seven separate constituencies, under proportional representation they would be elected in a single constituency using a formula like those introduced above. The people of Lincolnshire would therefore have their own representatives who could speak up for local concerns in Westminster.

If you are concerned about local representation, this is certainly an improvement on the nationwide version of proportional representation. But many would say that it still has problems. Voters will still be choosing parties rather than individual candidates. They will have no way of expressing support for one of a party's candidates but not another. Many forms of proportional representation seek to overcome these problems by allowing voters to choose not just between parties, but between candidates as well. In one simple version, voters first vote for a party, just as in the versions of proportional representation that we have already discussed. But then, if they wish, voters have the chance also to express a preference for one of the candidates standing for that party. It's these votes that determine which of the party's candidates win the seats that the party is entitled to.

To see how this works, we can look again at the North East region in the 2009 European Parliament elections, where, as you'll remember, three seats were up for grabs. Each of the significant parties put up three candidates in this region, though, as it turned out, only one candidate from each of the three main parties was elected. Because this was an election in which voters could choose only parties, not candidates, it was the parties that determined which of their candidates was the one to be elected. That is, before the election, each of the parties presented their list of candidates in order. Where a party's share of the votes was sufficient to secure one seat, the candidate at the top of that party's list was elected. Had one of the parties garnered sufficient support to capture two seats, the top two candidates on the party's list would have been elected.

If, by contrast, Britain had elected its MEPs by a system that allowed voters to determine the order of a party's candidates, the outcome could have been very different. Each voter would still have voted first for a party. Having backed the party, however, the voter would also have been able to choose one of that party's three candidates, and the candidate with most votes would have headed the party's list. Each party would have won just as many seats as under the actual system: this is determined by the party votes. But the voters could have given these seats to different candidates from those who actually won.

A proportional electoral system in which voters choose parties but not candidates is generally known as a 'closed-list' system: each party presents a closed list of candidates that cannot be altered by voters. A system that allows voters to change the order of the candidates on the list is known as an 'open-list' system. Here, the total set of candidates is generally decided by the party (though a few systems even allow voters to write in their own candidates), but voters decide the order in which those candidates are elected. Candidates thus have more of an incentive to build up a personal reputation with voters, and voters can punish a candidate who fails to live up to expectations without punishing that candidate's party as a whole.

As is so often the case with electoral systems, a range of further variants are possible. In many countries, for example, the order of the candidates on a party's list is determined partly by the party and partly by the voters. But such details need not worry us too much here. The key point is that systems can be devised that ensure a high level of proportionality in the representation of parties while also providing for local representation and giving voters the chance to select individual candidates.

Proportional representation around the world

Some form of proportional representation is used for national parliamentary elections in eighty-five countries around the world today. Some of these countries use the particular variants of proportional representation that we will be focusing on later. But the simpler versions of PR discussed in this chapter – which are known collectively as list PR – are used to elect the lower house of Parliament in seventy-five countries, making them the most widespread family of electoral systems in the world. Of the thirty-six countries we are using to make comparisons in this book, fifteen use some form of list PR. Thus, while simple proportional representation has rarely been seriously advocated for elections to the UK House of Commons, such systems are popular in many other parts of the world. It's time now to consider whether these systems really do have advantages that deserve our closer attention.

Rewarding popularity

The very simplest forms of proportional representation – in which seats are allocated on a nationwide basis – translate popularity into parliamentary representation in an entirely systematic way. There's no possibility for anomalous outcomes in which one party comes first in terms of votes but another party wins more seats. Once we move to systems that have constituencies, the possibility of this anomaly does arise: it is possible that the constituency-based results could add up in strange ways. But the likelihood that this will happen is much lower under proportional representation than it is under either first past the post or the alternative vote (partly because of the proportional allocation rules and partly because there are fewer constituencies). Furthermore, it is always possible to design a proportional system in order to eliminate this danger entirely: many systems, such as those used in Denmark, Norway and Sweden, allocate most seats in constituencies, but also allocate a small number of seats at the national level in order to even out any discrepancies. The danger that the wrong party might win an election can therefore easily be avoided.

The open-list version of PR introduces what might be thought of as a new type of anomaly: where a candidate is elected in a constituency even though another candidate has secured more votes. Consider the hypothetical example shown in Table 5. The top part of the table shows the share of the vote won by each party: party A won 40 per cent, party B 30 per cent, and so on. Supposing that this is a constituency that elects five MPs and that the d'Hondt method is used to allocate seats, this distribution of votes implies that parties A and B win two seats each, party C wins one seat, and party D wins no seats. The next step is therefore to work out which of each party's candidates fill these positions. In an open-list system, this is determined by looking at the number of votes secured by each of the candidates: the two most popular candidates from each of parties A and B will be elected, as will be the most popular candidate from party C. The lower part of Table 5 shows the share of the vote captured by each candidate from each party. For example, the 40 per cent of voters who voted for party A were able to pick one of the candidates on party A's list: candidates (a) to (e). 11 per cent chose candidate (a), 10 per cent chose candidate (b), and so on. The candidates who are elected are therefore candidates (a), (b), (f), (g), and (k). So candidate (k) is elected ahead of candidates (c), (d), and (h), even though each of the latter candidates secured more votes.

Table 5. Hypothetical voting figures in a five-member constituency

Party vote shares							
A 40%		B 30%		C 20%		D 10%	
Candidate vote shares							
a	11%	f	10%	k	6%	p	5%
b	10	g	9	l	4	q	2
c	9	h	8	m	4	r	2
d	7	i	2	n	3	s	1
e	3	j	1	o	3	t	0

This happens because, in electoral systems such as these, the principle of representing parties trumps the principle of selecting the most popular candidates. That may seem odd to British voters, who are used to voting for individual candidates. But the alternative is that the 20 per cent of voters who supported party C should go unrepresented, just because support within the party is spread across a range of candidates. Advocates of proportional representation would say that, despite appearances, there is no anomaly here at all: supporters of party C have been given their fair share of representation and have been able to choose which of their party's candidates will represent them in Parliament.

Fair representation in Parliament and government

Given all that we have said, it will come as no surprise that proportional electoral systems translate votes into parliamentary seats much more faithfully than does either first past the post or the alternative vote. Figure 12 repeats the information regarding disproportionality that we saw in Chapter 3, but this time it shades in the proportional systems (including those countries that use the forms of proportional representation that we'll be looking at in the next two chapters). It's very clear that the proportional systems are clustered towards the left of the graph. The most proportional election results have been in the Netherlands, where elections are decided in a single national contest with a low threshold of just 0.67 per cent. Denmark also has a low threshold (2 per cent) and, though it uses constituencies, it also, as we have noted, allocates some seats at the

Figure 12. Disproportionality of election results, 1945–2010: PR compared

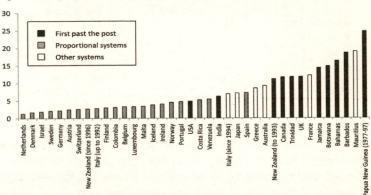

Note: The figures average across all elections since 1945 or since democratisation where that is later. See the Appendix for details of sources and how the numbers are calculated.

national level to ensure high proportionality overall. As we move further to the right and disproportionality begins to rise, we find systems that have higher legal thresholds or smaller constituencies. The least proportional of all the proportional electoral systems is the Spanish one: many constituencies there elect just three members, skewing the results in favour of the larger parties.

Systems of proportional representation also do better than first past the post or AV in fostering representation for women and minorities. Figure 13 picks out the cases of proportional representation in our earlier graph showing the proportion of female MPs across our sample of democracies. Some PR countries do remarkably poorly: Malta and Ireland rank among the countries where women's representation is weakest. But all the best performing countries use proportional representation.

Figure 13. Percentage of MPs who are women, 2010: PR compared

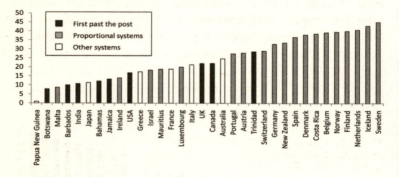

Note: Figures correct as of 31 July 2010. Source: Inter-Parliamentary Union (www.ipu.org).

As we've seen, however, opponents of proportional representation argue that all this talk of fair representation in Parliament is beside the point: what matters is fair representation in the corridors of power and fair influence over the actual policies of government. The danger under proportional representation, they argue, is that the tail can wag the dog: the smaller parties can exert far more power over government than they deserve. We began to look into this in

Chapter 3, but it's a complex issue, so more probing is required. Figure 14 repeats our earlier graph on the proportionality of power-holding, this time highlighting the countries that use proportional representation. Clearly, while many PR countries do achieve fairly high levels of proportionality between parties' popular support and their share of power, there are quite a few exceptions to this.

We need to burrow a bit further beneath the surface of the numbers represented in Figure 14 in order to see what's happening here. If the claim that the tail wags the dog is correct, the big differences between vote shares and participation in government in countries like Luxembourg and Italy should be attributable to over-representation of small parties in the corridors of power. In fact, however, that's not the case. In Italy, the main source of disproportionality was the fact that the Communists were largely excluded from power, even though they were one of the largest parties. A similar pattern explains most of the disproportionality in the French Fourth Republic (which ran from 1946 to 1958). In most of the other grey-shaded countries towards the right of Figure 14, most of the disproportionality comes from the over-representation of the largest party, not the smallest. In Luxembourg, for example, the Christian Democrats have averaged

Figure 14. Disproportionality of governing power since 1945: PR compared

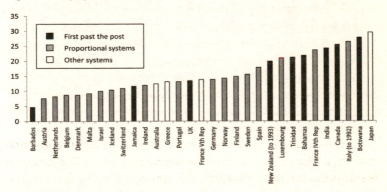

Note: The figures cover the period from 1945 (or democratisation if later) until the most recent election. See the Appendix for details of sources and how the numbers are calculated. Presidential countries (Columbia, Costa Rica, the United States and Venezuela) are not included. Data are not available for Mauritius or Papua New Guinea.

37 per cent of the vote but have held something like 60 per cent of the power in government. Only in a few countries – the most notable being Germany – is there strong evidence that proportional representation gives small parties too much power.

Nevertheless, it can fairly be said that Figure 14 fails to tell the whole story here. Over-representation in terms of actual government posts might not be the main problem. In Israel, for example, complaints are often raised about the power of tiny Orthodox parties. The concern that people voice is not primarily about the fact that these parties can secure a few seats around the cabinet table. Rather, the problem is that they have enough bargaining power to exert enormous veto power over certain key policy issues. Similarly, in the Scottish government today, the minor parties have no executive positions at all: the Scottish Nationalists hold office on their own. But because the SNP holds only a minority of seats in Parliament, it relies on the support of other parties in order to get its measures through. The smaller parties, if they play their cards effectively, can extract large concessions in the process.

In truth, the issue of whether the tail wags the dog under proportional representation is one on which we just don't have definitive answers. We have no way of measuring in general how much power small parties can exert. Certainly, we can come up with examples where they wield wholly disproportional power. Equally, however, there are situations where their bargaining power is much more limited.

So we cannot reject the argument that proportional representation can give disproportional power to small parties, but nor is the claim clearly correct. The possibility – but only the possibility – that the tail might wag the dog needs to be weighed against the advantages of fair parliamentary representation that proportional systems undoubtedly bring.

Effective, accountable government

We've seen evidence suggesting that governments under first past the post systems do last longer than those under systems of proportional representation, but that any differences between the systems in terms of economic performance are small. Countries such as Germany, Austria and Italy have seen growth rates far higher than those in the UK during the post-war era, though all have had proportional electoral systems for most or all of the period. New Zealand switched from first past the post to a form of proportional representation in 1996. Since then it has never had a single-party government backed by a parliamentary majority, and yet the country has prospered. So the doom-mongers regarding life under proportional representation are clearly overegging the pudding. Indeed, we might expect proportional representation to improve policy-making if it pushes politicians to cooperate and negotiate with each other before taking decisions.

But advocates of proportional systems have a harder time when it comes to accountability. Under first past the post or the alternative vote, most of the time, it's the voters who determine the composition of government. That is, most of the time one party wins a majority of the parliamentary seats and can therefore form a government on its own, and most of the time the party that wins the majority of the seats is the party with greatest support among voters. Under proportional systems, however, governments are often formed through post-election dealing between the parties. We caught a glimpse of this in May 2010 when, unusually, our first past the post system failed to deliver a clear result. The coalition talks were conducted with impressive efficiency, but they delivered an outcome that few voters (or even pundits) had expected. Such uncertainties, according to opponents of proportional representation, are the norm under PR, not the exception. Similarly, if the arithmetic is right, a party might be able to hold on to power despite a substantial loss of electoral support by doing a deal with new coalition allies.

Proponents of proportional representation can respond to these arguments in two ways. First, they can say that the problem can be contained. Pure PR can indeed engender a plethora of parties that form into ever-shifting alliances. But proportional representation within the limits of legal thresholds and moderately sized constituencies will produce fewer, more stable parties. We can't extrapolate from the events around the election of 2010 because they were a one-off: with PR, everyone would be expecting before the election that a coalition would need to be formed, and parties would need to signal the sorts of coalition deal they would be willing to make. Second, PR's supporters argue that coalition-building brings benefits as well as dangers: it encourages a more cooperative political spirit and a more deliberative style of debate. Exerting effective influence in that debate may require more of voters than that they simply cast a ballot every four or five years and leave the rest to the government they have thereby chosen, but that's no bad thing if it fosters a more active and engaged citizenry.

So there are legitimate arguments on both sides here. Pure forms of proportional representation can certainly generate problems in terms of effectiveness and accountability, but these problems are significantly mitigated if limits are introduced on the degree of fragmentation. Even so, problems of accountability can still arise when unexpected coalitions are formed or parties cling to power. We might or might not think these problems are compensated for by the more cooperative politics that results.

Voter choice and turnout

Under proportional representation, nearly all votes count. As we have seen, under first past the post or the alternative vote, only those who have voted for the single winning candidate in any constituency can claim to have influenced the result. Under proportional systems, by contrast, a range of parties will generally secure representation in each constituency, so the voice of far more voters will be heard. On this key aspect of voter choice – that our choices actually influence who is elected – proportional systems score very well.

Proportional systems also generally give voters a broad range of choices, in the sense that they encourage a diverse party system. As we've seen, first past the post and the alternative vote tend to concentrate competition on a few large parties that compete in the centre ground where most votes can be won. Parties that pitch their tent far from the political centre are unlikely to get very far. But proportional representation allows more parties to gain seats and influence. Britain's representatives in the European Parliament, for example, now include members from UKIP, the Green Party, and the BNP, as well as the three larger parties and the Scottish and Welsh nationalists. Voters who complain that the parties are all the same may welcome the chance to vote for a party that has a different message and might actually be able to exert some influence.

But proportional representation also has problems in terms of the choice criterion. We've just seen that there are significant questions over how far it allows the votes cast to determine the composition of government. Beyond this, as I've suggested before, a diverse party system can be a party system in which extremists are powerful. Parties conventionally thought of as belonging to the far right have gained significant influence in recent years in countries such as Austria, Belgium, Denmark, and the Netherlands. Few of us would welcome a similar development here.

Finally, the simple proportional systems that we have been discussing place tight limits on the degree to which voters can express their preferences. That's clearest in the case of closed-list systems, where voters can do no more than choose a party. If there's a particular candidate whom you want to support under such a system, you can of course do so by voting for their party, but that vote will count for the party's other candidates too. Open-list systems allow voters to choose among candidates, so you can increase the likelihood that your preferred candidate will be the one who fills a party's seat. Still, however, your vote counts for the party as a whole whether you support the party or just the candidate. That might not be a bad thing: the existence of cohesive political parties is more important to the effective operation of our democracy than many of us imagine, so an electoral system that encourages voters to think in terms of political parties may be desirable. But this does go against how many British voters want to engage with our political system.

The constituency link

The last point above feeds into the issue of the constituency link. The simplest proportional system, with closed lists and allocation of all seats at the national level, abandons the constituency link entirely and bases representation solely on the principle of partisanship. No one advocates such a system in the UK; everyone agrees that it would shift political competition too far away from candidates in favour of parties.

What, then, of proportional systems that have open lists and constituencies of, say, six or seven members? What of the system that I mentioned earlier in which Lincolnshire, for example, would form a single constituency from which seven MPs would be elected? This system would clearly have some disadvantages for the constituency link compared to first past the post. No longer would each MP have special responsibility for a particular area: instead, seven MPs would overlap, perhaps encouraging some of them to shirk their duties. These MPs might also feel more distant from voters. Each MP (or party) would presumably have one constituency office, and if these offices were all huddled in one part of the constituency, other areas might feel neglected.

On the other hand, this system would also have certain advantages over first past the post. At present, Lincolnshire is represented by seven Conservative MPs: no other party has any seats. That's despite that fact that just half of all those who voted in the election backed the Conservatives, while around a fifth backed each of Labour and the Lib Dems. Quite apart from the issues of fairness that we have already discussed, non-Conservative voters might want to turn to a local MP who shares their own political priorities, but that is currently impossible. A proportional system would change that: the d'Hondt method would have translated Lincolnshire's votes in the 2010 election into four seats for the Conservatives, two for the Lib Dems, and one for Labour. Lib Dem and Labour voters might then have felt that the constituency link was working more effectively for them.

So while open-list proportional representation with constituencies does dilute the relationship between one MP and one constituency, it also gives voters a range of local MPs to choose from when seeking redress on particular issues. While it places greater emphasis on party than first past the post, that might not be as bad a thing as many of us suppose.

Keeping MPs in check

One of the main arguments that advocates of electoral reform have made since the scandal over MPs' expenses broke in May 2009 has been that first past the post, with all its safe seats, encourages complacency among MPs, whereas a proportional system, by getting rid of these safe seats, would keep MPs on their toes. Clearly, much depends in this argument on which form of proportional representation we are talking about. A closed-list system of proportional representation would make safe seats even more impregnable than they are already: Lincolnshire, for example, is always going to elect several Conservatives, so the candidates occupying the top spots on the Conservatives' list would always be guaranteed their seats. But things are quite different under an open-list system: here, unlike under first past the post, an unpopular candidate could be voted out even if voters still want to support her or his party. No longer could MPs rely on their party label to secure their continuing re-election. PR with fully open lists would keep MPs on their toes.

This leads to the question that I raised in Chapter 2 of whether rules devised in response to the expenses scandal might just encourage other forms of misbehaviour. As I said there, there are two basic types of malfeasance: looting and cheating. The behaviour uncovered in the expenses scandal belongs to the category of looting: some MPs started to take advantage of public office for their own private benefit. There is considerable cross-national evidence that looting is greater where political competition is low. But there is also evidence that strong political competition encourages cheating – it increases candidates' incentive to abuse the system in order to capture the extra votes that they desperately need. Such abuses can involve true corruption, where candidates attempt directly to buy constituents' votes. Or it can take subtler forms, where politicians seek to funnel public spending into their constituency in ways that serve their personal prospects of election but not the wider public interest.

The evidence that we have on these issues – which is nicely summed up by Torsten Persson and Guido Tabellini in an article that you will find in the Further Reading – isn't conclusive. But it does warn against taking arguments about safe seats and open lists for granted. By solving one problem we might just end up creating another further down the line.

Summing up

Proportional electoral systems have the undoubted benefit of delivering an accurate translation of voters' preferences into parliamentary seats. Given that representation is the essence of modern democracy, that is a very significant plus. On the other hand, there's a question mark over whether such proportional representation equates to proportional influence over policy decisions that actually affect people's lives, and proportional systems also perform poorly in terms of the accountability of government. In addition, the simplest forms of PR, with nationwide seat distribution and no legal thresholds, encourage excess fragmentation, destroy the constituency link, reduce voter choice to supporting an anonymous list of party candidates, and limit voters' ability to keep individual MPs in check.

For all of these reasons, no one in the UK seriously argues for the adoption of the simplest forms of proportionality. Many would say that we need to strike a balance between accurate representation and effective and accountable government, and that this can best be achieved through a moderately proportional system that incorporates legal thresholds and constituencies in order to prevent undue fragmentation of the party system. Some would say that the use of open lists also adequately addresses concerns about voter choice, the constituency link, and the accountability of individual MPs.

Nevertheless, even with open lists, it's still impossible in simple PR systems for voters to support a candidate without also supporting that candidate's party and helping its other candidates win election. Given the UK's tradition of individual representation, most reformers have concluded that such a system would be unacceptable to the British public. They have therefore generally advocated forms of proportional representation that do allow voters to support just an individual candidate. Two branches of the proportional family tree achieve this (at least in part) and therefore attract particular attention: these are the so-called mixed systems on the one hand and the single transferable vote system (STV) on the other.

6. Mixed electoral systems

A mixed electoral system is simply a system in which some MPs are elected by one method while other MPs are elected by another method. Any two (or, indeed, more) kinds of electoral system could in principle be mixed and it is possible to mix them in a whole variety of different ways.

Under the most straightforward mixed systems, two or more methods of election simply operate in parallel with each other. In Japan, for example, the 480 members of the House of Representatives are elected through two separate systems. 300 of them are elected in single-member districts using first past the post, just as in the UK today. The remaining 180 are elected by a closed-list system of proportional representation in eleven regions across the country. There is no connection between these two components. Voters have two votes: one for their constituency representative and one for a regional party list. The overall result is therefore a halfway house between what you would get if all MPs were elected by first past the post and what would emerge if all were elected by proportional representation.

Parallel mixed systems such as this might look quite attractive: they seem to offer a compromise between the advantages of proportional systems on the one hand and majoritarian systems such as first past the post and the alternative vote on the other. Yet these systems have not attracted much attention in the UK. Quite why isn't very clear. But the fact is that they have not, and there's therefore not much point spending more time on them here.

The mixed systems that have attracted attention in the UK are different. Though they again contain both single-member constituencies and an element of proportionality, they combine these elements in a way that yields a result that is broadly proportional overall. They achieve this by linking the two parts: the results in the proportional part depend on the results in the single-member constituencies. The seats from party lists are allocated in order to compensate for any disproportionalities that arise in the constituencies.

That probably sounds slightly bamboozling when described in the abstract. But I promise it will get much clearer when we look at a practical example. Let's get on and do that now.

Compensatory mixed systems

Mixed systems that use the proportional seats to compensate for the disproportionalities in the single-member districts are known by a variety of names. Political scientists sometimes called them mixed-member proportional systems, or MMP. In the UK, they have often been referred to as additional member systems (AMS). But we'll keep things simple here by calling them compensatory mixed systems.

In order to see how such compensatory mixed systems differ from the straightforward parallel mixed systems, imagine a country with a parliament of two hundred MPs. One hundred of these members are elected in single-member constituencies by first past the post, while the remaining hundred are allocated to party lists based on proportional representation. Table 6 shows two possible sets of election results, first for a parallel and then for a compensatory system.

Table 6. Hypothetical results under two mixed electoral systems

Party	Votes won (%)	Parallel system			Compensatory system		
		Seats won in constituencies	Seats won from party lists	Seats won overall	Seats won in constituencies	Seats won from party lists	Seats won overall
Purple	41	57	41	98	57	25	82
Orange	32	35	32	67	35	29	64
Turquoise	19	8	19	27	8	30	38
Olive	8	0	8	8	0	16	16

Voters cast their votes in the same way in both cases: 41 per cent of them vote for the Purple Party, 32 per cent for the Orange Party, and so on. In both mixed systems, the results in single-member constituencies are determined in the same way, by first past the post. As usual, first past the post gives a bonus to the largest party and a smaller bonus to the next party, while significantly under-representing the smaller parties. Thus, the Purples win fifty-seven of the constituencies, the Oranges thirty-five, the Turquoises eight, and the Olives none at all.

Next we need to work out how many seats each party is allocated from its proportional list. In the case of the parallel system, this is very simple: these seats are allocated in proportion to the total vote won by each party. So the Purple Party, on 41 per cent of the vote, gets forty-one of the one hundred list seats, the Oranges get thirty-two, and so on. In order to work out the total number of seats won by each party, we just add together the seats won in constituencies and the seats won from the lists.

In the compensatory case, by contrast, the aim is that the distribution of all two hundred seats should be proportional. So the first step is to move to the final column of the table and work out the total number of seats that each party should win. With two hundred seats to be filled, the Purples, on 41 per cent of the vote, should get eighty-two seats overall. The Oranges, with 32 per cent of the vote, should receive sixty-four seats, and so on. Once we have these totals, we subtract the number of seats that each party has already won in the constituencies, and the number we are left with is the number of seats allocated to each party from its list.

Compensatory mixed systems are used to elect the national parliament in eight countries today, the best known examples being Germany and New Zealand. They are also familiar to millions of British citizens, as they are used in elections to the Scottish Parliament, the Welsh Assembly, and the London Assembly.

We can get some further sense of how compensatory systems work in practice by moving from the hypothetical to the real, in the form of an example from the Scottish Parliament elections of 2007. The Scottish Parliament has a total of 129 members (MSPs), of whom seventy-three are elected in single-member constituencies using first past the post and fifty-six are elected in eight regions from party lists. Each voter has two votes: one for their constituency MSP and one for a regional party list.

It's the votes cast for regional lists that basically determine the partisan composition of the Parliament, so we should look at these first. To take the example of the Highlands and Islands region, Table 7 shows each party's share of the regional list votes: the Scottish Nationalists came top on just over a third of the vote, followed by the Liberal Democrats and other parties. A total of fifteen seats were to be filled from the Highlands and Islands: eight of them from constituencies and seven from the regional lists. The first step is to work out how many of these fifteen seats each party was entitled to. That is done by applying the d'Hondt method that I discussed in the last chapter to the regional vote shares. Those of you who want to know the details of the d'Hondt method will find them in the Appendix (p. 177). The second column of Table 7 shows the results that this method produces: the SNP is entitled to six seats, the Lib Dems to four, Labour to three, and the Conservatives to two.

Table 7. Scottish Parliament election results, 2007: Highlands and Islands

Party	Share of regional list votes (%)	Total seat entitlement	Constituency seats won	Seats from regional lists
Scottish National Party (SNP)	34.4	6	4	2
Liberal Democrats	19.9	4	4	0
Labour	17.7	3	0	3
Conservatives	12.6	2	0	2
Green Party	4.6	0	0	0
Christian Party	3.4	0	0	0
Senior Citizens' Party	2.1	0	0	0
Others	5.4	0	0	0
Total	100	15	8	7

Source: www.electoralcommission.org.uk

These are the total numbers of seats that each of the parties is entitled to. As we know, however, some of these seats – eight of them – are won in the single-member constituencies using first past the post. So we need to subtract the number of seats that each party has won in the constituencies from the total number of seats it is entitled to. This gives us the number of seats filled from each party's regional list. Thus, the SNP was entitled to six seats but had already won in four constituencies; it therefore gained two extra seats from the party lists. The Lib Dems, by contrast, had already won their full entitlement of four seats from the constituencies, so they gained no seats from the list. Labour and the Conservatives were entitled to three and two seats respectively; having won no constituencies, all these positions were filled from the party lists.

In this way, each constituency elects its own MP by first past the post, but the disproportionalities produced in these contests are then evened out through the allocation of the seats from party lists. You might be wondering what happens if a party wins more constituencies than its total entitlement. What, for example, if (as would have been entirely possible) the Lib Dems had won an extra constituency seat but had still been eligible for just four seats overall? There are two different ways of dealing with this problem, and those of you who are interested will find them explained in the Appendix (p. 180). The rest of us can be content that this issue can be resolved, and even where it arises it rarely causes significant problems.

Evaluating the compensatory mixed system against our criteria

The compensatory mixed system is a proportional electoral system. Just as with other proportional systems, the precise degree of proportionality can be varied. Thus, legal thresholds can be used, the list MPs can be allocated in regions of varying sizes, and different allocation formulas can be employed. The proportion of seats that are filled through constituency contests and through party lists can also be adjusted – if the share of list seats is low, it will not be possible to compensate fully for disproportionalities in the constituency results, so the overall level of proportionality will be lower than if there had been a more even mix.

This means that, in terms of the criteria of rewarding popularity, delivering fair representation, and providing effective and accountable government, the compensatory system performs just like the simple proportional systems that we discussed in the previous chapter. A highly proportional version will reflect people's votes very accurately in the composition of Parliament and will avoid anomalous results, but it may score badly in terms of accountability and proportionality of influence in the corridors of power. A more moderately proportional version will produce more balance among these various criteria.

Where this system differs from the simple proportional systems that we looked at in the last chapter is in terms of the nature of the choices that voters can express and the nature of the connection between MPs and constituencies.

In typical compensatory systems, voters have two votes: one for a constituency MP and one for a party list. That means that it is possible, if you wish, to choose the candidate of one party in your constituency, but then to vote for a different party in the list section. The interesting thing to note is that doing this allows you to boost the chances of the individual candidate without in any way boosting that candidate's party as a whole. Remember that it's the votes cast for party lists that determine the overall distribution of seats in Parliament. You haven't cast your list vote for this candidate's party, so your vote does not add to its overall seat share. If the party's candidate wins in your local constituency because of your support, that will be offset by a reduction by one in the number of seats that the party gets from its list.

So if you like the job that your local MP is doing, but you don't much like her party, you can vote for her individually, without promoting her party. In this sense, the choice available to you as a voter is greater than under either first past the post or a simple system of proportional representation.

On the other hand, the list component of compensatory systems tends to employ closed lists. There is no necessity for this: open lists could equally well be used. But whether we look at Scotland or Wales or London or Germany or New Zealand, we find that, in the list part of the election, voters have the chance only to cast a ballot for a party; they cannot also express a preference as to the order of the candidates on the party's list. The reason for this seems simply to be a desire not to make the system too complicated: voters are already being asked to cast two votes; allowing them also to express preferences among list candidates might make the process of voting excessively confusing or burdensome.

The effect of using closed lists is that a substantial bloc of MPs – over two fifths of the total in the Scottish Parliament – are elected without individual backing from voters. As we saw in the last chapter, this is a significant disadvantage: it creates the impression that many MPs are representatives of the parties rather than of the voters, and it weakens voters' ability to keep their MPs in check. This has been a significant source of popular dissatisfaction with the compensatory system that was adopted in New Zealand in 1993 and first used there in the elections of 1996. It was also one of the most powerful arguments used by supporters of first past the post when they defeated a proposed move to a mixed system at a referendum held in the Canadian province of Ontario in 2007. So while compensatory systems in their commonest form promote voter choice in one respect, they also limit that choice in another.

This leads on to a further complaint that is often heard in places where compensatory systems are used, that they create two classes of MPs: some MPs are closely tied to a constituency; but others are freely floating. This complaint partly relates to the accountability issues that we have just looked at: the list MPs can seem like party stooges who get elected whether they have popular backing or not. But it also involves a concern that list MPs do not have a full job to do that could justify their hefty salaries. While constituency members are beavering away at their constituency caseloads, list members seem to have no role to play except to speechify and to act as lobby fodder for their party bosses.

In fact, it appears that many list MPs in Scotland and Wales do a great deal of constituency work. Many of them 'shadow' a single-member constituency – perhaps with a view to running in that constituency at the next election. They also respond to constituents who turn to them rather than to their representative in the single-member constituency. As we discussed in the previous chapter, it may be a good thing that citizens have such choice. On the other hand, regional members are often perceived as inferior to constituency member; as the political scientist Thomas Lundberg has shown, they are often seen as less accountable and sometimes (paradoxically) as less representative than their constituency colleagues. Furthermore, regional members who stood in a constituency but were defeated are often viewed as having weaselled unfairly into the chamber through a back door: if they were defeated, people say, they should not be sitting in Holyrood or Cardiff Bay. These perceptions reached such a level in Wales that it's now impossible for anyone to stand as both a constituency and a list candidate.

Whatever we think of such perceptions, they are a matter of concern. It is clearly a problem if some MPs are viewed as less legitimate than others: this may damage the credibility of the institution as a whole. On the other hand, the Welsh solution of banning dual candidacies makes no sense. In practice, despite the scope for choice that mixed systems create, most voters choose a local candidate on the basis of their party affiliation. So whether a candidate wins in a constituency depends mainly not on their personal qualities but on the local popularity of their party, and defeat is hardly a reflection of whether they would make a good MP at all. The effect of the ban will only be to diminish the quality of the candidates willing to run in constituencies where they have little chance of winning. A better solution would be to employ open rather than closed lists to fill the regional positions: that way, the accountability of list members can be greatly enhanced and those members have a strong incentive to work hard in their regions.

A final concern is that compensatory systems diminish the constituency link even for the members elected by first past the post, because they necessitate an increase in the size of constituencies. If, say, half of all MPs are elected in constituencies and half from lists (as in Germany), then, assuming the total number of MPs is not increased, the number of constituencies will have to be divided by two. Rather than representing an average of just over 70,000 electors, each constituency MP would represent an average of 140,000. That would not be particularly unusual in international comparison: each constituency member of the German Bundestag represents over 200,000 electors and the average member of the US House of Representatives represents over half a million. Still, the constituency service activities of British MPs are much greater than those of MPs in most other countries, and many people would be unhappy if this role were diluted.

Most electoral reformers in Britain would argue that compensatory mixed systems are better than either first past the post or the simple forms of proportional representation that we discussed in the last chapter. Indeed, it is often said that they offer 'the best of both worlds': they provide both local constituency representation, with all the advantages of individual accountability that this brings, and fair representation of a broad range of opinions about how best to run the country.

On the other hand, we should remember that compensatory systems are fully proportional. We should not be fooled by the mixture of different elements into thinking that they provide a halfway house between the disproportionality of first past the post and the proportionality of proportional representation. The Japanese parallel system that I mentioned at the start of the chapter does this. But the compensatory seat allocation process is designed so that the result is proportional overall. As I've said, limits can be placed on this proportionality by thresholds and other measures. If you think proportionality of representation is important, you are likely to find compensatory mixed systems very attractive. But if you don't like systems that are designed to achieve proportional outcomes, you should not like the compensatory system either.

In addition, this system retains the party lists that most British electoral reformers find problematic. Certainly, fewer MPs are elected from such lists than is the case under simple proportional representation. But the number of such MPs is nevertheless considerable and if usual practice is followed, these seats will be allocated through the undesirable mechanism of closed lists.

Overall, then, compensatory mixed systems do combine some of the advantages of first past the post and proportional representation: they provide for representation of opinion and of society in Parliament just as well as the simple PR systems, but they also retain a link between voters and at least some individual MPs. Yet they remain, like all electoral systems, imperfect. They retain the disadvantages of proportionality as well as the advantages, particularly by raising questions of accountability in coalition government. They dilute the constituency link provided by first past the post. And the combination of MPs of different types creates new tensions of its own.

AV+

There is one particular form of the compensatory mixed system that has had a special place in debates about electoral reform in the UK over recent years. This is the system called alternative vote plus (AV+). It shares its basic features with the standard compensatory systems that we have just explored. But it has a number of particular features that deserve separate attention.

AV+ has never been employed in any election anywhere in the world. It was invented by the Independent Commission on the Voting System, chaired by Lord Jenkins, which was set up by Tony Blair in 1997 to consider what system might best replace the first past the post system for electing the House of Commons. The Commission was asked to propose a system that satisfied as far as possible four criteria: 'the requirement for broad proportionality, the need for stable Government, an extension of voter choice and the maintenance of a link between MPs and geographical constituencies'. The system that it came up with was AV+.

As its name suggests, AV+ is based on the alternative vote system that we discussed in detail in Chapter 4. The Commission proposed that the great majority of seats – between 80 and 85 per cent – should be filled by this method. With a House of Commons of 650 members, as at present, this implies a total of around 520 to 550 individual constituencies. If the total number of MPs were reduced to 600, as the current government plans, there would be between 480 and 510 individual constituencies.

The 'plus' element of the system involves the allocation of compensatory seats, as in the systems we have just explored. But the Jenkins Commission proposed only a very limited compensatory element. First, only a small number of seats – between 15 and 20 per cent of the total – would be allocated from party lists if the Commission's proposals were adopted. Second, the Commission suggested that these seats should be allocated in small top-up regions. Specifically, it proposed the use of eighty top-up regions. In Scotland and Wales, these would correspond to the regions used in elections to the Scottish Parliament and Welsh Assembly. In England, they would mostly match the counties in non-metropolitan areas, while London, the West Midlands, and the urban strip from the Mersey to West and South Yorkshire would be divided into a series of pockets. Northern Ireland would receive two regions. Each region would typically contain six or seven constituencies and list seats would be allocated to compensate for disproportionalities. But the number of compensatory seats available in each region would be just one or two – too few to produce proportionality in the overall result.

We can see just how proportional this AV+ system would be by looking at simulated results for recent elections. As in previous cases, a stern health warning has to be attached to such simulations. They assume that voters would vote in the same way under different electoral systems, whereas in fact some would not. For the AV part, they also need to impute estimates for second and lower preferences based on limited survey evidence. Nevertheless, they provide us with a ballpark estimate of what might happen. Table 8 shows the simulated results for the 1997 election that the Jenkins Commission used in its deliberations and the Electoral Reform Society's estimates of the results AV+ would have produced in the 2010 election. It compares these to results under first past the post and pure proportional representation.

As can be seen, AV+ gets much closer to a proportional allocation of seats than does first past the post (or, indeed, the straight system of alternative vote), but it is still a long way from perfect proportionality. In 1997, under first past the post, Labour was hugely over-represented while other parties were under-represented. As we saw in Chapter 4, under pure AV these results would have been even more extreme. AV+ with a top-up of 15 per cent of the seats would have pegged Labour back but would still have left the Conservatives worse off than under first past the post. A 20 per cent top-up, by contrast, would have boosted the Conservatives slightly and the Lib Dems more significantly, though Labour would still have won

Table 8. Election results under AV+ compared to other systems

1997

	First past the post	AV+ with 15% top-up	AV+ with 20% top-up	Nationwide PR (LR–Hare)
Labour	419	378	360	285
Conservative	165	160	175	202
Lib Dem	46	88	90	111
Others	29	32	34	61

Source: AV+: Jenkins Commission report, Annex A; LR–Hare: my calculations.

2010

	First past the post	AV+ with 15% top-up	Nationwide PR (LR–Hare)
Conservative	307	275	235
Labour	258	234	189
Lib Dem	57	110	150
Others	28	31	76

Source: AV+: Electoral Reform Society website; LR–Hare: my calculations.

a substantial overall majority of seats. In 2010, the Conservatives and Labour were both over-represented by first past the post, while AV+ would have reduced this over-representation to the benefit of the Lib Dems. In neither election would AV+ have done much to overcome the under-representation of the minor parties. Almost all the minor-party seats under first past the post belong to the Scottish or Welsh nationalists or to the parties in Northern Ireland. AV+ would not greatly change their performance and it would be insufficiently proportional to give any top-up seats to UKIP, the Greens, or the BNP.

As I said, AV+ was invented by the Jenkins Commission in the late 1990s, but the proposal was never taken further. Though the Blair government originally planned to hold a referendum, in the end it got cold feet, and the referendum never happened. We should not be surprised by this failure: as Table 8 shows, AV+ would have cost Labour seats. So the fact that the Jenkins proposals didn't get anywhere doesn't in itself reflect badly on AV+. Indeed, some prominent politicians continue to argue that it's the best electoral system. Former Labour home secretary Alan Johnson, for example, argues that it would increase proportionality, maintain the constituency link and enhance voter choice, while still keeping small parties out of Parliament. Let's now consider whether these judgements are correct.

Evaluating AV+ against our criteria

As we have just seen, AV+ is what we might call a semi-proportional electoral system: it reduces the disproportionalities found under first past the post or the alternative vote, but it is far from delivering a fully proportional result. It promotes greater proportionality among large parties – and thereby reduces the chances of anomalous overall results – while also maintaining a high barrier to the entry of small parties. The Jenkins Commission argued that it provided a healthy compromise between the criteria of fair representation on the one hand and fair influence and effective and accountable government on the other. By boosting the Lib Dems, AV+ would increase the likelihood of hung parliaments compared to first past the post, so it would, for example, have produced a hung parliament in 1992. But it does not deliver perpetual coalition government. It permits a clean break in government when that is what voters clearly want.

As we would expect, however, opponents on both sides find this middling compromise unsatisfactory. Supporters of first past the post dislike coalition government at all times and therefore reject any reform that makes it more likely. Supporters of full proportional representation, by contrast, think it unacceptable that the electoral system should be designed systematically to favour large parties and argue that our political system would be much healthier if all shades of opinion were heard and subjected to searching scrutiny within the political system.

Both parts of AV+ would increase voter choice relative to first past the post. The AV part allows voters to express more of their preferences and increases the number of voters who contribute to the result of the election. The 'plus' part further ensures that more voters' voices are heard. Furthermore, the Jenkins Commission argued that the compensatory seats should be filled from open rather than closed lists. So voters would be able not only to split their vote between one party in their constituency and another in the top-up region, but also to select among party candidates in the region.

Because AV+ is so dominated by constituency MPs, it largely maintains the constituency link. Introducing it would require the number of constituencies to be reduced somewhat and therefore their size to be increased, but the changes would be fairly slight. Set against this, the AV part would, as we saw in Chapter 4, give more voters a sense of connection to their MP. And the proportional element would, as we saw in Chapter 5, give more voters the feeling that one of the people representing them shared their views. All in all, AV+ should not worry those who wish to maintain MPs' local connections.

Finally, AV+ would do no harm to voters' capacity to keep their MPs in check, but nor would it improve it. The constituency MPs would be just as easy in principle – but, in safe seats, just as hard in practice – to remove as under first past the post or pure alternative vote. Open lists in the top-up component would allow unpopular individuals to be removed – though with many regions electing just one top-up MP, the choice available would likely be minimal.

Overall, then, introducing AV+ would enhance representation and voter choice while leaving the constituency link and MPs' individual accountability largely unchanged. Our judgement on this system depends heavily on how far we want election results to be proportional or to promote single-party majority government. If we think proportionality of representation in Parliament is all important, we will not think AV+ goes far enough. If we strongly prioritise the certainties of single-party governments, then one of the purely majoritarian systems – first past the post or AV – will be more attractive. If, on the other hand, we consider both values to be clearly important, AV+ might provide the sort of compromise we are looking for.

One final aspect of AV+ needs to be considered. By adopting it, we would be introducing into the Westminster system the principle of electing some MPs by proportional representation. It would thereafter be much easier for that proportional element to be expanded if that were thought desirable. So if ever we are given the choice between a majoritarian system (first past the post or pure alternative vote) and AV+, supporters of full proportionality should certainly leap at the opportunity. Opponents of proportionality, meanwhile, will clearly want to keep that door firmly shut.

Summing up

Mixed electoral systems come in many shapes and sizes. Two versions are prominent in debates about electoral reform in the UK. Standard compensatory mixed systems are essentially a form of proportional representation that incorporates a substantial element of constituency representation. AV+, meanwhile, is much closer to the majoritarian system that we have now, but it dampens that system's resolute emphasis on facilitating single-party government in favour of seeking balance across our various criteria. Because they retain single-member constituencies, both of these systems are more likely to be adopted for elections to the House of Commons than are the simple proportional systems that we looked at in the last chapter.

7. The single transferable vote

For many of Britain's most ardent electoral reformers, the electoral system known as the single transferable vote – or STV – is the holy grail. The Electoral Reform Society has fought for this system since the nineteenth century. The Liberal Democrats, too, see STV as the best option. So what is this system, why are its supporters so passionate about it, and what should the rest of us think?

Describing the workings of STV can get a little bit complicated. Before we get too deep into the details, therefore, it's good to clearly see the basic principles upon which the system is based. STV is a proportional electoral system. It therefore has two basic features shared by all proportional systems: it allocates seats not in single-member constituencies but in larger regions that each elect several members; and this allocation is organised not to give all the seats to the most popular strand of opinion, but to spread the seats out across a range of opinions.

But STV is very different from the proportional systems that we've been looking at so far. The systems we have examined in the last two chapters – whether simple proportional systems or the proportional parts of mixed systems – are specifically designed in order to ensure proportional representation of political parties. In the first instance, they allocate seats to parties by adding up all the votes that each party has received. Only after that do they allocate these seats among each party's candidates. STV, by contrast, is based not on parties, but on candidates. Voters thus cast their ballots for individual candidates, and voting for one of a party's candidates in no way boosts the fortunes of other candidates from the same party. The overall result reflects the spread of opinion among the voters. So if voters think in partisan terms, the result will be broadly proportional across political parties. If, however, voters structure their votes around some other criterion – say gender or locale – then the results will generate proportional representation of men and women or of different parts of the region instead. STV's supporters therefore argue that this system produces results that reflect voters' wishes, rather than a preconceived notion that parties are what matter most.

So how does STV achieve all of this? The next section provides some details.

How STV works

STV looks quite like the alternative vote system that we examined in Chapter 4, except that it operates with multi-member rather than single-member constituencies. Thus, voters who go to a polling station receive a ballot paper that lists candidates. Because several MPs are elected from each constituency, the large parties will generally put up multiple candidates, so the total number of candidates will typically be much greater than we are used to in our first past the post elections. Just as under the alternative vote, voters mark the candidates in order of preference, placing a '1' next to their favourite candidate and working down as far as they wish to go.

We then turn to the process of counting these votes. This is a little complicated, so we'll go through the process in detail. The first step is to work out how many votes a candidate needs in order to secure election. We saw in Chapter 4 that, under the alternative vote, a candidate must win more than half of all the votes in order to secure election. But if you want to elect multiple candidates from the constituency, that clearly won't work: it's not possible for more than one candidate to get more than 50 per cent support. The logic of the 50 per cent quota in the alternative vote is that once a candidate has passed 50 per cent of all the votes, you know that no other candidate can possibly defeat them, as no other candidate can possibly gather more votes. We can apply the same logic to multi-member constituencies. If we are electing two MPs from a constituency, then the equivalent quota is one third of the votes: if two candidates have each surpassed a third of the vote, then these must be the most popular two candidates as there are too few votes left for anyone else to catch them. Similarly, in a constituency that elects three MPs, the quota must be passing a quarter of the vote, in a constituency with four MPs, winning candidates must surpass a fifth of the vote, and so on. However many seats there are to be filled in a constituency, you add one to that number and then divide this into the total number of valid votes cast within the constituency. Any candidate whose vote total is greater than this number is elected under STV.

The number of votes required to win here is known as the Droop quota. Like so many of the more arcane bits of electoral system terminology, the Droop quota is named after a mathematician – in this case a nineteenth-century British mathematician called Henry Droop. The mathematicians among you, meanwhile, will find the formula for the quota written out at p. 172 of the Appendix.

Having determined the quota, the next step is to count up all the first preferences, just as under the alternative vote. STV is already used for various elections in the UK: for most elections in Northern Ireland and for local elections in Scotland. So let's take a concrete example, the ward of Colinton and Fairmilehead from the Edinburgh local elections of 2007. Three councillors were to be elected in this ward and the total number of valid votes cast was 12,324. The quota was therefore calculated by dividing this number of votes by four, giving 3,081. Candidates had to exceed this – that

Table 9. Local council election results in the Collinton/Fairmilehead ward of Edinburgh City Council, 2007: First preferences

Candidates	First preferences
Elaine Aitken (Conservative)	2,877
Eric Barry (Labour)	2,332
Stuart Bridges (Lib Dem)	1,842
Thomas Kielty (SNP)	1,861
Robert Mathie (Scottish Socialist)	80
Jason Rust (Conservative)	2,815
Alastair Tibbitt (Green)	517
Total	12,324
Number of seats to be filled	3
Droop quota	3082

Table 10. Local council election results in the Colinton/Fairmilehead ward of Edinburgh City Council: Elimination of bottom candidates

Candidates	First count	Second count		Third count		Fourth count	
		Transfer	Total	Transfer	Total	Transfer	Total
Elaine Aitken (Con)	2877	+1	2878	+29	2907	+204	3111
Eric Barry (Labour)	2332	+9	2341	+101	2442	+316	2758
Stuart Bridges (LD)	1842	+3	1845	+175	2020	+569	2589
Thomas Kielty (SNP)	1861	+20	1881	+102	1983	excluded	
Robert Mathie (SSP)	80	excluded					
Jason Rust (Con)	2815	+1	2816	+28	2844	+150	2994
Alastair Tibbitt (Gr)	517	+29	546	excluded			
Non-transferable		+17		+111	128	+744	872
Total	12,324						
Seats to be filled	3						
Droop quota	3082						

is, to secure at least 3,082 votes – in order to win election. The first preference votes were distributed as shown in Table 9.

It is often the case in an STV election that one or more candidates pass the quota on first preferences. But that was not the case here: no candidate has reached the magic number of 3,082 votes. As under the alternative vote, therefore, the next step is to eliminate the bottom placed candidate – Robert Mathie – count up his voters' second preferences, and add these votes to the other candidates' totals. Table 10 shows this process. It also shows the exclusion of the next two lowest candidates, Alastair Tibbitt and Thomas Kielty. As might be expected, the most popular second choice among those who voted initially for Mathie (the Scottish Socialist candidate) is the Green Party, whereas only one of these second preferences goes to each of the Conservative candidates. The seventeen 'non-transferable' ballots are from voters who expressed one preference and no more. Similarly, when the Green Party's Alastair Tibbitt is excluded, his voters tend to transfer to the environmentally friendly Lib Dems.

The vote totals for each of the leading candidates rise with each round of counting, but the first two batches of transfers are insufficient to push anyone over the quota. It is only with the elimination of Thomas Kielty from the SNP that one of the candidates, the Conservatives' Elaine Aitken, squeezes past the quota and is therefore elected.

So far, everything looks just as in the alternative vote. Indeed, were this an AV election, we would stop here, and Elaine Aitken would be the new councillor for the Colinton and Fairmilehead ward. But we can't stop here, because we still have two more council posts to fill. We need to keep on counting until two more candidates meet the quota.

This is where things start to get slightly more complicated. The aim of STV is to ensure that the views of the whole electorate are fully reflected in the election outcome. That means that everyone's vote, so far as possible, should contribute to the result. But Elaine Aitken has ended up overshooting the quota: twenty-nine of her final tally of 3,111 votes were not needed to secure her election. Such a small surplus might seem trifling. But in other contests a

Table 11. Local council election results in the Colinton/Fairmilehead ward of Edinburgh City Council 2007: Transfer of Aitken's surplus

Candidates	Total vote after fourth count	Raw transfers from Aitken	Weighted transfers from Aitken	Total vote after fifth count
Elaine Aitken (Con)	3111	elected		2760.15
Eric Barry (Labour)	2758	+231	+2.15	2593.21
Stuart Bridges (LD)	2589	+452	+4.21	
Thomas Kielty (SNP)	excluded			
Robert Mathie (SSP)	excluded			
Jason Rust (Con)	2994	+2006	+18.70	3012.70
Alastair Tibbitt (Gr)	excluded			
Non-transferable	872	+422	+3.93	875.93
Total	12,324			
Seats to be filled	3			
Droop quota	3082			

popular candidate might sail way over the quota. If a candidate won two full quotas, for example, it would be unfair that all those voters collectively would secure just one council seat. So whenever a candidate is elected, we need to transfer their surplus votes to the other candidates who remain in the contest. Table 11 shows how this is done.

First we look at all the votes in Aitken's pile and count up the next preference for a candidate still in the race. As we would expect, most of these go to the other Conservative candidate, Jason Rust. But we can't transfer all of these votes: only twenty-nine out of the total of 3,111 are surplus. We therefore multiply each of the figures in the 'raw transfers' column by 29/3111 . This scales down the transfer to a total of just twenty-nine votes, as shown in the 'weighted transfers' column. For example, 2,006 of Elaine Aitken's 3,111 supporters gave their second preference to Jason Rust. The share of the twenty-nine surplus votes that we transfer from Aitken to Rust should be proportional to this. By multiplying 2,006 by 29/3111 we get the figure of 18.70: 18.70 as a share of twenty-nine is the same as 2,006 as a share of 3,111. So 18.70 votes are added to Rust's total. Doing the same for each of the surviving candidates gives the new totals shown in the column on the right.

We're inching closer to a final result here, but we're not quite there yet, as we still have two more councillors to elect. No candidate passed the quota when Aitken's surplus was transferred, so all we can do now is eliminate the bottom candidate, the Lib Dems' Stuart Bridges. This turns out to be the final step because, as Table 12 shows, once Bridges is excluded Eric Barry and Jason Rust both pass the threshold and are thereby elected to the final two positions.

So the three candidates elected are, Elaine Aitken and Jason Rust for the Conservatives and, for Labour, Eric Barry. It happens that these were also the three candidates who led in terms of first preferences. Equally, however, the order of the candidates could have changed in the course of the counting process, just as under the alternative vote. In this example, by the end, three candidates had passed the quota. But remember that some votes may become 'non-transferable' because the voter has expressed preferences only for candidates who have been eliminated. As the number of these

Table 12. Local council election results in the Colinton/Fairmilehead ward of Edinburgh City Council, 2007: Elimination of Bridges

Candidates	Total vote after fifth count	Sixth count	
		Transfers	Total
Elaine Aitken (Con)	elected		
Eric Barry (Labour)	2760.15	+878.88	3639.03
Stuart Bridges (LD)	2593.21	excluded	
Thomas Kielty (SNP)	excluded		
Robert Mathie (SSP)	excluded		
Jason Rust (Con)	3012.70	+582.51	3595.21
Alastair Tibbitt (Gr)	excluded		
Non-transferable	875.93	+1131.83	2007.76
Total	12,324		
Seats to be filled	3		
Droop quota	3082		

non-transferable votes builds up, it's possible to reach the end of the process with three candidates left but only one or two of them (or even none of them) over the quota. Where this happens, the last three candidates left standing are all declared elected.

STV is much rarer than the other forms of proportional representation that we have investigated in previous chapters: only Ireland and Malta use it to elect the lower (or only) house of their national parliament, while Australia uses a variant to elect its upper house. STV is also used in all elections in Northern Ireland except those for Westminster and, as we've seen, it has been used for local elections in Scotland since 2007. Outside the world of politics, STV has been used for elections within the Church of England since early in the twentieth century and is widely used in elections to student unions. It's the obvious system to choose if you want proportional representation of diverse views without having political parties.

As you can see from the preceding description, the mechanics of STV are a little complicated. Most of these complexities are of concern only to returning officers, not to ordinary voters: you don't need to understand exactly how transfer votes are counted in order to follow the essence of what is going on. Still, we might legitimately ask whether it's all worth the bother. So let's now look at how STV measures up against our various criteria of evaluation.

Rewarding Popularity

STV generally does a good job in terms of the basic criterion of rewarding popularity. The transfer of votes ensures that similar candidates cannot split the vote, thus allowing another candidate to be elected even though his views are less popular. Because it is a proportional system, the likelihood that the wrong party will win most seats nationwide is lower than under either first past the post or the alternative vote.

Nevertheless, two points of concern can be raised. First, though the likelihood of a wrong national winner is lower than under majoritarian systems, it's not eliminated. In fact, several recent elections in Malta have delivered a majority of votes for one of the main parties but a majority of seats for the other. This is possible because STV tends to be run with fairly small constituencies (in order to keep the ballot paper from getting too long), the national result is therefore an aggregate of lots of local results, and so some peculiar outcomes can arise. That said, it's possible to address this problem without too much difficulty. The Maltese solution has been to allow for the addition of a few extra MPs whenever the wrong party wins the election in order to ensure that the result overall is not grossly distorted.

The second problem is that of non-monotonicity. As we saw in Chapter 4 (and as is detailed further at p. 169 of the Appendix), it's possible under the alternative vote system for a candidate to be harmed by winning more votes. The same applies to STV. As we saw in the case of AV, however, while it's possible to construct hypothetical examples in which voters' preferences are structured in ways that generate bizarre results, in fact preference distributions like these are extremely unlikely. Some experts think that the mere possibility of a non-monotonic outcome is sufficient to render an electoral system unacceptable. As we've seen again and again in the course of this book, however, no electoral system is perfect, and it's always necessary to weigh benefits on some criteria against costs on others. Given that the likelihood that a candidate would be harmed by gaining extra votes is in practice extremely low, it would be perverse to reject STV on this basis alone.

Fair representation in Parliament and government

Whereas the proportional representation of political parties is designed into other proportional electoral systems, it's not designed into STV. Rather, STV promotes proportionality in terms of whatever it is that voters structure their votes by. Thus, if parties matter to voters, proportional representation of parties will result. In the example of the Edinburgh city council election that we looked at above, for example, many of the votes transferred as we would expect them to if voters were thinking in terms of parties: the lion's share of the leading Conservative candidate's supporters gave their second preference to the other Conservative candidate; Green supporters tended to give their second preference to the Lib Dem, presumably on the basis that the Lib Dems are the greenest of the three main parties. So long as voters behave in this way, proportional representation of parties will be high.

Some evidence on the proportionality of actual elections using STV is available if you turn back to Figure 12 on p. 89. You can pick out the two cases that use STV: Ireland and Malta. Election results in these countries are clearly more proportional than in any country that uses first past the post or the alternative vote. But they are towards the less proportional end of the range of countries

Figure 15. Scottish local council election results, 2003 and 2007

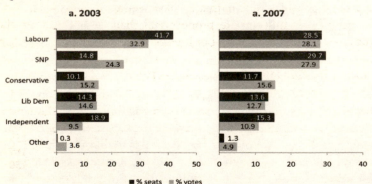

Source: David Denver and Hugh Bochel, 'A Quiet Revolution: STV and the Scottish Council Elections of 2007', *Scottish Affairs*, no. 61 (autumn 2007).

that use some form of proportional representation. More evidence comes from the Scottish local council elections of 2007. As I said above, these were the first Scottish elections to be conducted under STV: previous elections, up to 2003, had used first past the post. Figure 15 compares the election results before and after the change. It's pretty clear that the level of disproportionality – the gaps between vote shares and seat shares – fell quite markedly between the two elections. In fact, in terms of our disproportionality score, it fell from 11.6 in 2003 (making it similar to UK national elections under first past the post) to 5.0 in 2007 (comparable to the United States or Costa Rica).

We can also look at simulations of the effects that STV would have in elections to the House of Commons. Table 13 shows the Electoral Reform Society's simulations of the 2010 election results under STV, compared both to the actual results with first past the post and to fully proportional results. An especially big health warning is needed here: elections under STV are probably the hardest of all to simulate, as they are different in so many ways from elections using first past the post. Nevertheless, we can identify several features. STV would have greatly reduced the over-representation of the Conservatives and Labour. It would have over-represented slightly all three main parties (including the Lib Dems) at the expense of minor parties. Besides the Scottish and Welsh nationalists and the parties of Northern Ireland, minor parties would, on these estimates, have secured no seats at all.

So STV is much more proportional than either first past the post or the alternative vote, but it tends to be less proportional than

Table 13. Simulated 2010 election results under STV

	First past the post	Single transferable vote	Nationwide PR (LR–Hare formula)
Conservative	307	246	235
Labour	258	207	189
Lib Dem	57	162	150
Others	28	35	76

Source: STV: Electoral Reform Society website; LR-Hare: my calculations.

many other PR systems. The main reason for this is constituency magnitude. STV becomes too burdensome on voters if the number of seats available – and therefore the number of candidates – is too great. Thus, constituencies in Malta elect five MPs and those in the Republic of Ireland have between three and five. The STV system used to elect the Northern Ireland Assembly has six-member constituencies. In Scotland, each local council ward elects three or four councillors. In simulating the 2010 election results, the Electoral Reform Society assumed constituencies of three to five members. With constituencies of these sizes, the level of proportionality is necessarily constrained, and small parties will find it difficult to enter.

There are some reasons for doubting whether STV elections are as effective as other proportional systems in promoting the representation of women and minorities. As Figure 13 on p. 90 shows, of all the countries in our sample with some form of proportional representation, those using STV – Ireland and Malta – have the lowest share of women in parliament. The proportion of women in the Northern Ireland Assembly – at 15 per cent – is lower than the proportion of Northern Ireland's MPs at Westminster who are women – 22 per cent. The adoption of STV for local government elections in Scotland left the proportion of women councillors exactly the same as before. If voters continue to prefer (however subconsciously) to have male rather than female politicians, a system such as STV that gives voters a complete choice of candidates rather than just parties would indeed be expected to score badly on this criterion. The evidence is that this preference is declining, but not at a pace that will bring equal representation for women under STV any time soon.

We have already examined in detail the effects of proportional electoral systems upon the distribution of actual influence in the corridors of power, but we have found the evidence to be fairly inconclusive. Given the boost it would give to the Lib Dems, STV in the UK context would produce coalition government most of the time. That would raise fears that smaller parties would be able to hold the large parties to ransom – that the tail would wag the dog. These fears are reasonable, but, equally, the problem could easily not arise. We should factor this concern into our overall judgements, but we should be wary of giving it too much weight.

Effective, accountable government

The implications of proportional representation for the effectiveness and accountability of government are also mostly the same as for other forms of proportional representation. There's no clear evidence that a moderately proportional system such as STV harms the effectiveness of government, though there is some evidence that it weakens accountability.

Where STV differs from other proportional systems, however, is in the degree to which it emphasises the role of individual candidates over parties. I'll examine this in more detail shortly when looking at the constituency link. As we'll see, there is some reason to fear that STV might distract politicians too much from effective decision-making at the national level, encouraging them to focus too heavily on pleasing their local patch. The evidence is far from conclusive on this point, but it's certainly an issue that we need to keep in mind.

Voter choice and turnout

What many of STV's supporters like most about this system is the degree to which it enhances voter choice. Enid Lakeman, the doyenne of British electoral reformers, who chaired the Electoral Reform Society throughout the 1960s and 1970s, observed that 'The single transferable vote gives more freedom to the voter to choose his representative than is possible under any list system.' As we have seen, the voter can rank as many candidates as she or he wishes. In contrast to the alternative vote, where each party puts up just one candidate, under STV voters will typically be able to choose from multiple candidates running for their preferred party. In contrast to other proportional systems, voting for one of a party's candidates does not aid the election of its other candidates in any degree – unless, of course, the voter chooses to grant those other candidates his or her second and lower preferences. There seems little doubt that if our priority is to maximise the choice available to voters, we should opt for STV.

The Jenkins Commission agreed that STV 'maximises voter choice'. Yet it rejected STV in significant part on the basis of this very criterion. It found that, under STV, the choice available to voters could become too great: the system offered 'a degree of choice which might become oppressive rather than liberating'. It explained this judgement in words that deserve repeating for their panache as well as their content:

> it should be stated that the Commission sees the extension of voter choice as highly desirable up to the point at which the average voter is able and eager meaningfully to exercise choice, both between and within parties. But that where the choice offered resembles a caricature of an over-zealous American breakfast waiter going on posing an indefinite number of unwanted options, it becomes both an exasperation and an incitement to the giving of random answers. In voting rather than in breakfast terms exasperation may discourage going to the polls at all and randomness lead to the casting of perverse or at least meaningless votes.

Does STV really give voters a burdensome degree of choice? Certainly, as I have suggested, if constituencies are too large and ballot papers therefore too long, the problems that Jenkins described may arise. But is there any evidence of such problems from systems using moderately sized constituencies of three to six members? The claim that STV is too complex or too difficult for voters is commonly made, so it will be useful to investigate it in detail.

One way of doing so might be to look at figures on electoral turnout. As we have seen, however, while electoral systems do seem to have some impact on turnout, other factors are more important, so it's impossible to draw conclusions from the few cases of STV that we have around the world. Malta has long had exceptionally high turnout – higher even than in Australia, where voting is compulsory – whereas turnout in Ireland is very close to that in the UK. Evidence from local and other elections in Scotland and Northern

Ireland tells us little about what would happen to turnout were STV introduced for elections to Westminster, as turnout behaves very differently depending on the body that's being elected. So useful evidence on turnout is just not available.

An alternative source of evidence comes from the number of spoilt ballot papers. If more voters spoil their ballot paper under one electoral system than another, that might indicate that the first system is asking voters to make choices that they cannot deal with. Indeed, much hoopla followed the first STV elections in Scotland in 2007, when an increase in the proportion of spoilt ballot papers led some to argue that the new system was too confusing for voters. Specifically, the proportion of invalid votes rose from 0.6 per cent of the total in the last local elections using first past the post, in 2003, to 1.8 per cent in the STV elections of 2007. At the same time, however, the proportion of invalid votes cast in the simultaneous elections to the Scottish Parliament, using a compensatory mixed system, rose from 0.7 per cent to 2.9 per cent in the regions and from 0.7 per cent to 4.1 per cent in the single-member constituencies. So, whatever the problem was, STV was not its major source. In fact, detailed investigation by the Electoral Commission suggested that the main problem lay in the design of the ballot paper used for the Scottish Parliament election. The simultaneous use of multiple electoral systems for different elections didn't help. The political scientists David Denver and Hugh Bochel concluded, 'Given the unfamiliarity of STV for most people, 1.83 per cent of ballots rejected seems not an unreasonable figure. The vast majority of voters were clearly able to handle preferential voting.'

Evidence from other countries suggests a similar conclusion. The proportion of invalid votes cast in recent elections in Ireland and Malta has hovered around 1 per cent. This is exactly the level seen in first past the post elections in the UK: in the 2005 general election, invalid ballots made up 0.98 per cents of the total; in 2010, their share was 1.02 per cent. There is no evidence here that STV induces a state of mass confusion.

A final piece of evidence comes from how voters actually use their votes. Because each constituency in STV elects several MPs, each of the major parties will typically put up several candidates. How do voters decide which of these candidates to give their first preference to? If voters are genuinely thinking about the merits of individual candidates as well as of parties, we can expect the order in which they vote for candidates to be unrelated to the order in which those candidates' names appear on the ballot paper. If, by contrast, voters aren't really aware of who the candidates are, then they're likely to use some shortcut: most likely, they will vote for their preferred party's candidates in the order they appear on the ballot paper. So we can expect to see differences in how people vote depending on whether they're really using the opportunities for choice that the system provides. In fact, in the Scottish local elections of 2007, of all the cases in which a party put up two candidates, the candidate who appeared first on the ballot paper scored more votes than the candidate who came second 85 per cent of the time; in only 15 per cent of cases did the candidate lower down the ballot paper win more votes. That was despite the fact that candidates were simply listed in alphabetical order. This gives us pretty solid evidence that many voters were not taking full advantage of the choice available to them.

This last point suggests not only that voters do not make use of the choice that STV provides, but also that the excess opportunity for choice has undesirable consequences: it means that candidates whose names come low down in the alphabet are systematically disadvantaged. On the other hand, it's perfectly straightforward to address this problem: in a method known as Robson rotation that's used in parts of Australia, candidates' names can be randomly rotated on different ballot papers so that every candidate gets a bite at being listed first. Given the availability of this fix, we can say that, though not all voters are able to use the choice that STV provides effectively, no particular harm is generated as a result.

The constituency link

STV's supporters and opponents offer contradictory arguments regarding its impact on the constituency link. For opponents, STV dilutes the unique connection of one MP to one constituency. It also greatly increases the size of constituencies: if we were to use STV for Westminster elections, constituencies would be at least three times bigger than now, perhaps five or six times bigger. Unless special provision were made, constituencies in rural Scotland would be vast.

For supporters, by contrast, STV enhances the constituency link. As under other forms of proportional representation using constituencies, voters would have several MPs to turn to rather than just one, and the rules of STV would make MPs particularly responsive to voters' concerns.

Evidence from Ireland and Malta suggests that there is much merit in the STV supporters' arguments. In both countries, MPs are closely attentive to local issues and to individual voters' difficulties. In fact, there's a strong argument for saying that STV makes the constituency link *too* strong. Candidates have to compete not just against candidates from other parties, but also against other candidates from their own party. The easiest way they can differentiate themselves from their co-partisans is to devote themselves to constituency service, even to the extent of neglecting their crucial national roles of debating laws and holding the executive to account. It's often said that Irish politics is excessively parochial, and that effective national decision-making is harmed because politicians are too focused on local affairs. The policy failures that contributed to Ireland's crippling economic collapse in recent years have spurred widespread calls for political reform, often focused on enhancing parliamentary scrutiny of the government. The degree to which STV contributes to these problems is disputed, but it's not unreasonable to think that it plays some part.

Here we return to a point that I made back in Chapter 2. British voters increasingly demand that their MPs should focus their attentions locally: MPs are expected to live in the constituency and to return pretty much every weekend when Parliament is sitting. This is perfectly reasonable: we all want our local advocate in the corridors of power. But it also carries a cost: issues that powerfully affect all our interests but lack strong local resonance – such as regulating the banks or constraining carbon emissions or controlling the budget – can easily get neglected. STV does not guarantee such problems, but it does create dangers that we need to bear in mind.

Keeping MPs in check

Since the expenses scandal of May 2009, many electoral reformers have promoted STV as a means of preventing – or at least rendering less likely – the recurrence of such misbehaviour. The Electoral Reform Society boldly asserts that: 'There are no safe seats under STV, meaning candidates cannot be complacent.'

There is much validity in this claim. A safe seat is a seat that a candidate can be confident of winning, no matter his or her personal merits, on the basis of voters' party loyalty. As we've seen, however, STV requires a candidate to compete not just against other parties, but also against her co-partisans, so coming from a popular party isn't enough to win election. A candidate needs individual popularity too.

This argument works so long as the parties put up more candidates than they expect to win seats. In most real-world STV elections, that's exactly what parties do: in Malta, indeed, the main parties often put up many more candidates than there are seats available. If, however, a party puts up only as many candidates as it expects to win seats, then voters' capacity to kick out MPs they don't like is greatly diminished. This is what the Scottish parties did in the local elections of 2007 – if you look back to the example of Colinton and Fairmilehead, you can see that the Conservatives nominated two candidates and won two seats, while the other parties nominated just one candidate each. This is also the pattern followed by Northern Ireland's parties: they have each nominated just one candidate in recent European Parliament elections, though three seats are available; in elections to the Northern Ireland Assembly, they generally nominate between one and three candidates, though each constituency elects six members. If the parties were to follow this pattern in UK-wide elections under STV as well, then safe seats would be just as prevalent as they are today.

Summing up

STV has considerable merits. It delivers proportional representation but guards against extreme fragmentation. It does so without excessively empowering political parties and without eliminating the constituency link. It gives voters more choice than any other electoral system. It holds out the prospect of greatly reducing the number of safe seats.

On the other hand, followers sometimes appear to worship STV with a religious zeal that blinds them to its shortcomings. And STV, just like any electoral system, does have shortcomings. If you are unconvinced by the merits of coalition government, then STV is not for you. Even if you are relaxed on that point, you might wonder if the degree of choice that STV offers is really of value to many voters and you might reasonably worry that STV can encourage excessive parochialism among MPs. Finally, we need to recognise that the argument that STV eliminates safe seats depends on how our parties choose to behave. If they follow the pattern observable in those parts of the UK that already use STV for some elections, then it appears they will nominate insufficient candidates for this argument to work.

Whatever the merits of STV, however, we should remember that neither it nor any other proportional system will be available to us as an option in the coming referendum. Arguments about the merits of PR will lurk in the shadows throughout the referendum campaign. But the only options available on the ballot paper will both be non-proportional: first past the post and the alternative vote.

8. Before election day

We have been looking so far at the core of the electoral system: the rules that determine the sort of votes that we as voters can cast and the translation of those votes into parliamentary seats. But there's much more to the electoral system than this alone. The electoral process is not confined to what happens in the polling station and the counting hall, and the wider set of rules governing this electoral process can also be crucial in determining the composition of Parliament and the character of the political system.

In this chapter and the next one, we'll therefore explore some of these other rules.. We can't look at everything. But we can examine some of the issues that are likely to be high on the agenda over the next year or two.

When we are thinking about the period before election day, two issues matter most: how candidates are selected, and how the campaign is conducted. Whereas the core of the Westminster electoral system has remained largely constant for decades, both the procedures used to select candidates and the rules that govern campaigning have changed significantly, and further changes are on the cards. So let's tackle these two issues in turn.

How parties select their candidates

The selection of parliamentary candidates has traditionally been largely the preserve of local parties. In each of the major parties, it has been the constituency party that has decided who their candidate in the coming election should be. The typical pattern has been that a selection committee has whittled down all the applicants to a shortlist and local party members – either at a meeting or by postal ballot – have chosen among these. In addition, the parties' national headquarters have long vetted potential candidates for suitability and have maintained the right to veto a selection if they think it might damage the reputation or cohesion of the party as a whole.

There are two big issues of debate surrounding this selection process. One concerns the candidates who are selected. As we have seen, politicians in the UK are far from representative of the diversity of society: they are overwhelmingly white, male, and middle class. The core of the electoral system that we have looked at so far might have something to do with this, but changes to that core offer no panacea. The problem seems often to lie further back in the election process: a lack of diversity among candidates. So can the process of selecting candidates be improved in order to change this? The other issue concerns the people who are involved in making these selections. Candidate selection is an incredibly important part of our democratic system, yet it's currently controlled by a tiny proportion of the electorate. Is it possible – and would it be desirable – to open this process up to wider participation, notably through the use of American-style primaries?

Promoting diversity in the candidates selected

A total of 861 women stood for Parliament in 2010. That was a record high, but still women comprised only 21 per cent of all the candidates. Seven per cent of the three main parties' candidates were from minority ethnic backgrounds. This is close to these groups' population share, but the lower share of members of ethnic minorities among elected MPs – just 4 per cent – attests to the fact that many were nominated in seats that their party had little chance of winning. Despite considerable progress in recent years, therefore, equality remains a distant goal. Indeed, in terms of at least one criterion – educational background – Parliament was even less representative of the population after the 2010 election than it had been before. 37 per cent of the MPs elected for one of the three main parties in 2010 were educated in independent schools – the highest figure since 1992. Nine out of every ten MPs went to university, compared with around two in ten across the working-age population as a whole.

The parties have worked strenuously in recent years to improve the diversity of their candidates. All have extensive programmes for encouraging and helping candidates from under-represented groups and actively seek the nomination of women and minority candidates in seats they think they can win. The Labour government legislated to allow parties to draw up all-women shortlists when selecting their candidates. Though Labour is the only party to have used this provision, the other parties have been far from inactive: David Cameron's 'A list' of candidates was used to encourage (or, more accurately, force) the selection of women and minority candidates in winnable seats; the Lib Dems have made some use of gender-balanced shortlists in order to encourage the selection of more women.

The question arises, however, of whether further legislative changes would be desirable. A report prepared by three senior academics for the Hansard Society in 2005 concluded that, without firmer action, improvement would occur only at an unacceptably slow pace. They pointed to the fact that compulsory quotas for the number of women candidates have been found elsewhere to work in tackling under-representation, so long as they are properly enforced. It would be possible, for example, to require parties to select women in a certain number of seats. It would even be possible to legislate that a certain portion of these should be winnable.

There are clearly objections to such provisions. They do not square well with the traditional liberal idea that parties should be free to choose their own candidates as they see fit. They cause excluded potential candidates to feel unfairly treated. It is often argued that they demean women or members of minorities, leading those who are selected to be seen as token representatives who have not been chosen on merit. Supporters of firmer guarantees of diversity accept these points but argue that they are outweighed by the greater benefit that quotas would bring in overcoming huge injustice. They also suggest that such provisions would be controversial only in the short term: once diversity had increased, the culture of politics would change, women and minority candidates would more readily come forward and secure support, and quotas would naturally be met.

Whoever is right in this argument, further significant changes to the rules appear unlikely in the near future. The parties showed that they took the issue seriously (or, at least, that they wanted to be seen to take the issue seriously) by launching a Speaker's Conference in 2008 to investigate how diversity among elected politicians could be improved. A Speaker's Conference is a rarely used forum for cross-party deliberation on a subject of broad significance. It reported in early 2010 and made wide-ranging recommendations concerning not just the electoral system (however broadly conceived), but also the culture and working practices of Parliament itself. It endorsed all-women shortlists and argued for a similar provision allowing parties to restrict some shortlists only to members of ethnic minorities. It also explored means of overcoming barriers to candidacy for people with disabilities. But it stopped short of a recommendation that such constraints should be compulsory for parties.

Even these limited recommendations are not currently high on the political agenda. The Labour government toyed in its final years with the idea of allowing all-ethnic-minority shortlists, but ultimately chose not to pursue the idea. The only relevant words in the coalition agreement between the Conservatives and the Lib Dems say, 'We will introduce extra support for people with disabilities who want to become MPs, councillors or other elected officials.' The general view appears to be that existing measures have begun to bear fruit and that to force the pace more aggressively would provoke too much dissent from a variety of quarters.

The introduction of primaries

Big changes are, however, on the cards in the second aspect of candidate selection – measures to extend the range of people involved in making the selections. Almost all MPs are elected as the candidates of political parties, and traditionally they are selected by party members within the constituency. But party memberships have been declining steadily over recent decades: having peaked somewhere around four million in the 1950s, the total membership of the three main parties today probably stands at less than half a million, little more than 1 per cent of the total electorate. As we have seen in previous chapters, under the first past the post system – or, indeed, under the alternative vote system that might replace it – many seats are safe, meaning they are very likely to remain in the hands of the same party for the indefinite future. Where that is the case, the really important stage of the election is not election day itself – the result there is a foregone conclusion. Rather, it is the stage of candidate selection – it is here that the identity of the next MP is really decided.

With party memberships so small, that means that, in many constituencies, the most important democratic decision is being made not by the electorate as a whole, but by just a tiny minority. Indeed, given that, traditionally, many candidates are selected at meetings, and that even many party members don't bother to show up at such meetings, it can sometimes be that just a handful of people are involved in the effective selection of a constituency's next MP.

For this reason (and others that we will get to in a moment), there has been a recent burst of interest in choosing candidates by 'primaries' – mechanisms that, one way or another, expand the set of people involved in the selection process. The coalition programme, taking its cue from Conservative Party policy, says, 'We will fund 200 all-postal primaries over this Parliament, targeted at seats which have not changed hands for many years. These funds will be allocated to all political parties with seats in Parliament that they take up, in proportion to their share of the total vote in the last general election.'

Before we start to think about whether this is a good idea, we need to be clear on what exactly it means. What, in fact, is a 'primary'?

Three features of the candidate-selection process are relevant here. First, who is allowed to participate? Second, how can they participate? Third, who are the candidates they can choose from? In the traditional model for British parties, only party members can participate, they generally do so by attending and voting at a meeting of the constituency party, and they can choose among the candidates who have been chosen in advance by a shortlisting committee. Selection procedures with these characteristics are definitely not primaries. But each of these three features can be varied. It is possible to open up the right to participate beyond party members – either to voters who are willing to affirm that they are party supporters, or to anyone who is registered to vote in general elections in the constituency. Means of participation can be opened up to include voters who are unwilling or unable to attend a meeting – either by setting up polling stations, as in a general election, or by holding a postal ballot. Finally, the range of candidates whom participants can choose from can be opened up to any party member (or even anyone at all) who is willing to put themselves forward, perhaps with the requirement that they first receive a certain number of nominations from party members.

Primaries are most familiar from presidential elections in the United States: the early months of every election year are dominated by the caravan of candidates and trailing hacks moving from state to state as successive primaries are held to determine the Democrat and Republican candidates. These primaries vary between states: some are restricted only to party supporters, while others are open to everyone. But all these primaries are held using polling stations – selection meetings, which do happen in some states, are known as caucuses, not primaries. And in all of them candidacy is open: there is no prior process of shortlisting.

Two sorts of selection process have been labelled as 'primaries' in the UK. The first involve meetings, opened up either to party supporters or to any local voters. The second involve postal ballots, in which any voter in the constituency is allowed to take part. The difference between a meeting and a postal ballot is really important, as we shall see shortly, so it would be better to keep them separate in our minds. Following the American practice, I'll refer to the first as caucuses and the second as primaries. Caucuses or primaries are 'open' when any local voter can take part and 'closed' when only party supporters (whether party members or not) can do so. In all cases in the UK, the process of shortlisting has been retained: voters are typically given three or four possible candidates to choose from.

The first so-called 'primaries' in the UK were in fact caucuses.

They were held to select the Conservative candidates in Warrington South and Reading East in 2003. The Warrington caucus was open, while that in Reading was closed. Similar processes were used by the Conservatives in many more constituencies ahead of the 2010 election. A more radical step came during 2009, when the Conservatives held two genuine open postal primaries – one in the Devon seat of Totnes, the other in Gosport, on the shores of the Solent. So far, only the Conservatives have experimented with such innovations. But there is support on the left too. The longstanding Labour MP for Birkenhead, Frank Field, thinks he may have been the first British politician to advocate such a step, having made the suggestion in the early 1980s, when Labour risked capture from activists on the hard left. Both David and Ed Miliband came out in favour of the idea in the course of 2009.

What should we think of the government's plan to expand the use of primaries? To date, the constituencies in which caucuses or primaries have been held have clearly been chosen for partisan reasons. Warrington and Reading were seats that the Conservatives had lost but hoped to win back; they expected (correctly) that the innovation of caucuses would attract media attention and help them rebuild connections with voters. Many of the caucuses and both of the primaries held in 2009 took place in constituencies being vacated by MPs tarnished by the expenses scandal: Totnes was the domain of Anthony Steen, who declared that voters were jealous of his 'very, very large house'; Gosport was home to Sir Peter Viggers, the man with the infamous duck house. Conservative leaders saw primaries in these constituencies as means of wiping the slate clean and starting afresh.

But caucuses and (more especially) primaries also bring some clear benefits to the political system as a whole. They expand voter choice – particularly in safe seats, where choice on election day itself is largely meaningless. Under traditional selection procedures, local voters who do not wish to join the ruling political party have no real say over who their MP will be. Caucuses give them the right to a choice and primaries make it relatively easy for them to exercise that right. In consequence, a primary in which a broad section of the electorate participate can also enhance the legitimacy of the MP elected and strengthen his or her links with constituents. An MP selected in the traditional way by the dwindling band of faithful and then elected in a lifeless contest where the outcome is known in advance may have little opportunity or need to connect with voters. But an MP who has first had to fight a genuine contest in the public eye can reasonably expect to be better known and respected in the community. It is for these reasons that the coalition wants to target funding for primaries on safe seats.

More generally, primaries are a way of re-engaging voters with politics. Both David Cameron and David Miliband argued in the wake of the expenses scandal that they would help bridge the gulf that has opened up between politicians and those whom politicians are supposed to represent by giving voters more of a stake in the system. Open caucuses go some way to achieving this by opening what would otherwise be internal party debates to public participation. But the number of voters who actually attend even an open selection meeting never exceeds a few hundred. Open primaries can achieve far more. Over 16,000 voters took part in the Totnes primary – almost a quarter of the constituency's entire electorate. Another 12,000 – almost 18 per cent of eligible voters – participated in Gosport. This represents a huge increase in popular participation in the democratic process.

The case for primaries therefore sounds pretty compelling. But there are also major arguments on the other side – this is no open-and-shut case. The qualm that some politicians initially expressed is that allowing anyone a say will allow your opponents to engage in monkey business, deliberately saddling you with a weak candidate. Yet this objection need not be taken too seriously. Primaries in the UK will retain the shortlisting stage, which will still be conducted by local party activists. So voters' choice of candidates will be restricted to those whom senior figures in the local party think suited to the job. Further, if primaries are held to choose the incumbent party's candidate in safe seats, party supporters should in any case outnumber those who might be tempted to do mischief. A caucus could be swayed by an organised group able to mobilise a few hundred voters, but this will be very difficult in a full primary.

Nevertheless, several other arguments against primaries need more careful attention. One is that primaries deprive local party workers of the reward for their loyalty. They are therefore unfair to people who are willing to sacrifice their time in making our democracy work and they threaten to undermine local party organisation. The Conservative MP Julian Critchley observed in 1965 that 'The choice of a candidate is for the constituency party worker the reward of many years of hard, unglamorous work. It is a pleasure to be savoured.' That might seem a bit overblown, but it is a point made by contemporary critics of primaries as well. John Strafford, chair of the Conservative Campaign for Democracy, argues that primaries deprive ordinary party members of their last right in party decision-making and asks why anyone today would bother to become a member. Proponents of primaries – notably David Miliband – counter, however, that the traditional model of party membership is outmoded in a world where fewer and fewer people are willing to identify rigidly with a single political team. Parties, he contends, must seek new, more flexible forms of engagement with their supporters, and primaries encourage these.

Another argument concerns the effectiveness of our governing institutions. As I have suggested, effective and accountable government is possible in a parliamentary system such as ours only with cohesive and disciplined parties. Parliament should not be a slave to the executive, but if MPs disregard the party manifesto on which they were elected it is difficult for voters to exercise democratic control. With primaries, however, it may appear that MPs are no longer beholden to their party, but to voters more widely. An MP who has been chosen – not just as an MP, but also as her party's candidate – by local voters may feel she has a personal mandate that overrides the diktats of the party leadership. Opponents of primaries will point towards the United States, the country where primaries are most established. Congressmen there are notoriously independent-minded. In order to secure major legislation on healthcare reform and other issues, President Obama has had to plead with individual representatives and buy them off with special deals. Few of us would want our own government to be held thus to ransom.

How much credence should we place in these arguments? Certainly, if the independence of US representatives were to be translated into our parliamentary system, both democracy and governance would suffer. But is that likely? There are at least two reasons for thinking not. First, the greater independence of American congressmen compared to British MPs is not the product of primaries alone. Our parliamentary system creates pressures for party discipline that do not exist in the American presidential system: most MPs here would like to climb the ministerial ladder, so they need to keep their leader happy; MPs' electoral fate is much more bound up with the fate of the government in a system where Parliament and government are elected together. Second, primaries in the UK will be different from those in the US. As we have seen, party members will retain control of shortlisting, so excessively independent individuals will find it hard to get anywhere near the ballot paper. In addition, the plan is to use primaries only when a sitting MP retires, not for the reselection of existing MPs. This means that, for an MP looking ahead to the next election and beyond, it is support within the party that matters.

So the dangers to parliamentary discipline are there, but they should not be exaggerated. Other questions can also be raised about the sorts of MP that primaries are likely to produce. One concern is that primaries might be bad for the election of women and minorities: if there is bias among voters in favour of white, male politicians, primaries might import this bias into the process of selecting candidates. Indeed an article published by Robert McIlveen in 2009 seemed to offer evidence in favour of this view and concluded, 'Primaries may well advantage local favourite sons to the detriment of less well-known candidates. Local councillors seeking a seat in Parliament, who are predominantly men, could be expected to do best in open primaries due to their local profile, contacts, and indeed friends and neighbours, who would be eligible to vote without being party members.' But McIlveen's research was based on caucuses, not on true primaries, and in fact the two primaries that have now been held both led to the selection of women. General conclusions cannot be drawn just from two cases, but there is good reason to expect caucuses and primaries to behave differently: some of those who take part in primaries are likely to be people who feel disillusioned with politics as it stands, who would never think of attending a selection meeting, and who would be keen to support a non-traditional candidate for Parliament.

But this leads on to another concern: primaries may bias elections towards centrists who appeal to a broad range of voters and towards candidates who are unsullied by past involvement in politics. That might sound very good. But if we want more than a choice between Tweedledum and Tweedledee at election time, excessive centrism may be unattractive, and unsullied candidates might well lack the experience that is required to perform effectively in the tough world of Westminster. We just don't have sufficient evidence yet to judge such claims. Of the two candidates elected through primaries so far, one – Sarah Wollaston in Totnes – had very little political experience, while the other – Gosport's Caroline Dinenage – had been a councillor and had run for Parliament in 2005. Neither presented a strongly ideological pitch to voters, but only time will tell what positions they might adopt at Westminster.

Thus, though the case for primaries may at first seem very solid, in fact there are good reasons for questioning their value. They could harm as well as help the democratic system and the quality of government. In addition, the benefits they bring might end up more limited than they initially appear: while turnout has been decent in the two primaries held so far, it would be reasonable to expect it to decline as the novelty wore off. In truth, we don't know what long-term effects the spread of primaries would have on our political system.

On one final concern, however, we do have clear evidence: full postal primaries cost a lot of money. Based on experience in the two primaries held so far, the Conservatives estimate the cost per contest at £40,000. That is more than any British political party can afford in more than a handful of key seats. It is for this reason that the Conservatives have advocated and the coalition agreement promises that the state will fund 200 primaries between now and the next election, at a total cost of £8 million. This might be seen as a sign of healthy commitment to the democratic process. But many will find it outrageous that the state is going to pay for parties to choose their election candidates at a time when so many vital services are being cut to the bone. This moves us towards the final subject of this chapter, the costs of election campaigning.

Financing parties and campaigns

There are many aspects of election campaigning that we could look into. One rule that sets the UK apart from many other democracies is the ban on political advertising on television and radio. Whereas American TV viewers (at least, those living in marginal states) are bombarded with endless campaign commercials during election years, we in Britain are free from such invasions into our living rooms. The main parties are entitled to a certain quota of party election broadcasts, but the airwaves are otherwise left undisturbed. Another aspect of campaigning of current interest is the introduction of televised leaders' debates.

I'm going to concentrate here, however, solely on the issue of campaign finance: how much it costs to campaign for elected office and who pays the bills. There have been significant changes to the rules on this over the last decade or so, and all the major parties promised further reform in their 2010 election manifestos.

Regulation of campaign finance has a long history in the UK. It goes back, in fact, to 1883, when limits were first introduced on the amount candidates could spend on their campaign in their own constituency. Thereafter, despite sporadic anxieties, the system remained largely unaltered for over a hundred years. In the late 1990s, however, several developments came together to generate a consensus that further reform was badly needed. One of these developments was the gradual rise in the importance of national rather than constituency campaigning. Electioneering in 1883 was still mostly a local affair. Even in the early post-war years, election periods were not notably frenetic for party leaders: David Butler, leading observer of British politics for over half a century, recalls a four-hour meeting he had with Winston Churchill during the 1950 election campaign: 'twelve days before the election', Butler remarks, 'he had nothing to do but show off to a 25-year-old nobody'. In the age of television, however, the national campaign is very important indeed. Battle buses must be hired, photo ops staged, billboards plastered, and rallies held. It makes no sense to cap local campaign spending but allow the parties to lavish whatever resources they can get hold of on the national campaign.

This need became particularly apparent in 1997. At the 1992 election, the three main parties between them had spent £23 million on their national campaigns. In 1997, this leapt to £56 million – even in real terms, spending more than doubled in just one election cycle. Then, months after the 1997 election, further concerns were raised by the Ecclestone affair, in which it was perceived by many that the head of Formula One racing, Bernie Ecclestone, had secured his sport's exemption from the ban on tobacco advertising by donating £1 million to the Labour Party.

In the wake of these developments, an inquiry was held and fresh legislation was passed. The new rules – which entered the statute books in 2000 – overhauled the regulation of political parties and campaigns in many ways. For our purposes, three elements particularly stand out. First, donations from overseas were banned, with only organisations based in the UK or people eligible to vote in UK elections able to donate to parties or candidates. Second, donations of more than £5,000 (since raised to £7,500) had to be disclosed: we can all now read details of them on the Electoral Commission's website. Third, national campaign spending was capped for the first time: the limit for a party that contests every seat in Great Britain is just under £19 million.

Only fairly minor adjustments have been made to these rules since 2000. But it's almost universally agreed that further reform is needed. The spending limits that were introduced in 2000 have done much to control the expenditure 'arms race' that had begun to break out among the major parties, and the fact that the cap is not indexed to inflation means that real levels of spending will gradually be reduced from election to election. But the absence of any cap on donations means that concerns remain that the rich are able to buy political influence. Certainly, the fact that large donations must be publicly declared limits the scope for such influence: the blatant coincidence of a major donation and a significant policy change will be rapidly exposed in the media. Nevertheless, subtler forms of influence remain entirely possible.

So a further review was launched in 2006, led by the retired civil servant Sir Hayden Phillips. This reported in 2007 and recommended a cap on donations of £50,000. Phillips said 'Few would now dissent from the proposition that there should be a limit on how much any one donor may contribute to a party each year' – he reported that, of the parties he had consulted, only UKIP opposed this. While all the main parties agree to this in principle, however, they failed during talks following publication of the Phillips report to agree the details. In particular, they were unable to find compromise on how to treat donations from trade unions. As a result, no cap has yet been introduced.

Quite apart from these details – which have big implications for the parties but which most of us will be happy to let those parties resolve among themselves – one major difficulty does remain. If large donations are to be banned, how will the shortfall in parties' funding be plugged? The fact is that all the main parties are heavily dependent on big donors: the Electoral Commission has estimated that a £50,000 cap would have reduced the total value of donations to political parties between 2001 and 2003 from £68 million to just £22 million. It would be nice if the parties could instigate a wave of civic activism, enthusing millions of citizens to engage actively in politics and contribute to the democratic process – as Barack Obama succeeded spectacularly in doing during the race for the presidency in 2008. But there's no evidence that British parties are capable of this (or British citizens willing). Many people think that the only alternative is funding from the state.

The use of taxpayers' money to fund the activities of political parties is clearly controversial. When the polling organisation ICM asked voters in 2006, 'Do you agree or disagree that public money should be used to finance political parties?' more than three quarters – 77 per cent – said that they disagreed. At a time when politicians are in particularly low repute and public spending across the board is being slashed, few politicians are willing to make the case for it. Thus, though all the main parties backed further controls on political donations in their 2010 election manifestos, none explicitly called for state funding to make up the shortfall.

In fact, however, a strong case can be made for state funding of political parties. Indeed, though none of the parties was brave enough to put this policy to the voters in 2010, all had endorsed it in the preceding years. And research conducted for the Electoral

Commission in 2003 found that voters who participated in focus groups where arguments for and against state funding were discussed generally ended up supporting the idea.

The case for state funding begins with the argument – which I have already made in earlier chapters – that political parties are vital to the health of our democracy. Jack Straw, then Justice Secretary, wrote in his introduction to a government paper on party finance in 2008 that 'Political parties are integral to our democratic system. They make parliamentary government possible.' Andrew Tyrie, leading Conservative thinker on these matters, opened his own discussion of party funding in 2006 with the words, 'Democracy needs parties.' Hayden Phillips wrote in his review in 2007, 'Our Parliamentary democracy cannot operate effectively without strong and healthy political parties.' Without decent resources, however, parties cannot perform their essential democratic functions: they cannot develop policies or communicate those policies to voters or enthuse and mobilise their supporters to engage in the democratic process. If – as appears to be happening – we collectively decide that existing funding sources for parties are unacceptable, then it would seem reasonable that we should seek collectively to come up with some kind of alternative. No one has thought of an alternative besides state funding that looks likely to succeed.

Furthermore, the principle of state finance for political parties is already very widely accepted. It was apparently first applied in Uruguay in 1928. It spread to Europe – specifically, to Germany, in 1959, and it has since become an accepted part of most democratic systems. Even in the UK – where state funding remains limited – it is nevertheless already well entrenched. Funding for opposition parties' parliamentary offices was first introduced in 1975, and it is generally agreed that this is essential if the opposition is to be able to carry out its crucial function of scrutinising government. This so-called Short Money (along with more limited Cranborne Money in the House of Lords) will total almost £7 million in 2010/11. More recently, policy development grants have been introduced in order, as the name suggests, to assist parties in researching and developing new policy proposals. These grants, totalling £2 million a year, are distributed among those parties with at least two MPs sitting in the House of Commons. There's also limited public support for election campaigning: all parliamentary candidates are entitled to send out one election address without paying postage; and parties do not pay for the airtime devoted to their fixed allocation of party election broadcasts. The introduction of direct state funding for campaign spending and general party activities would not, therefore, constitute a radical departure from existing practices.

There is a widespread concern that funding parties through the state might cause parties' roots in society to wither. In the 1990s, the political scientists Richard Katz and Peter Mair argued that parties around the world were no longer acting as representatives of society in the state, but were increasingly the creatures of the state whose function was to reconcile voters with whatever the state decided to do. Michael Pinto-Duschinsky, one of Britain's leading experts on political finance, recently built on this point, arguing, 'If we go further down the road of state funding of political parties, we risk exacerbating the long-run trend that is converting parties from popular, democratic institutions into top-down bureaucracies.'

While there's no denying that political parties do appear increasingly remote from ordinary voters, however, there's some research that questions whether state funding can be blamed for this. Party memberships have collapsed across the old democracies, irrespective of the level of state support. Indeed, it's possible to design systems of state finance such as to encourage parties to develop their social base. Hayden Phillips, for example, recommended 'a matched funding scheme to encourage the parties to recruit paying supporters', suggesting that parties should establish online subscriber schemes – much like Barack Obama's – and that all donations of £5 or more would be matched by £5 (but never more) in public funding. In this way, the returns from building up a substantial activist base would be enhanced. So fears that enlarged state funding will sever parties' last links with the electorate may be overblown.

Still, there are also good arguments against state finance for parties. One is that our political parties already benefit handsomely from taxpayers' money. Pinto-Duschinsky argues that the official figures for state funding greatly underestimate the true level. He suggests that a sizeable portion of MPs' allowances support party and campaign work: MPs often rent constituency offices from their own party, for example, and MPs' constituency activities are clearly designed in significant part to boost their re-election prospects. Adding in all MPs' allowances, payments to councillors, funding for special advisers, and so on, Pinto-Duschinsky suggests that state funding for the activities of candidates and parties might be as high as £1.75 billion across a four-year electoral cycle. This is surely an over-estimate: even on the broadest definitions, MPs' allowances are not entirely devoted to constituency or party activity. Still, Pinto-Duschinsky does have a point: much as there is a strong case for funding core democratic institutions through the public purse, it isn't obvious that the obligation is not being fulfilled already.

In present circumstances, however, the main argument against extended state finance for parties is simply that limited public funds could better be devoted to other purposes. When funding for so much else is being cut, it's difficult to imagine how politicians could justify giving more money to themselves. The government justifies cutting the number of MPs in terms of the financial savings this will bring. It has cut ministers' pay in order to emphasise the same agenda. In this context it seems inconceivable that public funding for parties could be substantially increased. Whatever the merits of the case, there seems little likelihood of change any time soon.

But this has implications for plans to introduce a cap on donations to parties as well. The coalition agreement says the government will 'pursue a detailed agreement on limiting donations and reforming party funding in order to remove big money from politics'. But if a substantial increase in state financing is out of the question, it's difficult to see how the parties could cope with the sorts of donation limits that have been discussed. We can therefore expect no more than very slow progress on this agenda in the next few years.

9. After election day

We have just looked at aspects of the electoral rules that apply before election day itself. Even two years ago, there would have been no scope for a mirroring chapter looking at the electoral process after election day: once the election result had been declared, that was pretty much it until the next general election four or five years later.

But all that has changed with the sudden emergence on to the political agenda of the idea of recall: the idea that, provided certain conditions are met, voters in a constituency can demand an early election which their MP must win if he or she is to retain the seat. At the time of the 2005 election, the idea of introducing recall procedures in the UK was mentioned by no one. By 2010, it was shared orthodoxy among all the major political parties, and the government coalition has promised to press ahead with the policy.

So how exactly would recall work? What forces have caused it to burst on to the agenda in the last few years? And what would its effects be upon our democratic system?

Recall around the world

Recall provisions originated in the United States in the late nineteenth and early twentieth centuries. This was the 'progressive era' of American politics, when public disillusionment with the political system spurred a series of reforms designed to expand opportunities for civic participation. Recall was introduced first at the local level. The first state to adopt it was Oregon, in 1908, and others rapidly followed. Today, state-level politicians can be recalled in eighteen states, and local recall provisions exist in many more.

The idea of recall has spread only slowly around the world. Exact information on where recall procedures exist is hard to come by, though the most authoritative study, published in 2008, found twenty-two countries using them in some form at some level of government, but at least one case is missing from its list. We can be confident, however, that recall, particularly at the national level, is rare. Furthermore, some of the countries that enshrine it in the letter of the law – such as Belarus and Turkmenistan – are dictatorships in which we can assume it does not operate effectively.

Recall provisions allow voters to take action leading towards the dismissal of an elected politician before their term is up. Beyond this core, the rules of recall vary widely. In some cases, as in the United States, the power of recall lies entirely in the hands of voters: the process is initiated by a petition to which a specified proportion of eligible voters must add their names; this triggers a popular vote that determines whether the initiative is successful or not. In other cases, however, the power to initiate recall lies in the hands not of voters, but of politicians. In Austria, for example, the recall of the president can be initiated only by parliament; this move is then endorsed or rejected by voters. Where the right of initiative lies with voters, the number of signatures required is different from case to case. Among American states, the lowest threshold is in Montana, where the signatures of 10 per cent of eligible voters are needed to initiate the recall of some office holders. California also has permissive rules, with a 12 per cent minimum. But most states have thresholds around 25 per cent and a few set the minimum as high as 40 per cent.

There is also variation in the circumstances in which recall can be initiated. In most US states that allow for recall, no particular circumstances are required. But eight states require certain conditions to be met; to take just one example, the relevant law in Kansas stipulates that 'Grounds for recall are conviction of a felony, misconduct in office or failure to perform duties prescribed by law'. This means that it is not sufficient for voters simply to be unhappy with the policies that an office holder is pursuing – rather, she or he must be guilty of specific wrongdoing.

Finally, there is variation in what exactly happens once recall proceedings have been initiated. Sometimes there is a vote simply on the question of recall: voters are asked whether they agree that the politician or office holder should be recalled. If this is passed, a subsequent election is then generally held to choose a replacement. In other cases, the recall petition triggers, in effect, a by-election. The incumbent is allowed to stand; she or he must defeat other candidates in order to stay in office.

So there is no single procedure for recall: many widely varying mechanisms can be devised. These variations are extremely important when we come to judge whether the introduction of recall here in the UK would be desirable or not.

Debates over recall in the UK

The idea of recall is a very recent innovation on the British political agenda. The possibility of such procedures first came to wide attention in 2003, when California's governor, Gray Davis, was successfully recalled and replaced by Arnold Schwarzenegger. But this recall was messy and contentious, with even the normally sober *Financial Times* calling it 'a three-ring celebrity circus masquerading as a serious political debate'. While it sparked much comment in the UK, it created few converts for recall. Indeed, *The Independent* and *The Guardian* – both now eager crusaders for political reform – described recall as 'profoundly anti-democratic' and an exercise in 'mass escapism'. I have found no support at all from this period for the introduction of recall in the UK.

The bitter taste left by California's recall battle lingered for some time. In 2006, an independent group called the Power Inquiry, chaired by Baroness Helena Kennedy, published a report arguing for sweeping political reforms. It considered the option of proposing recall, and it acknowledged that the idea was popular with a panel of citizens which it consulted. Nevertheless, it concluded that other reforms to the core of the electoral system were more important and that these 'would render recall powers largely redundant'.

It was not until February of 2008 that the first significant intervention in favour of recall in British politics was made. In a prelude to the expenses scandal of 2009, the Conservative MP Derek Conway had faced allegations that he had paid his son Freddie over £45,000 for research assistance while Freddie was a full-time student hundreds of miles away. A committee of Mr Conway's colleagues found in January 2008 that these payments were excessive: there was no evidence that Freddie had been given enough work to justify such a salary. Mr Conway was subsequently thrown out of the Conservative Parliamentary Party and barred from standing as a Conservative candidate again. Yet he remained as an MP: no mechanism existed to remove him until the general election more than two years later. This understandably caused widespread outrage and the following month a group of twenty-seven first-term Conservative MPs wrote to the *Daily Telegraph* urging the adoption of recall in the UK.

Even then, however, the idea of recall did not really catch on. Nick Clegg endorsed it a week later, but thereafter it disappeared without trace for another year. It took the revelations about moat cleaning, duck islands, and all the rest in May 2009 for significant movement to occur.

The expenses scandal was the sort of problem for which recall leapt out as the obvious solution. Individual MPs had been found guilty of wrongdoing, but existing rules did not allow them to be properly punished. In the constituencies of some of the most tarnished MPs, petitions calling for their departure were signed by thousands of voters but had no legal status. Recall provisions would correct that fault in the system. The public could readily see this: a poll in *The Times* towards the end of May 2009 found that 82 per cent of respondents thought recall would improve the working of the political system; just 5 per cent thought it would make things worse. Not surprisingly, all the main party leaders were quick to follow the public's lead.

The plans for recall that the three main parties put forward at the 2010 election were very similar. The Conservatives said, 'a Conservative government will introduce a power of "recall" to allow electors to kick out MPs, a power that will be triggered by proven serious wrongdoing'. Labour promised that 'MPs who are found responsible for financial misconduct will be subject to a right of recall if Parliament itself has failed to act against them.' The Lib Dems said, 'We would introduce a recall system so that constituents could force a by-election for any MP found responsible for serious wrongdoing.' The coalition agreement mirrored these proposals and added a little further detail:

> We will bring forward early legislation to introduce a power of recall, allowing voters to force a by-election where an MP is found to have engaged in serious wrongdoing and having had a petition calling for a by-election signed by 10% of his or her constituents.

The recall provision that is proposed is therefore tightly restricted: voters will not be able to recall an MP just because they dislike his policies, for example. Nor will recall be possible if allegations of misbehaviour are made but not found to be justified. Details are yet to be announced, but it seems likely that the committee that found Derek Conway guilty of wrongdoing – the Commons Committee on Standards and Privileges – will be charged with ruling on whether an MP has violated the rules in such a way that recall is possible. Thus, opportunities for recall will be far rarer than in many US states. Thereafter, however, the barrier to the initiation of recall will be relatively low: gathering the signatures of 10 per cent of local voters is far from easy, but this is a lower threshold than currently exists in many jurisdictions.

The effects of recall

The immediate effect of the introduction of recall provisions is obvious: it greatly increases voters' capacity to keep politicians in check. It is very likely that recall procedures could have been used successfully against a number of MPs caught up in the 2009 expenses scandal as well as in earlier scandals such as the 'cash for questions' affair in the 1990s. In this way, corrupt MPs could have been removed by voters without the need to wait for another general election.

But just how effective would recall procedures be in achieving these goals? And would they be accompanied by any undesirable side effects? The limited spread of recall around the world means we don't always have as much evidence as we would like to answer these questions, but we can at least make some useful points.

All the available evidence on the operation of recall in practice suggests that it is very rarely used successfully. I have already mentioned the ejection of Gray Davis in favour of Arnold Schwarzenegger in California in 2003. But this was in fact only the second time a state governor in the United States had successfully been recalled, the only other instance having been in North Dakota in 1921. The National Conference of State Legislatures has found just seven cases in which a state legislator – equivalent to an MP – has suffered the same fate.

This points to the fact that the hurdles to recall are high. Gathering thousands of signatures is no walk in the park. Even when recall procedures are successfully launched, they're not always passed when it comes to the vote.

As I've just suggested, however, it's difficult to imagine that no recall initiatives would have passed in the wake of the 2009 expenses scandal. The point of recall is not that it should happen often – our politicians' failings are hopefully rarely so serious as to justify it – but that it should deter misbehaviour and provide a mechanism to remove MPs where that is really necessary. The fear that is more widely expressed is not that recall would be ineffective, but that it would be too effective, and that MPs would sometimes be removed without justification and would be hampered from doing their jobs properly. Scandals might be blown out of proportion. MPs might be subjected in effect to a kangaroo court. They might be removed for supporting policies that are tough but necessary. We already sometimes complain that MPs are slaves to focus groups, following what they think will make them popular rather than what they believe to be right. Recall provisions, some suggest, would only exacerbate this tendency. They would rock the basic principle of representative democracy: that we elect politicians so that they may exercise careful judgement on our behalf.

Fears such as these explain the negative British reaction to the Californian recall in 2003. *The Independent* opposed recall because it would constrain politicians from taking tough decisions: this facility, it warned, 'militates against the strong but unpopular action that governments have to take from time to time'. 'California needs reform', it added, 'but the recall will always make a governor wary of radical action'. It was often said that one successful recall campaign would only encourage political foes to deploy this tactic again, leading to paralysis and decline: 'California's government', said the *Financial Times*, 'could easily become prey to the seductions of the permanent campaign; hardly a recipe for more responsible government and better fiscal management.'

But any such dangers are avoided in the version of recall proposed for the UK by the requirement that it can be initiated only against an MP found guilty of misdemeanours. Kangaroo courts – or trial by media – will be impossible because allegations of wrongdoing will first have to be judged valid by the Committee on Standards and Privileges before proceedings can begin. Recall on the basis of policy will be ruled out entirely. Provision will presumably be included to ensure that a recall election that fails cannot be repeated unless fresh misdemeanours are uncovered and verified.

A further worry in 2003 was that recall could allow the rich to hold the political system to ransom. California's recall laws required around 900,000 signatures to be gathered before the process could begin. This was easily achieved because a rich Republican businessman hired over a thousand people to stand in shopping malls and other public places and paid them for each signature they collected. By shelling out an estimated $1.7 million, he could, in effect, buy himself a rerun of the previous year's election.

But this problem is not too difficult to avoid either. The restrictive conditions that are planned for the UK already greatly limit the circumstances in which the purchase of an election might be possible: a rich individual could not initiate recall just because she or he disliked the policies that a politician was pursuing. In addition, it would be a straightforward matter to extend the limits on donations and campaign spending that we discussed in the previous chapter to cover the costs of collecting signatures for a petition.

There seems, therefore, little conceivable argument against the claim that recall in the limited circumstances for which it is planned would strengthen our democracy. It would simply create the possibility that voters – if they wanted – could remove an MP found guilty of serious wrongdoing. Perhaps we could complain on grounds of cost – one estimate puts the cost of holding a by-election at £200,000. But if recall is used only rarely and in circumstances of genuine concern, such an outlay is surely justified.

If it is so clear that the planned recall provisions are not excessive, it is reasonable to ask if perhaps they are too limited. The restrictions that are to be imposed will prevent misuse of the recall mechanism, but will they also preclude recall in some circumstances where it would be entirely justified? I have suggested that there are good reasons for not allowing recall on the grounds of policy. Indeed, these reasons are even stronger when we are talking about the recall not of a directly elected governor – as in California – but of individual MPs. A policy maverick who occupies senior executive office might do serious damage. But the presence of mavericks on the parliamentary backbenches is surely to be welcomed unless we want political debate to become even more managed and constrained than it is already. In addition, to allow the recall of the Prime Minister by his local constituency on policy grounds would clearly be undemocratic: the good people of Witney are as entitled to their views as the rest of us, but the Prime Minister should be formulating policy for the country, not for one wealthy part of it.

Still, two points might be raised. First, besides wrongdoing, many will think it would be appropriate also to allow recall when an MP resigns from the party on whose ticket they were elected, particularly if that MP then joins another party on the other side of the house. Quentin Davies secured a healthy majority as the Conservative candidate for Grantham and Stamford in the 2005 election. Presumably few of those who voted for him intended to back the Labour government. Yet Davies defected to Labour in the week Gordon Brown became Prime Minister in 2007, and he later joined the government as a junior minister. It is reasonable to ask whether recall ought to be allowed in such a case.

Second, is it right that the gatekeepers of recall should be MPs themselves? The government has indicated that we will hear the details of their plans for recall only after the referendum on the alternative vote. So far, however, nothing has been said to suggest that the procedures for establishing wrongdoing will be changed dramatically from those already in place. As things currently stand, a veritable jungle of bodies are involved in overseeing MPs' conduct, including several independent entities and the committee of MPs that I have already mentioned – the Committee on Standards and Privileges. Until 2010 it was only the MPs' committee that could sanction a fellow MP for misconduct. The rules have been changed in the wake of the expenses scandal, such that one of the new independent regulators – who goes by the unwieldy and faintly Orwellian title of the Compliance Officer for the Independent Parliamentary Standards Authority – can now fine MPs found guilty of wrongdoing. But it is still for the committee of MPs to decide if an MP should be punished in a way that affects their ability to do their job, such as suspension from the House of Commons. The idea here is that only the people's elected representatives should be able to interfere with the people's choice of who will represent them. If that principle is maintained, it will be for MPs to decide whether the sanction of recall should be available to voters. Whether this needs to be changed is something that will be debated in the coming months.

Summing up

It's difficult to find any fault in the idea that voters should be able to recall an MP who has been found guilty of serious wrongdoing. The wider use of recall does raise important concerns about the representative system, the ability of politicians to get on with the crucial job of governing, and the potential undue influence of moneyed interests that have the capacity to organise a petition drive. But these worries largely evaporate when the opportunities for initiating recall are as limited as the government proposes. Nevertheless, questions of detail remain about whether the restrictions that are planned are slightly too tight and about who will determine whether an MP can be subject to recall or not.

10. Putting the pieces together

We have been looking at how electoral systems – particularly the core parts of electoral systems – measure up against a range of criteria. If one electoral system clearly performed better than all others on all of these criteria, we could by now have reached definite overall conclusions. But if such an electoral system existed, we wouldn't be having a big debate about it – we would all have agreed to use that system long ago. In fact, all the systems we have examined score well on some criteria but poorly on others.

Take, for example, the case of the alternative vote. AV is clearly better than first past the post at electing the most popular candidate in any given constituency. But it's clearly worse than first past the post in how it can exaggerate landslides and produce wholly indefensible under-representation of opposition parties. It's better than first past the post in terms of most aspects of voter choice – it allows us to express more than just one preference and it largely frees us from the need to make tactical calculations. But it might also weaken voter choice by encouraging even greater concentration of viable candidates around the political centre ground.

In order to come to any conclusions about which electoral systems are better or worse, therefore, we need not just to gauge each system against each criterion, but also work out how to make a comparison of the criteria themselves. Again, this is no simple task – if it were, we would have done it already and there would be very little to discuss. In fact, there's no single, ideal weighting scheme. How we weight our criteria depends partly on what it is that we're electing, and partly on our image of what democratic elections are all about.

Consider, for example, the election of individuals – whether they be presidents, party leaders, police commissioners, or *X Factor* winners. I suggested earlier that it might be inconsistent for a party that chooses its own leader by AV (or something very close to it) to oppose AV for elections to Parliament. But that was perhaps a little unfair: these positions need not be incompatible. What matters above all when choosing an individual in a democratic contest is that you choose the most popular person. AV does this better than first past the post. You don't need to worry about proportionality – you can't apportion one position to several candidates. When choosing Parliament, however, much as the fairness of each local result is important, we also need to attend to the overall result across all constituencies: proportionality and government effectiveness also weigh heavily. So it's perfectly consistent to argue that AV is the best system for choosing a party leader, but that, for parliamentary elections, the danger that it will generate overwhelmingly unfair results is just too great.

Similarly, the Blair government was widely criticised for introducing proportional representation for elections to the European Parliament but not to the House of Commons. This looked like brazen pursuit of self-interest: Tony Blair's power depended on his majority at Westminster, whereas it mattered little to him how many seats his party held in Brussels. This self-interest story is probably largely accurate. But it's possible to defend the divergence between the two institutions. The government depends on the support (the 'confidence') of the majority in the House of Commons. So the criterion of effective and accountable government is important when judging how the Commons should be elected. But no government relies on the confidence of Britain's members in the European Parliament, so the criteria relating to government don't really matter. In that case, the criterion of proportionality comes more to the fore.

A third example is provided by the House of Lords. Most Conservatives are vehemently opposed to the use of proportional representation in elections to the Commons. But they have now signed up, in the coalition agreement, to replacing the current House of Lords with a chamber elected 'on the basis of proportional representation'. Labour, too, is much more willing to accept PR for the Lords than for the Commons. These differences arise because the Lords is a very different sort of animal from the Commons. As in the case of the European Parliament, the government does not depend on the confidence of the Lords as it does on that of the Commons, so concerns about governability weigh far less heavily. Most people would also agree that the value of parties is much lower in the Lords than in the Commons: the Lords adds value because it is independent-minded, drawing on the individual expertise of many of its members. We are likely to want an electoral system that will help to preserve this.

Our key question, however, is how we should weigh the various criteria when deciding the electoral system for the House of Commons, as it's the Commons that primarily determines the character of politics in our country. This isn't straightforward, and on the face of things, all of the criteria have a strong claim to our attention. But we needn't despair. There are basically two possible ways forward. One is to nail our colours to the mast and advance a particular idea of what it is that matters most in a democratic system. The other is to accept that the world is a complex place and seek simply to balance out the various criteria as best we can. Let's look at these approaches in turn.

There's no doubt that there are different ways of looking at democracy. For some, democracy is, most fundamentally, a way of ensuring representation. Decisions should be made only after taking into account the interests of all members of the community. Parliament is there to assemble the people, and it should be filled with as diverse an array of voices as possible. For others, democracy is a way of ensuring popular control over those who make the key decisions. Power, as every schoolchild knows, corrupts. Elections are therefore needed to ensure that those who hold power do not get complacent, and that the people can throw them out if they prove not to be up to the job.

These two competing visions of democracy imply different priorities in choosing the electoral system. The first unsurprisingly lays stress on fairness and inclusivity of representation. It will therefore lead us to favour a proportional system of voting – whether simple

PR, the compensatory mixed system, or the single transferable vote. The second favours accountable and effective government, and points towards the retention of a majoritarian electoral system such as first past the post or the alternative vote. The first is therefore often called the proportional vision, the second the majoritarian.

Most people would agree that, in a highly diverse society, it's the proportional vision that ought to win out. If the majority were allowed to rule all the time, minorities might eventually conclude that they have no way of being heard except by violence. Thus, a key part of the process of ending apartheid in South Africa in the early 1990s was the negotiation of a proportional electoral system that would ensure all groups could be included in democratic politics. Proportional representation has for decades been used for most elections in Northern Ireland for the same reason: there would be no hope for peace if majority rule were maintained.

In a truly homogeneous society, by contrast, the majoritarian vision would make more sense. Here, society's interests are not much disputed: there is broad agreement on what government ought to deliver. The main danger is not that some voices will be excluded, but that those in power will fail to live up to the demands of their job. In this case, the niceties of representation are not too important; what matters is that the people should be able to kick the rascals out and appoint a new team in their place.

The trouble is that there is no consensus on which of these models best applies to the UK today. In many ways, we are a much more diverse society than once we were. The conformism and unity that characterised the middle decades of the twentieth century have been replaced by a more atomised ethos in which each of us expects to be able to pursue our own goals and ideals. Women's interests are no longer subordinate to men's. The young are no longer expected to defer to the old. We are much more diverse than before in our religions, our ethnicities and our sexualities. We are more unequal in our incomes.

In other ways, however, we are much less diverse. Far fewer of us than in the past embrace a fixed class identity. Ideological passion has withered. No longer do political parties present competing visions of how the world should be. No longer do they nurture deep roots in one part of society. Rather, they seek to appeal across the spectrum. They appeal to our shared interests – prosperity, stability, security, freedom. Political competition today is much more about competence than about ideas.

Either vision, therefore, is defensible in the UK today; it's conceivable that Britain could be or become the sort of country that best suits either the proportional or the majoritarian ideal. Much depends on what sort of country we want the UK to be.

So our preferences regarding the electoral system can ultimately be bound up in our deepest aspirations for the country in which we live. On the other hand, choices about voting procedures are also, in many ways, much more prosaic. For one thing, the overarching contrast between two competing visions hardly helps us in making many of the detailed choices that we have been looking at in preceding chapters. It doesn't tell us much about the choice between open or closed lists or between alternative mechanisms for drawing constituency boundaries. Most importantly at the current time, it doesn't give us much help in deciding whether we should vote for first past the post or the alternative vote – both of which, after all, are firmly majoritarian in character. In addition, visions are all very well, but we need also to be thinking about what electoral system is best for the country that we are actually living in today. And that is a country in which neither the proportional nor the majoritarian vision has any obvious monopoly of truth.

The alternative approach to weighing up our many criteria is therefore to say simply that we need balance: each of our criteria takes us in a particular direction, but going too far in that direction will knock us off course on some other criterion. All that we can reasonably do is seek the best combination available.

We might begin by seeking balance between proportionality and accountability. Our current system of first past the post is quite heavily skewed in favour of accountability rather than proportionality. On the other hand, the strongly proportional systems that some reformers favour are clearly heavily skewed the other way. So perhaps we should favour something in between – such as the AV+ system recommended in 1998 by the Jenkins Commission, or a proportional system in which the number of seats per constituency is kept quite low.

But then what does this choice do for other criteria? What, for example, of the balance between encouraging independent-mindedness in our MPs and ensuring that political parties are strong enough for the parliamentary system to work? Our first past the post system – or, indeed, the alternative vote – already achieves a fair balance here, whereas closed-list systems clearly lay too much emphasis on parties, and STV might in some circumstances leave parties too weak. How could we devise a system that achieves better balance in terms of the first dimension without losing what we already have in terms of the second? And then what happens when we add in third, fourth and fifth dimensions?

As I said right at the start of this book, my goal is not to give you answers, but to help you work towards your own answers. You will have your own views on which criteria matter more or less. You will have your own feelings on whether fundamental choices about our democratic system are better made on the basis of vision (which you might view as virtuous idealism or as blockheaded single-mindedness) or of current practicalities (which might be sensible and grounded or myopic and nit-picking).

I will take my own contribution to your thinking no further than this. I hope I have raised many issues that you will want to ponder and pointed in directions that that pondering might take. But the final answers have to be yours rather than mine.

The point we have reached

Still, there are three points that I'd like to be clear on before closing. First, the electoral system that we choose really matters. It shapes the nature of our democracy and the character of our government. It influences the role that we, as voters, can play in the political system, and it moulds the relationship that we have with our MPs. We should care about the choices that we and others are going to make in the months and years to come.

Second, however, changing the electoral system is no panacea. Some changes might do a little to restore electoral turnout towards previous levels, but they would trigger no new age of democratic activism: disillusionment with politics is high across the democratic world, no matter what the electoral system in place. Electoral systems other than the status quo might reduce the likelihood of abuses such as those we have seen with MPs' expenses, but they would also create fresh dangers of their own. A different electoral system might allow our views to be represented more accurately in Parliament, but it could also, if we're not careful, weaken our capacity to determine who forms the government.

Third, therefore, we should choose the electoral system carefully and calmly. There will be a lot of shouting in the coming months. Some will claim that only a 'yes' vote in the referendum will save our democracy from a self-serving and isolated political elite. Others will insist that a 'yes' vote would be the first step on the road to ruin and that only the status quo can ensure that our ancient rights are maintained. None of this is true. There are pros and cons on both sides. In order to decide what system to support, we should begin by thinking about what it is that we want from that system. Then we should look carefully through the evidence. Finally, each of us can come to our own measured judgement.

Appendix: the techie bits

I have tried to keep the main text of the book clear of obscure technicalities. Electoral systems matter, and it is important that we can understand how they matter without getting buried in unnecessary details. Still, you might be interested in the details, or you might find that obscure language is being used by those who find it amusing or useful to bamboozle you. This Appendix therefore contains some further details for those who wish them. They all relate to matters that come up in the text and they follow the same order here as there.

Electoral disproportionality

Gallagher's index of disproportionality, devised by the Irish political scientist Michael Gallagher, is calculated using the following formula:

$$\text{Gallagher index} = \sqrt{\frac{1}{2}\sum_{i=1}^{n}(v_i - s_i)^2}$$

where v_i is the vote share of the ith party and s_i is its seat share, both expressed as percentages. In 2010, for example, the Conservatives won 36.1 per cent of the votes and 47.2 per cent of the seats. We subtract one of these from the other (getting 11.1) and square this (123.2). We do the same for all of the parties: for Labour, the number we get is 114.3, for the Lib Dems it is 202.5, and so on. We then add up all these numbers (getting 458.5), divide this by two (229.2) and take the square root (15.1).

The data regarding proportionality in Figures 1 and 12 are mostly taken from Gallagher's own website, available at www.tcd. ie. A few of Lijphart's thirty-six countries are, however, missing from this source. I've calculated the missing numbers from three main sources: Dieter Nohlen (ed.), *Elections in the Americas: A Data Handbook* (Oxford University Press, 2005), pp. 322–30, 339–44, 569–74, and 576–8; Dieter Nohlen, Michael Krennerich, and Bernhard Thibaut, *Elections in Africa: A Data Handbook* (Oxford University Press, 1999), pp. 614–18; and Dieter Nohlen, Florian Grotz, and Christof Hartmann, *Elections in Asia and the Pacific: A Data Handbook* (Oxford University Press, 2001), vol. 2, pp. 772–4. Because of various problems with the data, the figure I give for Papua New Guinea in the chart is only an estimate.

Disproportionality of power-holding

The index of disproportionality that I use in Figures 3 and 14 relates each party's average vote share across all elections since 1945 (except the most recent one) to its share of government office since 1945 (up to the most recent election). The average vote share is just the average of the party's share in all the elections included. The share in government office is based on the time, in days, that each party has spent in government. As I said in the main text, we really want to know how much power each party actually wields within government, but this is impossible to work out without examining each case in enormous detail. It is reasonable, however, to suppose that a party that occupies government on its own and that has a majority in Parliament exerts more power than a party that is part of a governing coalition. In order very roughly to capture such differences, I therefore weight the time that each party spends in office according to its governing role. Each day that a party spends as the sole party in a majority government is multiplied by three. Each day it spends as the only party in a minority government or as the party holding the premiership in a coalition is multiplied by two. Each day it spends as a party in a coalition without holding the premiership is left as it is. Where information is available, I also include days spent supporting a government but not holding seats within it, multiplied by one half. Having calculated each party's weighted time in government, I plug this, along with each party's average vote share into a formula equivalent to Gallagher's index of disproportionality in order to obtain the figure for disproportionality of power-holding in each country.

Much more could be said about measuring proportionality of power-holding than I have had space for here. See, especially, P. J. Taylor, 'The Case for Proportional Tenure: A Defense of the British Electoral System', in Arend Lijphart and Bernard Grofman (eds.), *Choosing an Electoral System: Issues and Alternatives* (Praeger, 1984), pp. 53–8; Jack Vowles, 'Electoral Systems and Proportional Tenure of Government: Renewing the Debate', *British Journal of Political Science*, vol. 34, no. 1 (January 2004), pp. 166–79; Adrian Blau, 'The Effective Number of Parties at Four Scales: Votes, Seats, Legislative Power and Cabinet Power', *Party Politics*, vol. 14, no. 2 (March 2008), pp. 167–87.

The main sources I have used for data are Jaap Woldendorp, Hans Keman, and Ian Budge, *Party Government in 48 Democracies (1945–1998): Composition, Duration, Personnel* (Kluwer, 2000), and Thomas T. Mackie and Richard Rose, *The International Almanac of Electoral History*, 3rd edition (Macmillan, 1991). I have updated these sources mostly using annual reviews of political developments in the *European Journal of Political Research* and the Inter-Parliamentary Union's Parline Database, available at www.ipu.org.

Non-monotonicity

A substantial segment of writing about electoral systems explores a range of logical or mathematical criteria that electoral systems ought to meet. No electoral system meets all of these criteria in all circumstances – it's actually been proved through some very clever mathematics that this is impossible. I don't talk about all of the criteria in this book – for more on them, see Michael Dummett, *Principles of Electoral Reform* (Oxford University Press, 1997). But

I do talk about two: the Condorcet criterion (that a candidate who would defeat all the other candidates in head-to-head contests should win); and the monotonicity criterion (that an increase in support should not reduce your chances of election). The Condorcet criterion doesn't need any further elaboration here. But the monotonicity criterion does. How can an increase in support possibly harm a candidate's electoral prospects?

Failure of monotonicity – that is, non-monotonicity – can occur under either the alternative vote or the single transferable vote. Because STV is just an extension of AV in which multiple candidates are elected, it will be enough to show an example under AV. Suppose that we have a constituency in which four candidates are running – call them Amy, Brian, Carol, and David. For simplicity's sake, let's assume that there are just four types of voter (A, B, C, and D) and that all the voters within each type order the candidates in exactly the same way. Table A1 shows a possible distribution of voters and preferences.

Table A1. Non-monotonicity under the alternative vote

Type of voter	Number of voters in type	Order of preferences among candidates
A	18,000	Amy, Brian, Carol, David
B	15,000	Carol, Amy, Brian, David
C	12,000	Brian, Carol, David, Amy
D	6,000	David, Brian, Amy, Carol

At the first count, Amy wins 18,000 votes, Brian 12,000, Carol 15,000, and David 6,000. No candidate has an absolute majority, so the bottom candidate – David – is eliminated. All of David's votes transfer to Brian, who therefore now has 18,000 votes. Still no candidate has an overall majority, so Carol is now eliminated. All of Carol's votes transfer to Amy, and Amy is therefore elected, with 33,000 votes to Brian's 18,000.

So far so simple. Now, however, suppose that the election campaign had gone slightly differently. Amy did something that transformed her image among voters who supported David, so that now all the voters who originally intended to vote for David in fact voted for Amy. This means that, in terms of first preferences, Amy scores 24,000 votes, Brian scores 12,000, and Carol scores 15,000, while David has no votes at all. No one has an overall majority and eliminating David makes no difference, so Brian is now eliminated. All of Brian's votes transfer to Carol, and Carol is therefore elected by 27,000 votes to Amy's 24,000. Thus, though Amy was probably mighty pleased to have transferred a substantial block of voters into her support base during the campaign, in fact, the effect of this increase in support was to deny Amy victory.

This paradox arises because of the rather haphazard way in which AV and STV count lower preferences: these preferences are taken into consideration only once higher-preference candidates are eliminated. The order in which candidates are eliminated makes a difference to which lower preferences are counted and can therefore affect who gets elected in perverse ways. Supporters of AV and STV tend to respond to this problem by saying that it will occur very rarely – we need to construct a fairly improbable distribution of preferences before we can generate such a result. Indeed, estimates by Crispin Allard (in *Representation*, vol. 33, no. 2, 1995) suggest that the probability of non-monotonicity in any one constituency at any one election is something like 0.00028. That implies that, if STV were used in the UK, a failure of monotonicity would occur less than once a century. Michael Dummett (in the book mentioned above) thinks this a 'surely ludicrous underestimate'. While acknowledging that the probability is low, he argues that a low probability is still too great a probability for such a serious error.

The details of proportional representation

As we see in Chapter 5, there are various different ways of allocating seats to parties in systems of proportional representation. Among list PR systems, there are two basic approaches: those based on the principle of largest remainders and those based on the concept of highest averages.

Largest remainders systems are the first that I describe in Chapter 5. All such systems involve two steps. First, you define a quota of votes and allocate seats to parties according to the number of times they fulfil that quota. Then you give out any seats that haven't yet been allocated to the parties with the largest remainders – the largest numbers of votes left over after subtraction of the quotas. The particular version of this system that I describe in Chapter 5 uses the simple or Hare quota. This is (unsurprisingly) called the largest remainders system with the Hare quota, though you might occasionally see it also referred to as the Hamilton method. The Hare quota is the total number of valid votes divided by the number of seats available in the constituency:

$$\text{Hare Quota} = \frac{v}{s}$$

Looking again at the results from the European Parliament election in the South East region in 2009, Table A2 shows how the results using largest remainders with the Hare quota would be calculated. First, all the valid votes are added up and divided by the number of seats available. This gives the quota, shown in the bottom left-hand corner. We then see how many full quotas each party's vote total contains: the Conservatives' total contains three full quotas, the next three parties' one each. For each full quota, a party gets one seat, so six of the ten seats can be allocated this way. The next step is to look at how many votes for each party are left over. The Conservatives' three quotas come to 700,458 votes. If we subtract this from the Conservatives' total of 812,288 votes, we end up with a remainder of 111,830. Similarly, we subtract one quota from the vote totals of each of the parties that have been allocated one seat. For the parties that have not yet won any seats, all of their votes remain in play. We then allocate the four remaining seats in order of the size of the remainder votes until no seats are left: so we give a seat to UKIP, then to Labour, then to the Conservatives, and finally to the BNP. The final seat totals are shown in the rightmost column.

The Hare quota is not, however, the only quota that can be used. The most notable alternative is the Droop quota (discussed in Chapter 7), which defines the lowest possible quota that cannot be exceeded by more candidates than there are seats. The Droop quota is defined as:

$$\text{Droop Quota} = \frac{v}{s+1} + 1$$

Table A2. Largest remainders with the Hare quota in the European Parliament elections, South East region, 2009

	Votes	Number of quotas	Remainder	Additional seats	Total seats
Conservative	812,288	3	111,830	1	4
UKIP	440,002	1	206,516	1	2
Lib Dem	330,340	1	96,854		1
Green	271,506	1	38,020		1
Labour	192,592	0	192,592	1	1
BNP	101,769	0	101,769	1	1
English Democrats	52,526	0	52,526		0
Others	133,835	0			0
Total valid votes (v)	2,334,858				
Seats available (s)	10				
Hare quota (v/s)	233,486				

ignoring any fractions. Suppose, for example, that 100 votes were cast in a constituency where three seats were to be filled. The Droop quota would then be

$$\frac{100}{3+1} + 1$$

which comes to 26. It's not possible for more than three candidates to win 26 votes: once three candidates have 26 votes, only 22 votes remain for everyone else. But it would be possible for more than three candidates to secure 25 votes: four candidates could score exactly 25 votes each.

Table A3 shows how the calculations work for the South East region in the European Parliament elections if this quota is used. The first difference compared to the Hare method comes in the number of seats that are allocated by full quotas. Because the Droop quota is smaller than the Hare quota, UKIP's vote total now contains two quotas rather than one. But this doesn't actually matter for the overall result: it just means that UKIP has a much smaller remainder, so it doesn't pick up an extra seat at the second stage. Much more interesting is what happens further down. Because the quota that is subtracted for winning a seat is smaller than the one we used when looking at the Hare quota, the Lib Dems, who still have only one full quota, end up with a bigger remainder than when the Hare quota is used. And this is sufficient to take the Lib Dems over the BNP when remainders are compared – such that the Lib Dems win two seats and the BNP none. This is a general pattern. For each seat that you win, one quota is subtracted from your vote total. Because the Droop quota is lower than the Hare quota, each seat you win costs you fewer votes. This makes it easier for parties that have already won some seats to win more, so the system tends overall to be more favourable to larger parties.

Many countries use largest remainders systems – most commonly with the Hare quota – to allocate seats among parties. As I mentioned in Chapter 5, however, these systems are capable of generating weird results. The seeming injustices that I mentioned in the main text are mild in comparison with what is possible. In particular, there is something called the Alabama paradox, which is a version of the

Table A3. Largest remainders with the Droop quota in the European Parliament elections, South East region, 2009

	Votes	Number of quotas	Remainder	Additional seats	Total seats
Conservative	812,288	3	175,508	1	4
UKIP	440,002	2	15,482		2
Lib Dem	330,340	1	118,080	1	2
Green	271,506	1	59,246		1
Labour	192,592	0	192,592	1	1
BNP	101,769	0	101,769	1	1
English Democrats	52,526	0	52,526		0
Others	133,835	0			0
Total valid votes (v)	2,334,858				
Seats available (s)	10				
Droop quota ($\frac{v}{s+1} + 1$)	212,260				

Table A4. Highest averages (d'Hondt) in the European Parliament elections, South East region, 2009

	Con.	UKIP	Lib Dem	Green	Labour	BNP	Eng Dem	Others
Votes	812,288	440,002	330,340	271,506	192,592	101,769	52,526	133,835
÷ 1	**812,288**	**440,002**	**330,340**	**271,506**	**192,592**	101,769	52,526	
÷ 2	**406,144**	**220,001**	**165,170**	135,753	96,196			
÷ 3	**270,762**	146,667	110,113	90,502				
÷ 4	**203,072**	110,001	82,585					
÷ 5	162,458	88,000						
÷ 6	135,381							
÷ 7	116,041							
÷ 8	101,536							
Seats	4	2	2	1	1	0	0	0

non-monotonicity problem that I discussed above. This paradox was discovered in the United States in the nineteenth century. A largest remainders system was being used to work out how many seats each state should have in the House of Representatives. It was found, however, that the state of Alabama was entitled to eight seats in a House of 299 members, but only seven seats in a House containing 300 seats. This clearly makes no sense at all.

The other family of PR formulas – based on highest averages rather than largest remainders – are able to avoid such problems. The simplest such system, which I briefly described in Chapter 5, is the d'Hondt system (occasionally also known as the Jefferson method). The logic here is that you want the average number of votes required to win a seat to be as similar as possible across all parties. The easiest way to do this is to hand out each seat according to which party at that point has the highest average number of votes per seat. We can see how to go about doing this in Table A4.

First we imagine how many votes each party would have per seat if every party had one seat. Clearly, that's just each party's vote total (or its vote total divided by one). We give the first seat to the party with the highest number here – in this case, the Conservatives. If we allocated another seat to the Conservatives, its votes per seat would now be its vote total divided by two. That's less than UKIP's votes per seat if UKIP has one seat, so UKIP gets the next seat. But the third seat goes again to the Conservatives: doing so leaves the Conservatives on 406,144 votes per seat, which is higher than if we give the seat to any other party. The next two seats go to the Lib Dems and then the Greens. Then we go back to the Conservatives: giving them a third seat leaves them with 270,762 votes per seat, whereas giving this seat to any other party would leave it averaging fewer votes per seat. So we go on until we have allocated all ten seats. In effect, all that we do is pick the ten largest numbers from Table A4 – the numbers in bold – and give the seats to the parties to which these numbers belong.

D'Hondt is the most obvious system based on the logic of highest averages, but it's not the only one. D'Hondt divides each party's vote total by a series of divisors that is simply the series of whole numbers (1, 2, 3, 4, ...). But we can use other divisor series. Another system (known as Sainte-Laguë or, occasionally, the Webster method) uses the series of odd numbers (1, 3, 5, 7, ...). This produces the results shown in Table A5.

In this particular case, the number of seats allocated to each party ends up being the same as under d'Hondt. But that won't always hold. I've included some extra numbers in Tables A4 and A5 so that you can see for yourself what would happen if the number of seats to be filled were increased beyond ten. With Sainte-Laguë, the eleventh seat would go to the BNP and the twelfth to the Greens. With d'Hondt, by contrast, the next two seats would go to the Conservatives and UKIP. You would need to have eighteen seats available before one would be picked up by the BNP.

This fits the general pattern. Sainte-Laguë reduces a party's vote by more than d'Hondt does when that party wins a seat, making it easier for small parties to win seats. The numbers used in Sainte-Laguë look quite arbitrary – there's no obvious logic for using this series of divisors. In fact, however, it can be shown that Sainte-Laguë does make a lot of mathematical sense and that it yields the most proportional results of any PR formula. D'Hondt, by contrast systematically over-represents larger parties – though not, of course, by anything like as much as first past the post or the alternative vote.

If, therefore, you want the most proportional system possible, you should go for Sainte-Laguë in a single nationwide district with no legal threshold. If you think there should be some extra reward for building a wide support base, or if you're worried about excessive fractionalisation of Parliament, you can use d'Hondt or smaller constituencies or a legal threshold – or some kind of combination of all of these.

PR in constituencies: some details for Table 4

Table 4, on p. 82, simulates the results of the 2010 general election using various forms of proportional representation. The calculation of the seat numbers for nationwide PR is straightforward: you just apply the formulas described above to the national vote totals. The precise seat numbers for PR in constituencies depend, however,

Table A5. Saint-Laguë in the European Parliament elections, South East region, 2009

	Con.	UKIP	Lib Dem	Green	Labour	BNP	Eng Dem	Others
Votes	812,288	440,002	330,340	271,506	192,592	101,769	52,526	133,835
÷ 1	**812,288**	**440,002**	**330,340**	**271,506**	**192,592**	101,769	52,526	133,835
÷ 3	**270,762**	**146,667**	**110,113**	90,502	64,197			
÷ 5	**162,458**	88,000	66,068					
÷ 7	**116,041**	62,859						
÷ 9	90,254							
Seats	4	2	2	1	1	0	0	0

on how many constituencies there are and where you draw the boundaries. The more constituencies you have, the fewer seats will be available for allocation in each one, so the lower will be proportionality overall. Even if you keep the number of constituencies the same, there might be some small differences in the results depending on exactly where the boundaries lie.

The simulations in Table 4 use a map of eighty constituencies. These are based on the eighty constituencies proposed by the Jenkins Commission in 1998 for the allocation of top-up seats in the AV+ system, which you will find described in Chapter 6. The constituencies are built up from parliamentary constituencies as they existed at the 2010 election. Boundary reviews since 1998 mean that their borders today are sometimes slightly different from those used by Jenkins.

You might be interested to know where the minor parties pick up seats when the largest remainders system is used in constituencies. The one Green seat is in East Sussex (which includes the Brighton constituency that party leader Caroline Lucas really did win in 2010). The two independents are both in Northern Ireland. When no thresholds are employed, the BNP wins one seat in each of eight constituencies: Barnsley, Birmingham, London North East, London South East, Sheffield, Essex South West, Leicestershire, and Staffordshire. UKIP, meanwhile, wins seats in Devon, Essex South West, Cambridgeshire, Humberside, Nottinghamshire, Surrey, and West Sussex. If a 5 per cent threshold is applied, the BNP is reduced to two seats, in Barnsley and Sheffield, while UKIP retains three, in Cambridgeshire, Devon, and West Sussex. You might notice the curiosity that, when there is no threshold, the BNP wins more seats than UKIP, even though UKIP won more votes. That happens because the BNP vote is heavily concentrated in a few areas, whereas UKIP's support is much more widely spread.

Compensatory mixed systems: what happens when a party wins too many single-member constituencies?

Chapter 6 works through the process of allocating seats in a compensatory mixed system using the example of the 2007 Scottish

Parliament elections in the Highlands and Islands. The result in that region worked out as it should have done: each party ended up with as many seats as it was entitled to using the d'Hondt method. But what would have happened if – as was entirely possible – the Lib Dems had picked up an extra constituency seat, such that their constituency tally exceeded their total seat entitlement? One approach might be somehow to deny the Lib Dems one of their constituency seats. But that would be a violation of the principle that every constituency should be able to choose its own MP, and no one wants that. In fact there are two possible approaches.

One is simply to allow the Lib Dems to hold on to their extra seat and to increase the overall size of the Parliament in order to accommodate this. The total seat entitlements would remain as shown in Table 7 on p. 103. The Lib Dems would have five constituency seats and the SNP (having lost one to the Lib Dems) three. Regional list seats would be allocated to the parties in order to make up the shortfalls. The SNP now would win three list seats rather than two, so the total number of list seats available would be increased to eight.

This is the solution used in Germany and New Zealand. It has the advantage that it ensures that all the other parties besides the one with the extra constituency still get the seats that they are entitled to. But it also means that the region concerned gets more seats than it deserves. And it requires an increase in the number of MPs – which is hardly likely to go down well with voters. In the German elections of 2009, a record twenty-four extra seats – so-called 'overhang seats' – needed to be created because of excess constituency wins.

The alternative approach – which is the approach actually used in Scotland and Wales – is, in effect, to take the extra seats away from other parties. The result is calculated by using the same sort of procedure as I used in Table A4 to show results under d'Hondt. But the starting point is the number of seats that the parties have already won in constituencies. In our hypothetical example, shown in Table A6, the Lib Dems have won five constituency seats and the SNP three. As always with d'Hondt, we start off with divisors one greater than the number of seats the parties already have. So

Table A6. Hypothetical results in the Scottish Parliament election for the Highlands and Islands

	SNP	Lib Dems	Lab	Con	Green	Others
Votes won	63,979	37,001	32,952	23,334	8,602	19,905
Constituency seats won	3	5	0	0	0	0
1st divisor	4	6	1	1	1	1
1st quotient	**15,995**	6,169	**32,952**	**23,334**	8,602	
2nd quotient	**12,796**		16,476	**11,667**		
3rd quotient	10,663		**10,984**	7,778		
4th quotient	9,140		8,238			
Regional seats won	2	0	3	2	0	0
Total seats won	5	5	3	2	0	0

we start with six for the Lib Dems, four for the SNP, and one for each of the other parties. With these figures, the first regional seat goes to Labour and the second to the Conservatives. The next highest number is again Labour's. Then we get two seats for the SNP, a second seat for the Conservatives, and, finally, a third seat for Labour.

The final outcome, then, is that it's the SNP who are deprived of a seat as a result of the Lib Dems' good fortune. Of course, it was also the SNP that lost a constituency seat. But it could equally easily have been one of the other parties that lost out in the final reckoning. This way of dealing with excess constituency wins has the advantages of keeping the total number of seats constant and preventing over-representation of certain regions. But it also increases disproportionality: not only are the Lib Dems over-represented; in addition, the SNP is left without its full entitlement.

Further reading

The readings given here are selective: they include a few general sources of particular value for the issues discussed and those materials that I mention in the text or use as sources of specific information.

The best all-round introduction to electoral systems is David Farrell, *Electoral Systems: A Comparative Introduction*, 2nd edition (Palgrave Macmillan, 2010). Briefer but good discussion appears in Arend Lijphart, *Patterns of Democracy: Government Forms and Performance in Thirty-Six Countries* (Yale University Press, 1999). Useful analysis of the effects of electoral systems on a variety of criteria is given in Pippa Norris, *Electoral Engineering: Voting Rules and Political Behavior* (Cambridge University Press, 2004). Good introductions to many aspects of elections appear in Lawrence LeDuc, Richard G. Niemi, and Pippa Norris (eds.), *Comparing Democracies 3: Elections and Voting in the 21st Century* (Sage, 2010).

A very helpful overview of the electoral systems that exist around the world is Andrew Reynolds, Ben Reilly, and Andrew Ellis, *Electoral System Design: The New International IDEA Handbook* (International IDEA, 2005). Good discussions of how electoral systems operate in a variety of countries around the world, including the UK, appear in Michael Gallagher and Paul Mitchell (eds.), *The Politics of Electoral Systems* (Oxford University Press, 2005).

For a history of recent developments in the British electoral system, see John Curtice, 'The Electoral System', in Vernon Bogdanor (ed.), *The British Constitution in the Twentieth Century* (Oxford University Press, 2003), pp. 483–520. Much insight into recent debates over electoral reform can be gained from official documents. Most important is the report of the Jenkins Commission (the Independent Commission on the Voting System), which can be read online or found as Command Paper Cm 4090–I (1998). A recent overview of issues that need to be thought about when choosing an electoral system, written from a British perspective, is Simon Hix, Ron Johnston, and Iain McLean, *Choosing an Electoral System* (British Academy, 2010).

I mention the coalition agreement between the Conservatives and the Liberal Democrats at various points throughout the book. It is available from programmeforgovernment.hmg.gov.uk.

Chapter 1

The information on the number of countries enforcing compulsory voting comes from the International Institute for Democracy and Electoral Assistance, at www.idea.int.

Figures for postal voting come from Colin Rallings and Michael Thrasher, 'The 2005 General Election: Analysis of the Results' and 'UK General Election 2010: Turnout and Administrative Data', both www.electoralcommission.org.uk.

Chapter 2

The subject of what criteria we should use in evaluating electoral systems is discussed interestingly in Adrian Blau, 'Fairness and Electoral Reform', *British Journal of Politics and International Relations*, vol. 6, no. 2 (May 2004), pp. 165–81, and Michael Gallagher, 'Conclusions', in Michael Gallagher and Paul Mitchell (eds.), *The Politics of Electoral Systems* (Oxford University Press, 2005), pp. 535–78. A more formal, mathematical approach is taken by the Oxford philosopher Michael Dummett in his *Principles of Electoral Reform* (Oxford University Press, 1997).

Information on the number of women in Parliament is given in two papers from the House of Commons Library: 'Women in Parliament and Government' (30 June 2009) and 'General Election 2010' (8 July 2010). Both of these are available from the

Parliament website (www.parliament.uk). The latter also gives data on MPs from ethnic minorities (and much else besides).

The Power Inquiry report was published as *Power to the People: The Report of Power: An Independent Inquiry into Britain's Democracy* (2006) and is available at www.powerinquiry.org.

The Hansard Society report that looked (among other things) at the proportion of MPs' time spent on constituency work was called *A Year in the Life: From Member of Public to Member of Parliament* (2006), available at www.hansardsociety.org.uk.

The article by Benjamin Nyblade and Steven R. Reed is 'Who Cheats? Who Loots? Political Competition and Corruption in Japan, 1947–1993', *American Journal of Political Science*, vol. 52, no. 4 (October 2008), pp. 926–41.

Chapter 3

The quotation about our 'centuries-old' electoral system is from Macer Hall, 'Cameron faces split on vote reform poll', *Daily Express*, 3 July 2010. The quotations from Bernard Jenkin and David Davis are both from the debate held in the House of Commons on 6 September 2010 on the government's Parliamentary Voting System and Constituencies Bill (see *Hansard* col. 85 and 71)

Data on the numbers of countries using first past the post and (in later chapters) other electoral systems are all based on Andrew Reynolds, Ben Reilly, and Andrew Ellis, *Electoral System Design: The New International IDEA Handbook* (International IDEA, 2005) and updated through my own research.

Detailed analysis of proportionality and bias in the UK electoral system is provided in Ron Johnston, Charles Pattie, Danny Dorling, and David Rossiter, *From Votes to Seats: The Operation of the UK Electoral System since 1945* (Manchester University Press, 2001). Further exploration of how best to measure bias appears in Adrian Blau, 'A Quadruple Whammy for First-Past-the-Post', *Electoral Studies*, vol. 23, no. 3 (September 2004), pp. 431–53. For recent analysis of bias and boundary reviews, see Galina Borisyuk, Ron Johnston, Colin Rallings, and Michael Thrasher, 'Parliamentary

Constituency Boundary Reviews and Electoral Bias: How Important Are Variations in Constituency Size?', *Parliamentary Affairs*, vol. 63, no. 1 (January 2010), pp. 4–21.

Information on the number of second places for each party in 2010 and also on the total number of candidates is from the House of Commons Library's report 'General Election 2010' (8 July 2010), available from www.parliament.uk.

See the Appendix for sources regarding Gallagher's index of disproportionality.

For further discussion of the relationship between the electoral system and the representation of women, see Pippa Norris, *Electoral Engineering: Voting Rules and Political Behavior* (Cambridge University Press, 2004). The research that I refer to on the representation of ethnic minorities appears in Didier Ruedin, 'Ethnic Group Representation in a Cross-National Comparison', *Journal of Legislative Studies*, vol. 15, no. 4 (2009), pp. 335–54.

Ann Widdecombe's article, 'General Election 2010: This shambles must never happen again', appeared in the *Daily Express* on 12 May 2010.

The most widely regarded discussion of accountability is contained in G. Bingham Powell, Jr., *Elections as Instruments of Democracy: Majoritarian and Proportional Visions* (Yale University Press, 2000). See also a recent symposium on 'Voters and Coalition Government', edited by Jeffrey A. Karp and Sara B. Hobolt, in *Electoral Studies*, vol. 29, no. 3 (September 2010), which offers several contrasting perspectives. John Curtice's analysis appears in 'Neither Representative Nor Accountable: First-Past-the-Post in Britain', in Bernard Grofman, André Blais, and Shaun Bowler (eds.), *Duverger's Law of Plurality Voting: The Logic of Party Competition in Canada, India, the United Kingdom, and the United States* (Springer, 2009), pp. 27–45. This is updated to take account of the 2010 election results in John Curtice, Stephen Fisher, and Robert Ford, 'Appendix 2: An Analysis of the Results', in Dennis Kavanagh and Philip Cowley, *The British General Election of 2010* (Palgrave Macmillan, 2010), pp. 385–426.

The *Daily Mail*'s article on the effects of a hung parliament was 'Hung vote "could tilt Britain into Greek financial turmoil"', by James Chapman, 29 April 2010. The poll by the Chartered Institute for Securities and Investment was reported in *The Times*, 5 May 2010.

A good overview of research on the relationship between the electoral system and the economy is given by Torsten Persson and Guido Tabellini, 'Electoral Systems and Economic Policy', in Barry R. Weingast and Donald A. Wittman (eds.), *The Oxford Handbook of Political Economy* (Oxford University Press, 2006), pp. 723–38. Specific studies include Torsten Persson and Guido Tabellini, *The Economic Effects of Constitutions* (MIT Press, 2003), Torsten Persson, 'Forms of Democracy, Policy, and Economic Development', NBER Working Paper Series 11171 (2005), and Torben Iversen and David Soskice, 'Electoral Institutions and the Politics of Coalitions: Why Some Democracies Redistribute More than Others', *American Political Science Review*, vol. 100, no. 2 (May 2006), pp. 165–81.

A helpful review of research findings on the relationship between electoral systems and electoral turnout is given in André Blais, 'What Affects Voter Turnout?', *Annual Review of Political Science*, vol. 9 (2006), pp. 111–25.

Evidence on the impact of the 1999 change in the system used to elect British MEPs appears in David M. Farrell and Roger Scully, *Representing Europe's Citizens? Electoral Institutions and the Failure of Parliamentary Representation* (Oxford University Press, 2007), pp. 163–96.

The information about citizens' contact with and knowledge of MPs comes from the 2010 edition of the Hansard Society's annual *Audit of Political Engagement*, available at www.hansardsociety.org.uk. This found that 44 per cent of respondents were able correctly to name their local MP, while 10 per cent gave an incorrect name and 46 per cent gave no name.

Figures on the size of constituency electorates are from the Electoral Reform Society: www.electoral-reform.org.uk/blog/, 25 June 2010.

Detailed analysis of the government's plans for changing the process of boundary setting is given in Michel Balinski, Ron Johnston, Iain McLean, and Peyton Young, *Drawing a New*

Constituency Map for the United Kingdom: The Parliamentary Voting System and Constituencies Bill 2010 (British Academy, 2010). Further information on the campaigns against the proposals in the Isle of Wight and Cornwall can be found at www.onewight.org.uk and keepcornwallwhole.org. The description of the government's plans for boundary review is taken from Peter Hain's speech in the House of Commons in the debate on the Parliamentary Voting System and Constituencies Bill of 6 September 2010 (see *Hansard* col. 124). Similar claims have been made by many other leading Labour figures.

Chapter 4

The simulations of election results under the alternative vote in Figure 10 use two methodologies. The first set (labelled 1) are based on surveys that ask voters to express their first and second preferences. Those from 1983 to 2005 have been calculated by John Curtice in a paper called 'Recent History of Second Preferences', available on the BBC website. Those for 2010 are reported in John Curtice, Stephen Fisher, and Robert Ford, 'Appendix 2: An Analysis of the Results', in Dennis Kavanagh and Philip Cowley, *The British General Election of 2010* (Palgrave Macmillan, 2010), pp. 385–426. The second set (labelled 2) are based on surveys that ask voters to fill in a mock AV ballot paper. The 1992 simulation is reported and discussed in Patrick Dunleavy, Helen Margetts, and Stuart Weir, 'How Britain Would Have Voted under Alternative Electoral Systems in 1992', *Parliamentary Affairs*, vol. 45, no. 4 (October 1992), pp. 640–55. The numbers from 1997 are in Patrick Dunleavy, Helen Margetts, Brendan O'Duffy, and Stuart Weir, 'Remodelling the 1997 General Election: How Britain Would Have Voted under Alternative Electoral Systems', *Journal of Elections, Public Opinion, and Parties*, vol. 8, no. 1 (1998), pp. 208–31. The 2010 figures are in David Sanders, Harold Clarke, Marianne Stewart, and Paul Whiteley, 'Simulating the Effects of the Alternative Vote in the 2010 UK General Election', paper presented at the EPOP Annual Conference, University of Essex,

10–12 September 2010. I have added the Thirsk and Malton result to their figures and assumed it would have been won by the Conservatives.

For elections producing the wrong winner in South Australia, see Jenni Newton-Farrelly, 'Wrong Winner Election Outcomes in South Australia: Bias, Minor Parties, and Non-Uniform Swings', South Australian Parliament Research Library, 1 April 2010.

For the Winston Churchill quotation, see *Hansard House of Commons Debates*, 2 June 1931, col. 106. See also the excellent paper from the House of Commons Library, 'AV and Electoral Reform' (28 July 2010), available at www.parliament.uk, which gives much useful background to the current debate about AV.

Daniel Kawczynski expresses his case against AV in a number of articles, including 'The AV electoral system would unfairly create two classes of voter' on the Conservative Home blog (conservative-home.blogs.com), 7 July 2010.

Julian Huppert is the Lib Dem MP who claimed that AV would eliminate safe seats. He made the claim in the debate on the Parliamentary Voting System and Constituencies Bill in the House of Commons on 6 September 2010 (see *Hansard* col. 42).

Chapter 5

The results of the 2009 European Parliament elections in the UK are reported in full on the website of the Electoral Commission (www.electoralcommission.org.uk).

For the debate about the relationship between the electoral system and corruption, see Benjamin Nyblade and Steven R. Reed, 'Who Cheats? Who Loots? Political Competition and Corruption in Japan, 1947–1992', *American Journal of Political Science*, vol. 52, no. 4 (October 2008), pp. 926–41; Torsten Persson and Guido Tabellini, 'Electoral Systems and Economic Policy', in Barry R. Weingast and Donald A. Wittman (eds.), *The Oxford Handbook of Political Economy* (Oxford University Press, 2006), pp. 723–38.

Chapter 6

On the relationship between list and constituency MPs in mixed systems, see Thomas Carl Lundberg, *Proportional Representation and the Constituency Role in Britain* (Palgrave Macmillan, 2007).

The main source on AV+ is the report of the Jenkins Commission (the Independent Commission on the Voting System), published in October 1998 (HMSO, Cm 4090–I), and available in full online.

Alan Johnson has argued for AV+ in several articles, including 'Labour Must Embrace Electoral Reform', *Independent*, 8 July 2009.

Chapter 7

The quotation from Enid Lakeman comes from her classic book, *How Democracies Vote: A Study of Majority and Proportional Electoral Systems* (Faber and Faber, 1970), p. 214.

The long quotation from the Jenkins Commission appears at paragraph 95 of the Commission's report (see above for the report's bibliographical details).

Much valuable analysis of the operation of STV in the Scottish local government elections of 2007, including the figures cited in the text, appears in David Denver and Hugh Bochel, 'A Quiet Revolution: STV and the Scottish Council Elections of 2007', *Scottish Affairs*, no. 61 (autumn 2007), and Ron Gould's report for the Electoral Commission, *Independent Review of the Scottish Parliamentary and Local Government Elections, 3 May 2007*, available at www.electoralcommission.org.uk.

On the operation of STV in Ireland, Malta, and elsewhere, see David M. Farrell, *Electoral Systems: A Comparative Introduction*, 2nd edition (Palgrave Macmillan, 2010) and Shaun Bowler and Bernard Grofman (eds.), *Elections in Australia, Ireland, and Malta under the Single Transferable Vote: Reflections on an Embedded Institution* (University of Michigan Press, 2000). Data on invalid ballots cast in the UK come from Ministry of Justice, *The Governance of Britain: Review of Voting Systems: The Experience of New Voting Systems in the United Kingdom since 1997*, Cm 7304 (HMSO, 2008), p. 112, and

'UK General Election 2010: Turnout and Administrative Data',
www.electoralcommission.org.uk.

Chapter 8

Excellent and wide-ranging discussion of the use of quotas for
women in the UK and around the world appears in Mona Lena
Krook's book, *Quotas for Women in Politics: Gender and Candidate
Selection Reform Worldwide* (Oxford University Press, 2009).

Figures on women candidates are from the House of Commons
Library's report 'General Election 2010' (8 July 2010), available
from www.parliament.uk. Figures on ethnic minority candidates
are from Afua Hirsch, 'If Britain is really post-racial, why is the
election so white?', *Guardian*, 27 April 2010, and Labour Party,
Fairer Britain, Your Choice (2010), at www.labour.org.uk. Figures
on MPs' educational backgrounds are from the Sutton Trust, 'The
Educational Background of Members of Parliament in 2010', May
2010, available at www.suttontrust.com.

The Hansard Society report mentioned in the text is Sarah
Childs, Joni Lovenduski, and Rosie Campbell, *Women at the Top
2005: Changing Numbers, Changing Politics?* (Hansard Society,
2005), available at www.hansardsociety.org.uk.

Estimating party memberships is an inexact science, particularly
for the Conservative Party, which does not publish figures. An
overview of available figures and estimates is given in a recent paper
by the House of Commons Library, 'Membership of UK Political
Parties' (17 August 2009), available at www.parliament.uk.

The report of the Speaker's Conference on Parliamentary
Representation (10 March 2010) is available at www.parliament.
uk.

The case for primaries was put by David Cameron in his speech
'Fixing Broken Promises' (26 May 2009), available at www.
conservatives.com. Frank Field argued for them in *Back from Life
Support: Remaking Representative and Responsible Government in
Britain* (Policy Exchange, 2008), available from www.policyex-
change.org.uk. On David Miliband, see Francis Elliott, 'David

Miliband calls for Labour to select candidates with primaries', *The Times*, 8 August 2009. On Ed Miliband, see George Eaton, 'Ed Miliband backs open primaries', New Statesman blog, available at www.newstatesman.com.

Information on the primaries that have been held to date is given in the House of Commons Library paper 'Candidate Selection – Primaries' (23 September 2009), available at www.parliament.uk, and in the Conservative Party policy document 'Big Ideas to Give Britain Real Change' (2010), available at www.conservatives.com. The latter also gives details of Conservative plans for the future of primaries.

The remark by Julian Critchley is quoted in Peter G. J. Pulzer, *Political Representation and Elections in Britain* (Allen & Unwin, 1967), p. 65. John Strafford criticises open primaries in the article 'The decline and death of party membership: Why should anyone now be a member of the Conservative Party?', at conservativehome. blogs.com, 20 August 2009.

The article by Robert McIlveen is 'Ladies to the Right: An Interim Analysis of the A-List', *Journal of Elections, Public Opinion, and Parties*, vol. 19, no. 2 (May 2009), pp. 147–57, at p. 154.

David Butler's comments on his meeting with Winston Churchill are in 'Going with the Swing', *Oxford Today*, vol. 22, no. 3 (Trinity 2010), p. 13.

Figures on national campaign spending in 1992 and 1997 are from Michael Pinto-Duschinsky, *Paying for the Party: Myths and Realities in British Political Finance* (Policy Exchange, 2008), available at www.policyexchange.org.uk. Other references to Pinto-Duschinsky's work are based on the same source.

The Phillips review of party funding, *Strengthening Democracy: Fair and Sustainable Funding of Political Parties* (March 2007) is available at www.partyfundingreview.gov.uk.

The Electoral Commission's estimates for the impact of a donation cap are given in its report *The Funding of Political Parties* (December 2004), available at www.electoralcommission.org.uk.

The results of the 2006 poll on state funding are discussed in Justin Fisher, 'Research in Support of the Committee's 11th Enquiry: Review of the Electoral Commission' (June 2006). The focus group research is reported in *Attitudes towards the Funding of Political Parties*, published by the Electoral Commission in 2004 and available at www.electoralcommission.org.uk.

Jack Straw's words about the importance of political parties are in the government white paper *Party Finance and Expenditure in the United Kingdom* (June 2008, Cm 7329), p. 4. Andrew Tyrie's similar words appear in his paper *Clean Politics* (March 2006), p. 1, available at www.conservatives.com.

Useful overviews of cross-national patterns in party finance rules are given in Ingrid van Biezen, 'Party and Campaign Finance', in Lawrence LeDuc, Richard G. Niemi, and Pippa Norris (eds.), *Comparing Democracies 3: Elections and Voting in the 21st Century* (Sage, 2010), pp. 65–97, and in the International Institute for Democracy and Electoral Assistance's *Funding of Political Parties and Election Campaigns* (2003), available at www.idea.int. Richard Katz and Peter Mair set out their arguments about the changing nature of political parties in 'Changing Models of Party Organisation and Party Democracy: The Emergence of the Cartel Party', *Party Politics*, vol. 1, no. 1 (January 1995), pp. 5–28.

Figures for Short and Cranborne Money come from the House of Commons Library's note 'Short Money' (1 July 2010), available from www.parliament.uk.

Chapter 9

Much information on recall provisions and how they vary around the world is provided in *Direct Democracy: The International IDEA Handbook*, which can be downloaded at www.idea.int. The missing case that I allude to in the text is British Columbia. Further information in relation to the US is given on the website of the National Conference of State Legislatures: www.ncsl.org.

The Kansas law cited can be found at Kansas Statutes Annotated 25–4302.

The newspaper articles quoted in relation to the Californian recall of 2003 are 'A no vote for California's recall – And no to Arnold Schwarzenegger as governor', *Financial Times*, 7 October

2003; 'A Hollywood triumph, but a depressing day for the democratic ideal', *Independent*, 9 October 2003; 'California – Groping for victory', *Guardian*, 9 October 2003; 'Partial recall – California's latest initiative goes too far', *Financial Times*, 1 July 2003. The Power Inquiry report, *Power to the People: The Report of Power: An Independent Inquiry into Britain's Democracy* (2006), is available at www.powerinquiry.org.

The MPs' letter supporting recall, 'Sanctions against MPs' appeared in the *Daily Telegraph* on 29 February 2008. Nick Clegg's support for the idea is reported in Nicholas Watt and Patrick Wintour, 'Clegg calls for US-style recall system for discredited MPs', *Guardian*, 6 March 2008.

The *Times* poll was reported in Philip Webster, 'Poll suggests voters want radical reform of Parliament', *The Times*, 30 May 2009. Full details are available in 'The Times Poll – May 2009', at www.populus.co.uk.

Chapter 10

On contrasting visions of democracy and their implications for electoral systems, see especially Richard S. Katz, *Democracy and Elections* (Oxford University Press, 1997) and G. Bingham Powell, Jr., *Elections as Instruments of Democracy: Majoritarian and Proportional Visions* (Yale University Press, 2000).

Index

Also available from Biteback

BIG BROTHER WATCH

THE STATE OF CIVIL LIBERTIES IN MODERN BRITAIN

EDITED BY ALEX DEANE

with a foreword by Tony Benn

Big Brother Watch
The state of civil liberties
in modern Britain

edited by Alex Deane
with a foreword by Tony Benn

Big Brother is watching us.

We now live in a state that takes a disturbingly close interest in our everyday lives. The government enjoys an array of powers over individual freedoms unprecedented in a democratic nation and inconceivable to our forebears.

Big Brother Watch charts the encroachment of a surveillance culture and the erosion of civil liberties in the UK. The aim of its expert contributors is to highlight the increasingly illiberal nature of life in modern Britain, and the terrible consequences this could have for us all.

336pp paperback, £9.99

Available from all good bookshops or order from
www.bitebackpublishing.com